David Mitchell

CONTEMPORARY CRITICAL PERSPECTIVES

Series Editors: Jeannette Baxter, Peter Childs,
Sebastian Groes and Kaye Mitchell

Guides in the *Contemporary Critical Perspectives* series provide companions to reading and studying major contemporary authors. They include new critical essays combining textual readings, cultural analysis, and discussion of key critical and theoretical issues in a clear, accessible style. Each guide also includes a preface by a major contemporary writer, a new interview with the author, discussion of film and TV adaptation, and guidance on further reading.

Titles in the series include
Ali Smith edited by Monica Germana and Emily Horton
Andrea Levy edited by Jeannette Baxter and David James
Hilary Mantel edited by Eileen Pollard and Ginette Carpenter
Ian McEwan (2nd Edition) edited by Sebastian Groes
J. G. Ballard edited by Jeannette Baxter
Julian Barnes edited by Sebastian Groes and Peter Childs
Kazuo Ishiguro edited by Sean Matthews and Sebastian Groes
Salman Rushdie edited by Robert Eaglestone and Martin McQuillan
Sarah Waters edited by Kaye Mitchell
Don DeLillo edited by Katherine Da Cunha Lewin and Kiron Ward

Forthcoming titles
John Burnside edited by Ben Davies

David Mitchell

*Edited by Wendy Knepper
and Courtney Hopf*

BLOOMSBURY ACADEMIC
LONDON · NEW YORK · OXFORD · NEW DELHI · SYDNEY

BLOOMSBURY ACADEMIC
Bloomsbury Publishing Plc
50 Bedford Square, London, WC1B 3DP, UK
1385 Broadway, New York, NY 10018, USA

BLOOMSBURY, BLOOMSBURY ACADEMIC and the Diana logo are trademarks of
Bloomsbury Publishing Plc

First published in Great Britain 2019
Paperback edition published 2021

Copyright © Wendy Knepper and Courtney Hopf, 2019

Wendy Knepper and Courtney Hopf have asserted their right under the Copyright, Designs and Patents Act, 1988, to be identified as Authors of this work.

Cover design: Eleanor Rose
Cover image © Getty Images

All rights reserved. No part of this publication may be reproduced or transmitted in any form or by any means, electronic or mechanical, including photocopying, recording, or any information storage or retrieval system, without prior permission in writing from the publishers.

Bloomsbury Publishing Plc does not have any control over, or responsibility for, any third-party websites referred to or in this book. All internet addresses given in this book were correct at the time of going to press. The author and publisher regret any inconvenience caused if addresses have changed or sites have ceased to exist, but can accept no responsibility for any such changes.

A catalogue record for this book is available from the British Library.

Library of Congress Cataloging-in-Publication Data
Names: Knepper, Wendy, editor. | Hopf, Courtney, editor.
Title: David Mitchell / edited by Wendy Knepper and Courtney Hopf.
Description: London; New York, NY: Bloomsbury Academic, 2019. | Includes bibliographical references and index.
Identifiers: LCCN 2018059578| ISBN 9781474262101 (hb) | ISBN 9781474262125 (ePDF) | ISBN 9781474262118 (epub)
Subjects: LCSH: Mitchell, David (David Stephen)–Criticism and interpretation.
Classification: LCC PR6063.I785 Z57 2019 | DDC 823/.914–dc23
LC record available at https://lccn.loc.gov/2018059578

ISBN: HB: 978-1-4742-6210-1
PB: 978-1-3502-1541-2
ePDF: 978-1-4742-6212-5
eBook: 978-1-4742-6211-8

Series: Contemporary Critical Perspectives

Typeset by Deanta Global Publishing Services, Chennai, India

To find out more about our authors and books visit www.bloomsbury.com and sign up for our newsletters.

CONTENTS

Series editors' preface vii
List of contributors viii
Chronology of David Mitchell's life xi

David Mitchell: An introduction Wendy Knepper and
   Courtney Hopf 1

1 Globalization in David Mitchell's *Ghostwritten*: Minding
   'the reality gap' Hugh Charles O'Connell 23

2 Questing for the post-postmodern: David Mitchell's
   number9dream Nick Bentley 39

3 'What was knowledge for, I would ask myself': Science,
   technology and *pharmakon* in David Mitchell's *Cloud
   Atlas* Martin Paul Eve 53

4 Witnessing transhistorical trauma in *Cloud
   Atlas* Jason Howard Mezey 69

5 Raids on the inarticulate: The stammering narrative of
   Black Swan Green Courtney Hopf 85

6 History, globalization and the human subject in
   The Thousand Autumns of Jacob de Zoet William
   Stephenson 101

7 Voicing tragedy in David Mitchell's libretti: *Wake* and
   Sunken Garden Rose Harris-Birtill 117

8 David Mitchell's representations of environmental crisis and ecological apocalypse *Treasa De Loughry* 133

9 *The Bone Clocks* and the mud of humanity: The Anthropocene *Bildungsroman* *Chris Koenig-Woodyard* 149

10 David Mitchell as world-builder: *The Bone Clocks* and *Slade House* *Wendy Knepper* 165

Creating a fictional universe: An interview with David Mitchell *Courtney Hopf* 183

Further reading 195
Index 206

SERIES EDITORS' PREFACE

The readership for contemporary fiction has never been greater. The explosion of reading groups and literary blogs, of university courses and school curricula, and even the apparent rude health of the literary marketplace indicate an ever-growing appetite for new work, for writing which responds to the complex, changing, and challenging times in which we live. At the same time, readers seem ever more eager to engage in conversations about their reading, to devour the review pages, to pack the sessions at literary festivals and author events. Reading is an increasingly social activity, as we seek to share and refine our experience of the book, to clarify and extend our understanding.

It is this tremendous enthusiasm for contemporary fiction to which the Contemporary Critical Perspectives series responds. Our ambition is to offer readers of current fiction a comprehensive critical account of each author's work, presenting original, specially commissioned analyses of all aspects of their career, from a variety of different angles and approaches, as well as directions towards further reading and research.

Our brief to the contributors is to be scholarly, to draw on the latest thinking about narrative, or philosophy, or psychology, indeed whatever seemed to them most significant in drawing out the meanings and force of the texts in question, but also to focus closely on the words on the page, the stories and scenarios and forms which all of us meet first when we open a book. We insisted that these essays be accessible to that mythical beast, the Common Reader, who might just as readily be spotted at the Lowdham Book Festival as in a college seminar. In this way, we hope to have presented critical assessments of our writers in such a way as to contribute something to both of those environments, and also to have done something to bring together the most important qualities of each of them.

Jeannette Baxter, Peter Childs,
Sebastian Groes and Kaye Mitchell

CONTRIBUTORS

Nick Bentley is Senior Lecturer in English Literature at Keele University in the UK. He is author of *Contemporary British Fiction: A Reader's Guide to Essential Criticism* (Palgrave Macmillan, 2018), *Martin Amis: Writers and Their Work* (Northcote House, 2015), *Contemporary British Fiction* (Edinburgh University Press, 2008), *Radical Fictions: The English Novel in the 1950s* (Peter Lang, 2007); editor of *British Fiction of the 1990s* (Routledge, 2005); and co-editor with Nick Hubble and Leigh Wilson of *The 2000s: A Decade of Contemporary British Fiction* in The Decades Series (Bloomsbury, 2015). He has also published journal articles and book chapters on Martin Amis, Julian Barnes, Kazuo Ishiguro, Doris Lessing, Colin MacInnes, Ian McEwan, David Mitchell, Zadie Smith, Sam Selvon, Alan Sillitoe, the city in postmodern fiction, fictional representations of youth subcultures and working-class writing. He is currently working on a monograph titled *Making a Scene: Youth Subcultures in Postwar and Contemporary Fiction*.

Hugh O'Connell is Assistant Professor of English at the University of Massachusetts Boston. His current research examines the relationship between speculative fiction and speculative finance. Recent essays on British and postcolonial science fiction have appeared in *Postcolonial Literary Inquiry*, *Modern Fiction Studies*, *CR: The New Centennial Review*, *Paradoxa* and *The Los Angeles Review of Books*. His essay on Amitav Ghosh's *The Calcutta Chromosome*, 'Mutating towards the Future', received Honorable Mention for the 2013 Science Fiction Research Association's Pioneer Award for excellence in scholarship.

Martin Paul Eve is Professor and Chair of Literature, Technology and Publishing at Birkbeck, University of London. He is the author of three books: *Pynchon and Philosophy* (Palgrave, 2014); *Open Access and the Humanities* (Cambridge University Press, 2014); and *Password* [a cultural history] (Bloomsbury, 2016), as well as many journal articles. Martin is also a founder and director of the Open Library of Humanities and is well known for his work on open-access policies.

Rose Harris-Birtill is Post-Doctoral Researcher at the University of St Andrews, where she also teaches and lectures. Her current research investigates post-secular literature, examining the Buddhist influences that draw David Mitchell's novels, short stories and writing for opera into an interconnected ethical world. Her monograph, *David Mitchell's Post-Secular World: Buddhism, Belief and the Urgency of Compassion*, with Bloomsbury Academic is due in 2019. Rose's other publications on Mitchell's works include '"A Row of Screaming Russian Dolls": Escaping the Panopticon in David Mitchell's *number9dream*' (*SubStance* 44.1 136, 2015) and '"Looking down Time's Telescope at Myself": Reincarnation and Global Futures in David Mitchell's Fictional Worlds' (*KronoScope* 17.2, 2017) and articles on *The Bone Clocks* and *Slade House* (*Foundation* 44.1, 2015; 45.2, 2016). Rose was the lead organizer for the David Mitchell Conference 2017; she also guest-edited a related special issue of *C21 Literature* on his writing (2018).

Courtney Hopf is Lecturer in Writing and English as well as Programme Manager of Creative and Liberal Arts at New York University's London campus. She has published on David Mitchell previously, with her chapter 'The Stories We Tell: Discursive Identity through Narrative Form in *Cloud Atlas*' in *David Mitchell: Critical Essays* (Gylphi, 2011). She has also published articles on narrative and social media in *Rhizomes* ('Story Networks: A Theory of Narrative and Mass Collaboration') and *Alluvium* ('Social Media Memory'). Her wider research interests include twentieth- and twenty-first-century Anglophone literature, narratology, collaborative literatures and experimental novels.

Wendy Knepper is a visiting scholar at the Department for the Comparative History of Ideas at University of Washington. She is the author of two books: *Patrick Chamoiseau: A Critical Introduction* (University Press of Mississippi, 2012) and *Postcolonial Literature* (York Notes Companion, 2011). Her edited collections include special issues on Andrea Levy in *EnterText* (2012), Wilson Harris in *Journal of Postcolonial Writing* (2013) and 'Experimental Writing in a Globalizing World' in *ARIEL* (2016). She has published widely in the field of world/postcolonial literatures, including contributions to *Small Axe*, *PMLA*, *Journal of Postcolonial Writing*, *The Journal of Commonwealth Literature* and *ARIEL*. Her research focuses on twentieth-century and contemporary postcolonial/world literatures as well as feminist/gender studies.

Chris Koenig-Woodyard teaches eighteenth- to twentieth-century literature at the University of Toronto, with a focus on fantasy, the Gothic and science fiction. He is the co-editor of *Transatlantic Romanticism: An Anthology of American, British, and Canadian Literature, 1767–1867* (Longman, 2006), '*Sullen Fires across the Atlantic*': *Essays in British and American Romanticism* (Romantic Circles, 2006) and an issue of the *University of Toronto Quarterly* on 'Monster Studies'. He is a contributing editor and writer to *The Broadview Anthology of British Literature*. He has published on British, American and transatlantic romanticism, the pedagogy of literary studies, the digital humanities and the Gothic. His current research focuses on posthumanism and monster studies, and he is the founding director of the Monster Studies Lab.

Treasa De Loughry is Lecturer in Global and World Literatures at the University of Exeter. She has articles published or forthcoming in the *Journal of Postcolonial Writing*, the *Journal of Commonwealth Literature* and *Green Letters* and chapters in various edited collections. Her monograph, *The Global Novel and Capitalism in Crisis – Contemporary Literary Narratives* is under contract with the Palgrave Macmillan Series 'New Comparisons in World Literature', and examines how novels by Salman Rushdie, Rana Dasgupta, David Mitchell and Rachel Kushner evolved new aesthetics to represent global economic and ecological crises. Her research interests include postcolonial and world-literary studies, petro-cultures and the Green Revolution.

Jason Howard Mezey is Associate Professor of English at Saint Joseph's University in Philadelphia, Pennsylvania, where he teaches courses in postcolonial literature and theory as well as South Asian, South African, Israeli and Palestinian, and contemporary British fiction. He has published on Salman Rushdie, Arundhati Roy, Raja Rao and Paul Scott, and his work has appeared in *Interventions: International Journal of Postcolonial Studies*, *Studies in the Novel*, the *South Asian Review* and the *Journal of Commonwealth and Postcolonial Studies*. His first essay on *Cloud Atlas* was published in *Modern Language Studies*, and he is grateful for the opportunity to revisit Mitchell's novel in this collection.

William Stephenson is Associate Professor of Modern and Contemporary Literature. His academic books include *Gonzo Republic: Hunter S. Thompson's America* (Continuum, 2011) and *Fowles's The French Lieutenant's Woman: A Reader's Guide* (Continuum, 2007). He has contributed articles on Hunter S. Thompson, Alex Garland, Bret Easton Ellis and J. G. Ballard to *Critique: Studies in Contemporary Fiction*. He has published three collections of poetry, the latest of which is *Travellers and Avatars,* forthcoming from Live Canon Poetry Press.

CHRONOLOGY OF DAVID MITCHELL'S LIFE

Date	Event
1969	David Mitchell is born in Southport in Lancashire (now Merseyside), England, on 12 January
1976–81	Lives in Hanley Swan, Worcestershire
1976	Develops a stammer at age seven
1982–87	Hanley Castle High School, Hanley Castle, Upton-upon-Severn, Worcestershire
1987	Backpacks through India and Nepal
1987–90	Studies BA English and American Literature at University of Kent, where he was a member of the Keynes Duck Appreciation Society and the bell-ringing club
1990–91	Studies MA in Comparative Literature at University of Kent
1991–92	Lives and works in Catania, Sicily
1994–2002	Lives and works as an English teacher in Hiroshima, Japan
1997	Completes manuscript of first novel and receives a harsh rejection letter from Harper Collins
1999	Publishes *Ghostwritten*, which goes on to win the John Llewellyn Rhys Prize (for best work of British literature written by an author under thirty-five) and is shortlisted for the Guardian First Book Award
2001	Publishes *number9dream*, which is shortlisted for The Man Booker Prize
2002	Settles with his wife and family in Clonakilty, a seaside town in County Cork, Ireland
2003	Publishes 'January Man', selected as one of Granta's Best of Young British Novelists

2004	Publishes 'What You Do Not Know You Want' in *McSweeney's Enchanted Chamber of Astonishing Stories*
2004	Publishes *Cloud Atlas*, winner of the Geoffrey Faber Memorial Prize, the South Bank Show Literature Prize and Richard and Judy Best Read of the Year as well as shortlisted for The Man Booker Prize and the Commonwealth Writers' Prize
2006	Publishes *Black Swan Green*, shortlisted for the Costa Novel Award Prize and longlisted for The Man Booker Prize
2007	Listed among *Time* magazine's '100 Most Influential People in The World'
2008	Publishes 'Judith Castle' in *New York Times* and Zadie Smith's edited collection, entitled *The Book of Other People*
2009	Publishes 'The Massive Rat' in the *Guardian*
2010	Publishes *The Thousand Autumns of Jacob de Zoet*, which wins the 2011 Commonwealth Writers Prize (South Asia and Europe Region, Best Book)
2010	Production of *Wake*, an opera based on the 2000 Enschede fireworks disaster, with libretti by Mitchell and music by Klaas de Vries, performed by *De Nederlandse Reisopera*Publishes 'The Siphoners' in *I'm With the Bears: Short Stories from a Damaged Planet*
2011	Release of 'The Voorman Problem', a BAFTA-nominated short film, starring Martin Freeman, based on a segment from *number9dream*
2011	Contributes a short story, entitled 'The Gardener', to 'The Flower Show' exhibit by Kai and Sunny
2012	Adaptation of *Cloud Atlas* for the screen by the Wachowski siblings
2013	Co-publishes with Keiko Yoshida the translation of *The Reason I Jump:One Boy's Voice from the Silence of Autism*, a book written by Naoki Higashida, a thirteen-year-old Japanese boy with autism
2013	Production of *Sunken Garden*, with libretti by Mitchell and music composed by Michel van der Aa, by the English National Opera
2013	Contributes 'Lots of Bits of Star' to the exhibit 'Caught by the Nest' by Kai and Sunny

2014	'Variations on a Theme by Mr Donut' *Granta* 127: Japan, Spring
2014	Publishes *The Bone Clocks*, longlisted for The Man Booker Prize and eventual winner of Best Novel at the 2015 World Fantasy Awards in Saratoga Springs, NY
2014	Publishes 'The Right Sort' as Twitter fiction
2014	Portrait of David Mitchell displayed at National Portrait Gallery as part of Carl Randall's 'London Portraits' exhibition, depicting Mitchell in the Whispering Gallery in St. Paul's Cathedral
2015	Publishes Twitter fiction under the handle '@I_Bombadil'
2015	Publishes *Slade House*, which expands upon 'The Right Sort'
2016	Contributes 'My Eye on You' to Kai and Sunny exhibition, entitled 'Whirlwind of Time'
2016	Contributes 'From Me Flows What You Call Time' to *The Future Library Project* (2114)
2017	'A Forgettable Story' published in *Silkroad*
2018	'Start with the Map: A Writer's Lessons in Imaginary Cartography' in *The New Yorker*

David Mitchell: An introduction

Wendy Knepper and Courtney Hopf

Introduction

With the publication of *Ghostwritten* (1999), David Mitchell inaugurated a fictional universe that imaginatively chronicles world history and complicates the story of human life. Since then, the author's ever-expanding narrative universe has grown considerably across novels, libretti, short stories, a novella and digital fiction as well as through adaptations of his work. Together, these works imagine a world that extends back through the long history of planetary life, ranges through the rise of globalization and reaches forward to imagine a future shaped by capitalist crisis, environmental destruction, post-apocalyptic struggles to survive and exile from planet earth. To date, *The Bone Clocks* (2014) sets out in the most explicit fashion the author's fantastical cosmology of warring powers, establishing a millennia-old war between beings who quite literally fight for the souls of humanity. Somewhere between historical realism and fantastical alterity, David Mitchell has created an intricately imagined literary universe that both resembles our own and departs from it to speculate on the possibilities of the world as it is and might be. Mitchell's oeuvre interweaves diverse forms and traditions of storytelling to craft a vastly ambitious and distinctive literary world. This collection seeks to map and investigate Mitchell's creative cosmos, introducing readers to the author's multi-scalar world of interconnected fictions, the critical debates surrounding his work and the author's ideas surrounding world-building. Altogether, the contributors to this collection make the case for David Mitchell as a socially committed world author whose fictions intervene, ethically and politically, to critique the realities of inequality and imagine alternative pathways for social transformation.

Overview of David Mitchell's oeuvre

Mitchell is a rare novelist: one whose work achieves both popular success in the marketplace and critical acclaim. Rarer still, he gained that reputation with his first published novel, *Ghostwritten* (1999), an award-winning global fiction that was lauded for its deftly drawn characters, mixed genres and planetary sweep. This novel may have been an overnight sensation, but the same can hardly be said for the author who confronted creative challenges and setbacks as he struggled to find a novelistic form that could convey the scale and complexity of his vision. His first novel, *The Old Moon*, which remains unpublished to this day, was rejected by twelve agents and six publishers, partly because of its overwhelmingly complex narrative structure (Mason 2010). *The Old Moon* takes place over a period of 365 days, involving 20 subplots and dozens of characters. Mike Shaw, a literary agent, told a reporter, 'I could see the talent … . David could write, but the book was out of control and over the top. No structure, many characters. I'd never seen anything so extreme as that first typescript from David. So god-awful in one sense and so promising in another' (Mason 2010). In the face of critique, Mitchell worked to devise creative strategies that would balance his desire to tell it all in one ambitious story with the need for a tightly written, gripping fiction that would appeal to readers in the contemporary literary marketplace.

Commenting on his early literary aspirations, Mitchell observes: 'When I started writing … I wanted to put a lot of things into my books, and this idea of weaving different shorter narratives together, gluing shorter novellas together, was the only structure I have ever stumbled upon that lets me do that' (Keating 2014). *Ghostwritten* demonstrated Mitchell's ability to assemble and unify exhilarating and terrifying tales of global life in an interconnected world: to tell a wide-ranging story while gesturing towards a world of narratives as yet untold. Following the success of *Ghostwritten*, Mitchell published *number9dream* (2001), a novel inspired in part by the work of Haruki Murakami and which was shortlisted for The Man Booker Prize. For his third novel, *Cloud Atlas* (2004), an epic tale of global development ranging from the nineteenth century to a post-apocalyptic future, which was again shortlisted for The Man Booker Prize, Mitchell was awarded the Richard and Judy Best Read of the Year. While the former brought prestige, the latter award boosted his reputation and sales among the mainstream reading public. Named one of Granta's twenty 'Best Young British Novelists' in 2003, he would later go on to be listed as one of *Time* magazine's 100 most influential people in 2007 – a list on which few novelists appear.

These global novels were followed by works on more intimate scales, with a narrower focus on characters' life experiences. *Black Swan Green* (2006), a *Bildungsroman* based loosely on the author's own life, won the Best Book for Young Adults from the American Library Association, as well as being nominated for the Costa Award and appearing on various lists as a notable book of the year. *The Thousand Autumns of Jacob de Zoet* (2010), set in 1799 on the tiny Japanese trading island of Dejima off the coast of Nagasaki, debuted at the number one position on the *Sunday Times* hardback sale list, before it went on to win the Commonwealth Writers' Prize for South Asia and Europe in 2011. With *Thousand Autumns*, Mitchell's work took a dark fantastical turn that gave expression to a bleaker, less celebratory, view of globalization as a historical process: one shaped by inequality, uneven development and cultural difference. Where the celebratory ending of *Cloud Atlas* highlights the historical challenge to slavery and seeds the hope of collective resistance, *Thousand Autumns* acknowledges the historical constraints that limit the possibilities for emancipation as well as impede cross-cultural relations. Yet, *Thousand Autumns* signals clearly Mitchell's cosmological ambitions, while at the same time revealing that his entire oeuvre belongs to a single literary universe, where atemporal beings, such as the recurring character of Marinus, draw readers into a long history of development.

Mitchell's literary universe overlaps with our own as evidenced in its history and vast array of characters, but it also projects a fantastical moral order, alternative constructions of life and death, and a timeline of events that hurtle earth and its inhabitants towards an apocalyptic future. *The Bone Clocks* (2014), which chronicles the life of protagonist Holly Sykes, was longlisted for The Man Booker Prize and was the winner of Best Novel at the 2015 World Fantasy Awards, highlighting Mitchell's work's capacity to navigate across genres and audiences. This work sets Horologists, supernatural beings who reincarnate and flit from body to body, against Anchorites, humans who steal souls to prolong their lives, revealing a long and secret war pitting the predators against the protectors of human life. This war is expanded upon in the author's shortest novel to date, *Slade House* (2015), which takes the form of a Gothic tale that explores the soul-destroying conditions and conflicts that haunt everyday life in contemporary times. Finally, it will be some time before awards, if any, are given for Mitchell's 'From Me Flows What You Call Time', his 2015 submission to the Future Library Project in Norway. Not until 2114 will the story be printed on paper made from trees in the Norwegian forest.

Mitchell's creative talents extend to social and cultural criticism, Twitter fiction, short stories and essays. As a cultural critic, he is a frequent contributor to the *Guardian* and the *Telegraph*, with essays and articles that discuss opera, autism, historical fiction, life in Japan and reflections on culture. He has participated actively in several academic conferences, among them two dedicated events about 'David Mitchell' studies at St Andrews (2009 and 2017) and a conference hosted by the International Society for the Study of Time (2016). New York University in London also hosted a symposium on the author's work in 2014, which subsequently led to this collection. While Mitchell is careful to avoid engaging in scholarly debates about the global novel, post-postmodernism or other specialist topics, he nonetheless offers clearly articulated views about literary history, generic influences, world-building and genre fiction. Through discussions of his role as a creative writer as well as reflections on artists, film-makers, musicians and other writers, his work considers the role and function of the imagination and creativity.

The author's creative output and influences also extend across media. Mitchell has written the libretti for two operas, *Wake* (2010) and *Sunken Garden* (2013); consulted with the Wachowski siblings on their 2012 film adaptation of *Cloud Atlas*; assisted in the writing of season two of the Wachowskis' Netflix series, *Sense8* (2016); translated two memoirs by a teenaged Japanese boy with autism (2013's *The Reason I Jump* and 2017's *Fall Down Seven Times, Get up Eight*); published a story on Twitter ('The Right Sort', 2014); inspired exhibitions of work by visual artists, notably Kai and Sunny; and contributed dialogue to *Before the Dawn* (2014), the triumphant return to the stage of Kate Bush. Speaking of her influence, Mitchell says she 'transforms [him] into a deranged fan', observing that 'it's hard to think of a novelist, let alone another singer-songwriter, who takes on such diverse narrative viewpoints with Bush's aplomb' (Mitchell 2011). Surely, if there is someone to rival Kate Bush in this regard, it is Mitchell himself. Not only is his artistry wide-ranging in its production, each work itself shows a relish for diverse and pluralistic vantage points and demonstrates Mitchell's talent for 'channeling voices' (Iyer 2014). Fittingly, Carl Randall's portrait of the author, entitled 'David Mitchell and the Whispering Gallery, Novelist' (on exhibit at the National Portrait Gallery as part of a series of fifteen paintings of people who have contributed to British society and culture), depicts Mitchell as an auditor and visitor to St Paul's Cathedral – standing in the Whispering Gallery, listening to the voices of his characters as they resonate.

Mitchell's Literary Universe: Inspiration and Influences

Mitchell asserts that his diverse and wide-ranging oeuvre constitutes one story, one timeline and one universe – a work he has called 'the Übernovel'. Mitchell has described this universe with evolving terminology and through a variety of metaphors. Once termed a 'macronovel' by him (Mason 2010), it later became the 'Über-book' (Finney 2014 and others) and most recently, in the interview at the end of this volume, Mitchell coined the term 'biblioverse' (Hopf 2019: 183). The metaphors are as numerous as the epithets. Sarah Dillon (2011) introduced Mitchell's universe as a 'twenty-first-century house of fiction' (6), and Mitchell himself has picked this up, calling it 'a mad old rambling house with a new extension added on every time I publish, though which is the main house and which the extension or wing becomes obscured over time' (Hopf 2019: 184). Further models include auditory figurations like the syncing up of 'the white noise of the background of short stories'

(Birnbaum 2006), an atlas of clouds and a series of postcards (purchased by Jason Taylor in *Black Swan Green*) that can be lined up so that the individual images join up to create a single, larger picture. Elsewhere, Mitchell himself has referred to LEGO® building blocks: 'Basically I write novellas and I line them up and Lego them together to turn them into something bigger' (Keating 2014). The building blocks of smaller stories are interlinked to create larger narrative structures that together combine to create a literary universe, one that remains under construction. An organic idea of world-building emerges from Mitchell's reference to the Tolkienesque endeavour to generate new life from the 'compost heap' (Mitchell 2014) of culture and history, suggesting that discarded and eroded materials, peripheral and residual presences, inform storytelling as an art of reclamation and regeneration. In the interview contained in this book, Mitchell describes his 'biblioverse' as 'a large stage of time and space made mostly of blur and possibilities and potential, but with small islands of detail and clarity where my novels occur' (Hopf 2019: 184). What is notable about each of these metaphors is how they emphasize the processes of rumination, expansion and interlinking in a vast network. Mitchell himself is unsure which new island or wing or image will come into focus next; he just knows that it will be plotted in the space of a vast yet coherent background of time and event.

Many literary worlds have influenced the author as his own universe has evolved. That the young David Mitchell was a fan of J. R. R. Tolkien is well documented, and he has talked at length about his realization, in a conversation with his editor, that he was building his own Middle Earth (MacLeod 2015). Ursula Le Guin and George R. R. Martin also number among those writers who have inspired his act of world-building, as Mitchell remarks: Le Guin's 'Earthsea is an archipelago, dense with islands at its centre and sparser at its edges, and after my first reading, it joined Tolkien's Middle-earth to form an elite fantasy-world super-league of two (George R. R. Martin's Westeros has since made it three, but C. S. Lewis's Narnia feels too fey and allegorical to qualify)' (Mitchell 2015). An oeuvre that consists of a single universe is attractive to him, because, in his own words, 'It lets me be the maximalist I dreamed of being when I was a kid, but also the "minimalist" writer making each book an island unto itself' (Hopf 2019: 184). This marrying of planetary scope with a human scale is perhaps also a result of Mitchell's childhood enjoyment of *Dungeons and Dragons*. The role-playing game allows a group of people to collectively imagine a universe while also working collaboratively to complete a quest, and Mitchell highlights this focus on human cooperation and friendship: 'It was a collaborative art form. It's something you all made. It was noncompetitive. It was based on cooperation, and you only won if you worked together ... it was simply the vehicle for the human interaction that made the whole thing so very enjoyable' (*Nightmare Magazine* 2016). Such comments highlight the author's early preoccupation with writing as a mode of creation that challenges and critiques violence.

Mitchell's literary influences extend far beyond fantasy, with key figures like Haruki Murakami, Italo Calvino and Hari Kunzru among the many authors for whom he has voiced admiration. The stamp of Murakami is so evident in *number9dream* that Mitchell has expressed his concern that the novel be more than just an 'homage or an imitation of Murakami – but I'm not the best person to make that judgment' (Begley 2010). Still, without Murakami we might never have seen the flowering of Mitchell's biblioverse – as he describes in the interview in this volume, it was admiration of Murakami that led Mitchell to write his first crossover character: 'I think I put Suhbataar the Mongolian gangster from *Ghostwritten* into *number9dream* because I thought it was cool how Haruki Murakami had the Sheep Man and a character called Noboru Watanabe appear in several of his novels. No motive further-reaching than "cool", really' (Hopf 2019: 183). Indeed, pure enjoyment and fascination seem to be the emphasis when Mitchell discusses his literary influences. He has described being 'magnetized' by Calvino's *If on a Winter's Night a Traveller* and calls the novel's intertextuality 'giddying' (Mitchell 2004). With its numerous interrupted and unfinished narratives, the novel is an acknowledged precursor to *Cloud Atlas*. Mitchell has discussed how his disappointment with those unfinished narratives, though they were, 'of course, the whole point of the book', eventually led him to the mirrored narrative structure of his third novel (Begley 2010).

Mitchell is an omnivorous reader, with an appetite that ranges across fiction and non-fiction as well as genres of literature. To offer one example, in a 2012 interview for the *Sunday Book Review*, Mitchell spoke of his great admiration for Chekov, Isaac Bashevis Singer, Dorothy Parker, Sylvia Townsend-Warner and Katherine Mansfield ('David Mitchell: By the Book'). In the same interview, he discusses young adult fiction, noting the importance of Philip Pullman, J. K. Rowling, Lemony Snicket, Michael Morpurgo and Neil Gaiman. At that time, his bedside reading included *Postwar* by Tony Judt; David Finkel's *The Good Soldiers*, an account of US forces in Iraq; and a proof of Nadeem Aslam's forthcoming book, *The Blind Man's Garden*. He cites Halldór Laxness's *Independent People* and Kevin Powers's *The Yellow Birds* as works he admires. In retrospect, it's not difficult to see how the author's interests in young adult fiction, the war in Iraq, fantasy writing, and Iceland ultimately came to shape *The Bone Clocks*. Tracking Mitchell's engagements with the literary marketplace remains an area where further research is needed in order to map and better assess the author's creative output, processes and influences.

Film is another significant reference point for Mitchell, whose works often make use of montage techniques or cuts that are informed by cinematic literacy and storytelling. Mitchell argues that 'film has altered the imagination of people', such that we 'imagine more visually ... in terms of a large projected rectangle' (Lopez 2010). When thinking about scenes in his own work, he mentions that sight is a dominant perception, which he attributes to movie watching. Among his influences, he cites the plotting of Alfred Hitchcock, the Wachowski's *The Matrix* as an existentialist action film and the storytelling of *The Wire* (Lopez 2010). The transmedia influence of cinematic and prose storytelling techniques can further be seen in *The Voorman Problem* (2013), directed by Mark Gill, which is adapted from the 'Panopticon' chapter of *number9dream*, a sequence that is presented as an action film. Similarly, *Cloud Atlas* contains a reference to a film entitled *The Ghastly Ordeal of Timothy Cavendish*, thus complicating the reader's engagement with that section of the narrative. Finally, it is notable that when Sonmi~451 appears in her orison form, it is reminiscent of Leia Skywalker's appearance in *Star Wars*, when a message from her is stored and replayed by R2-D2.

Disability has shaped Mitchell as a writer, both as a stammerer and parent of an autistic child. Mitchell observes, 'While I wouldn't say that stammering drove me to become a writer – this impulse comes from elsewhere – it did influence the type of writer I have become. What feels like a curse when you're younger can prove to be a long-term ally' ('David Mitchell: By the Book' 2012). Stammering appears to have heightened Mitchell's awareness of the words we choose, sometimes driving the author himself to find alternative ways to express himself. This verbal creativity is visible in *Black Swan Green*'s Jason Taylor, Mitchell's nominally autobiographical protagonist. Living with a disability involves coming up with creative strategies which can enable new insights and capacities to emerge, thus leading to alternative ways of expressing oneself that might not otherwise come into being. Persons with a disability can also encourage us to question the norms of coexistence and engage more empathetically with others. Initially, Mitchell and his wife translated *The Reason I Jump*, the work of autistic writer Naoki Higashida, for their son's therapists because it

> dissolves the lazy stereotype that people with autism are androids who don't feel. On the contrary, they feel everything, intensely. What's missing is the ability to communicate what they feel. Part of this is our fault – we're so busy being shocked, upset, irritated or looking the other way that we don't hear them. Shouldn't we learn how? (Mitchell 2013)

As a way of living, of confronting inequality and discrimination, disability has influenced Mitchell's creative strategies as well as his ethical perspective on human existence and capabilities. Arguably, this author's commitment to tackling social injustice and understanding of creativity stem, in part, from the influence disability has had on his own life.

Mitchell's literary universe has been profoundly influenced by his experiences as a voyager and map-maker: as a writer born in England, who has travelled and lived elsewhere, both through his imagined adventures in-and-across literary worlds as well as life experiences in Sicily, Japan and Ireland, among other places. In 'Start with the Map: A Writer's Lesson in Imagined Cartography' (2018), Mitchell remarks that 'the map itself becomes the blueprint for the fiction, so that, once you've worked out your map, the section of the story it depicts is pretty much plotted out' (Mitchell 2018). His fascination with map-making continues to this day, informing his creative processes. Mitchell's writing notebooks are filled with maps that help him to construct the plot, imagine characters, create scenes and understand 'the language and world view of the people' (Mitchell 2018) he represents. Such maps serve as navigational tools for discovering truths about the world:

> You lose yourself in them and find if not factual truth, then other kinds. You meditate upon them. You meet yourself in them. You co-opt them and set stories of your own there, or fragments of stories, at least. Fictitious maps give form to a thing – the imagination – that has no form. They are mysteries and answers to those mysteries. (Mitchell 2018)

His reflections on the role of cartography, such as that exemplified by the medieval *Mappa Mundi*, suggest that maps reveal historical mindsets and construct worldviews. Mitchell is keenly aware that one's map of the world need not remain fixed: that cartography itself is open to change and transformation, and thus might posit alternative mappings of the world. A shift in position, whether geographic, historical, cultural or subjective, can generate productive gaps, altered perspectives and fresh relations. This idea of cognitive mapping may be further extended to the author's efforts to map world-historical transformation, intervene in the literary field and engage in world-making activities, all of which are indicative of an author committed to storytelling as a transformative art and social practice. As such, any map – whether real, imaginary or a composite mixture of known and unknown geographies – represents an imaginative revisioning of the world.

Reception of Mitchell's work

Both Mitchell's admirers and detractors acknowledge the ambitious scope of his work. Daniel Mendelsohn called *Ghostwritten* 'sprawling and intimate … an intricately assembled Fabergé egg of a novel' (1999), emphasizing once again how Mitchell's storytelling places carefully observed human experience against a universe-sized backdrop. Sixteen years later, Pico Iyer described Mitchell in similar terms as a 'novelist who's always close to the soil and orbiting the heavens in the same breath' (2014). A. S. Byatt said *Ghostwritten* was 'the best first novel I have read in a long time' (1999); she praised Mitchell's skill in wrangling the vastness of his ideas: 'For all his plot's dazzling complexity, his writing which has many styles is always simple and elegant' (1999). Speaking of *Cloud Atlas*, she wrote:

> David Mitchell entices his readers on to a rollercoaster, and at first they wonder if they want to get off. Then – at least in my case – they can't bear the journey to end. Like Scheherazade, and like serialised Victorian

novels and modern soaps, he ends his episodes on cliffhangers and missed heartbeats. But unlike these, he starts his next tale in another place, in another time, in another vocabulary, and expects us to go through it all again. Trust the tale. He reaches a cumulative ending of all of them, and then finishes them all individually, giving a complete narrative pleasure that is rare. (2004)

Referring to Mitchell's oeuvre more generally, Kazuo Ishiguro remarks, 'We often get into the reflex of "this is important because", relegating literary worth to some secondary function. But when reading David for the first time, I was exhilarated – the exhilaration of being swept along into another, different world. It's sheer joy' (cited in Mason 2010). Many readers share Ishiguro's sense of wonder and delight in the vibrancy, richness and diversity of Mitchell's artistry.

Mitchell has been praised for his deft mastery of first-person narration and various popular literary genres and modes, but other stylistic choices have sometimes drawn criticism. Some readers have been less enthralled by Mitchell's work when he departs from first-person narration or his signature 'bravura displays of voice' (Boddy 2010), as was the case with *Thousand Autumns*. One reviewer remarked that the novel simply tried to pack in too many ideas, with the result that 'the characters function primarily as pieces on a literary board' (Boddy 2010). Other critics are wary of Mitchell's ideological tendencies. For instance, Fredric Jameson critiques *Cloud Atlas*, a novel which he admires in many ways, on account of the author's apparent desire for a story that offers a moral message 'as a sop to the reader who still needs "meanings"' (2015: 312). Jameson protests against the novel's plotting of the future, exclaiming, 'We have escaped the inevitable, inescapable peril, and the doom of history's desperate and repeated emprisonments, and are still alive!' (312). While this critic admires the historical novel that awakens a 'multitudinous coexistence in History itself' (313), he seems doubtful that Mitchell entirely achieves this aim. Similarly, one of Mitchell's most ardent admirers, A. S. Byatt, has been more cautious in her view of his recent work, *The Bone Clocks*, observing that 'Mitchell's novel just has too much material that is *ad hominem*: there are too many jokes about his other books or references to characters from his other work' (Walker 2014). *The Bone Clocks* won the World Fantasy Award (2015), but some critics have questioned the author's emphasis on world-building. James Wood claims that there is no doubt that Mitchell is a 'superb storyteller', but he is less convinced by the cosmological turn in his fiction: 'His cosmology seems an unconscious fantasy of the author-god, reinstating the novelist as omniscient deity, controlling, prodding, shaping, ending, rigging' (Wood 2014). Such criticisms begin to indicate possible pitfalls for an author striving to create an ever-expanding universe with each novelistic outing, and the insistence on keeping that universe singular and unified could prove more difficult as more publications appear.

At the heart of these debates lies the question of agency: whether the characters, however richly imagined and charismatic, are merely players in a preordained literary universe. Are the lives of characters and the plotting of history overdetermined by the larger plotting of history? One might well argue that Mitchell's work represents a sort of revival of Greek mythology and epic, a reversion to a world of divine intervention in which the course of events is shaped by warfare among the gods, battles between the forces of good and evil or supernatural conflicts. However, we suggest this is not the case, partly because Mitchell's cosmology is populated by figures who are closer to the superhuman heroes and villains of comic book universes, those who have either seized power through violence or been granted special gifts as a result of supernatural events. In Mitchell's case, the Anchorites have gained power through violent deeds of extraction and accumulation, while the Horologists have been granted the powers of reincarnation that they might bear witness to and intervene in long cycles of social change. Yet, both superhuman forces remain vulnerable participants within a larger drama of social transformation: no one figure or collective can determine the outcome of history. The story of social transformation is not one that can be easily contained within the span of a single human life. Through an account of interwoven narratives and cosmological forces, Mitchell reveals a larger narrative vision of the uneven dynamics, power struggles and affiliated moments of resistance that combine and coalesce to effect social change.

We thus find Mitchell at his most compelling when he projects a world of ongoing conflicts without resolution, ruminates on the volatile politics of storytelling and ambivalently encodes the problem of agency as an enduring human problem. *Ghostwritten* suggests: 'We all think we're in control of our lives, but really they're pre-ghostwritten by forces around us' (1999: 287). Another character laments, 'There's no future in stories. Stories are things of the past, things for museums. No place for stories in these market-democracy days' (1999: 172). Yet, another view suggests that storytelling enframes human existence: 'The human world is made of stories, not people. The people the stories use to tell themselves are not to be blamed' (1999: 378). Similarly, *Cloud Atlas* sets acts of failed and successful resistance against the backdrop of a long history of circulating stories that inspire and transform their readers or auditors. *The Bone Clocks* offers a satiric view of contemporary world literature, including its mocking account of the radical political hopes of Third World writers striving to find viable ways to resist neo-liberal globalization. In *Slade House*, a character observes that 'legends and stories are as full of dirty tricks as life is, and however much time has gone by nothing has changed, and all I have are memories' (2015: 132–3). Yet, in that novel, it is the objects, warnings and fragmentary memories transmitted between the victims that ultimately overthrow the perpetrators of violence. Stories, it seems, might exercise agency as they circulate through the world and gain traction, even when humans fail to master the course of their own narratives.

Unsurprisingly, Mitchell's work has emerged as a touchstone for debates about the role of fiction in our global era. *David Mitchell: Critical Essays* (2011) discusses the relationship between narrative and social change through its critique of Mitchell's first three novels, *Ghostwritten*, *number9dream* and *Cloud Atlas*. As the editor, Sarah Dillon, notes: 'The consensus seems to be that while Mitchell employs postmodern literary techniques, he does not adhere to the apolitical and antisocial nihilism of postmodernity with its ironic take on modern life and its paradoxical insistence on the inadequateness of narrative' (18). Instead of postmodern exhaustion, thus, Mitchell demonstrates 'the fertility, power and sustenance of fiction' (18). Peter Childs and James Green offer a compelling account of the planetary dimensions of Mitchell's work through its mappings of 'the fluid networks of globalization' (43) and thematic concerns with the interconnectedness of 'transmigratory dreamscapes' (44). An emphasis on narrative as a tool for forming identity is central to Courtney Hopf's discussion of 'the power and possibilities of life *as* narrative and narrative *as* life' (2011: 122), which highlights especially the ways in which history unfolds through acts of storytelling and narration. Literature's capacity to intervene in the world to express alternative imaginaries emerges as an important line of critique in postcolonial (Dunlop 2011), utopian (Edwards 2011) and Marxist-derived readings (Stephenson 2011) of the author's early fictions.

Tensions between the subject and the world, the local and the global, have been central to debates about Mitchell's representations of community in a global era. In *The Cosmopolitan Novel*, Berthold Schoene argues that Mitchell's novels 'rehearse the world-creative repercussions of attempting to reconcile individual singularity with communal incorporation' (2009: 122). He views *Ghostwritten* as representing a shift towards renewal of the novel as a cosmopolitan form of 'imagining the world instead of the nation' (Schoene 2010: 43). We see this stance reflected soon after in discussions of Mitchell as part of the 'cosmodern' turn, which positions his work in opposition to postmodernism's Eurocentrism and indeterminacy. Theo D'haen, for example, acknowledges that, formally, *Cloud Atlas* has 'an impeccably postmodern pedigree' (2013: 275) but argues that the narrative is rooted in representations of 'acts of belief ... that underwrite a truly "cosmic" humanity appropriate to our new age of "planetarity"' (280), and thus highlights Mitchell's synthesis of postmodern narrative technique with humanist concerns. A special issue of *C21 Literature: Journal of 21st-Century Writings* (2018), edited by Rose Harris-Birtill, has further contributed to the analysis of cosmopolitanism and cross-cultural reading practices. Kristian Shaw emphasizes the ethical dimensions of Mitchell's 'fantastical cosmopolitanism' as a way to confront global inequalities and corrosive ecological practices, while exploring 'individual and communal ethical agency' (2018: 16), while Ryan Trimm argues that 'spiritual bonds between characters: ghosts, reincarnations, and migrating spirits help bridge disparate story lines' (2018: 1), such that a more complex understanding of the world in its materiality and alterity comes into being. Rose Harris-Birtill's *David Mitchell's Post-Secular World* (2019) offers an incisive analysis of the author's Buddhist-inspired poetic universe, with particular attention given to the mandalic mappings at work in the author's macronovel.

Some critics consider border-crossing moments in Mitchell's works, analysing how his fictions traverse time and space, cross cultures and transgress established boundaries. For instance, Douglas Coupland views Mitchell as a writer of a new genre of 'translit novels', which 'cross history without being historical; they span geography without changing psychic place' (2012). According to Coupland, 'Translit collapses time and space as it seeks to generate narrative traction in the reader's mind. It inserts the contemporary reader into other locations and times, while leaving no doubt that its viewpoint is relentlessly modern and speaks entirely of our extreme present' (2012). However, Coupland's argument overlooks the fact that Mitchell seeks to interrogate and remediate the present through his engagements with history across cultures. His works are fraught with political and ethical self-consciousness: creativity is harnessed as an active form of world-making activity. Forays into other places and times, across borders, can also work to reimagine temporality, particularly through Mitchell's reliance on translation as a trope that enables a plurality of readings and writings to surface through complex processes of circulation and reinscription (Walkowitz 2015; Larsonneur 2018). Likewise, Eva-Maria Schmitz shows how Mitchell's representations of islands serve to reimagine the world as a space of relation and interconnection through time and space (2018). Mitchell's works do not merely project contemporary anxieties onto history or collapse time and space; they also reimagine contemporary world horizons through efforts to expand knowledge about specific and related moments of exchange, translation and reception.

The study of time and alternative temporalities offers ethical and political critiques of Mitchell's efforts to represent history as well as speculate on the future of the planet. Patrick O'Donnell's monograph, *A Temporary Future: The Fiction of David Mitchell* (2015), reflects on the apocalyptic futures imagined in the author's work as well as the future of fiction. Beginning with *Ghostwritten* and ending with *The Bone Clocks*, this single-author study offers both a diligent overview of the interconnections between Mitchell's novels. Paying tribute to commonly invoked frameworks like cosmopolitanism and planetary fiction, O'Donnell also suggests new theoretical linkages in his discussions of temporality by emphasizing a psychogeographic tendency in Mitchell's work. Temporality, O'Donnell argues, is contingent for both Mitchell's protagonists and his readers, precisely because 'each party navigates narrative terrains that continuously shift in terms of affect, relationality, and connectivity' (13). As Mitchell's novels meander through time and space, they 'engender a certain temporality of reading' (28), driven partly by readers' recognition of intertextual elements. Further consideration of Mitchell's work with relation to time is evident in a 2015 special issue of *SubStance*, edited by Paul Harris and entitled 'David Mitchell and the Labyrinth of Time'. As Harris notes in his introduction to the issue: 'His work is mapping the deep past of the human species; its evolution into an active force in natural history; and its future prospects in light of its technological innovations and the voracious exploitation of resources that comes with them' (2015: 5). Contributors to this special issue consider Mitchell's 'thought-experiments in a laboratory of time' (2015: 5), with an emphasis on the critique of post-human temporality (Boulter 2015), responses to Big History (Shoop and Ryan 2015) and the cultural politics that arises from the disruption of linear temporality (Hooks 2015; Harris-Birtill 2015; Parker 2015; Ng 2015; Larsonneur 2015). Discussions of slow time (Harris 2018), historical/alternative temporalities (Eve 2018; Parker 2018; Polanki 2018) and the (post)apocalypse (Mitchell and Faber 2014; Bayer 2015; Hicks 2016; De Cristofaro 2018; Dimovitz 2018) further develop this trajectory of analysis.

Another important strand of criticism considers Mitchell's work in the context of world-literary debates surrounding the textual politics of creativity, publishing, translation, dissemination and reception in our global era. Three readings of *Cloud Atlas* exemplify this kind of interpretive approach. Martin Paul Eve (2016) presents a comparative analysis of how different editorial practices in America and Britain resulted in the publication, dissemination and circulation (via French translation) of markedly variant editions of *Cloud Atlas* across media. Eve argues for world-literary reading practices that accommodate the various interpretations arising from textual variants as they 'alter various political, historical, intertextual and characterological elements of the text and particularly affect the pacing and degree of foresight available to the reader' (Eve 2016: 16). Critics have remarked on the global and/or planetary dimensions of Mitchell's work from the start, but Jason Mezey (2011) inaugurated a world-literary critique of *Cloud Atlas* when he drew on the work of Immanuel Wallerstein to demonstrate that this 'epic of globalization' (30) tracks 'multiple short cycles recursively operating within longer cycles' (31) to expose the processes of transformation, such that active reading processes foreground the ethics 'implicit in narrative creation and consumption' (31), both as represented in the text and as enacted in the world. Wendy Knepper (2016) extends this kind of epic reading of *Cloud Atlas* to argue for the radical politics of Mitchell's work as it experimentally challenges the inequalities associated with combined and uneven development. Her work demonstrates that Mitchell's world-making fiction fosters new critical world literacies and alternative knowledges. Where Eve tracks the impact of publishing and circulation on the dissemination of *Cloud Atlas* as a work of world literature, Knepper considers how Mitchell seeks to create change in the world by disseminating alternative accounts of social transformation.

As a creative artist and cultural critic, David Mitchell has emerged as an active participant in the revival of world literature in a global era.

His work shares much in common with those radical political writers of world literature today – such as Orhan Pamuk, Roberto Bolaño, Margaret Atwood, Amitav Ghosh, Yan Lianke, Nnedi Okorafor, Hari Kunzru, Chimamanda Ngozi Adichie, Alexis Wright, Edwidge Danticat and China Mieville, to name a few – who strive to democratize world culture, challenge hegemonic development, stake claims on behalf of the oppressed and dispossessed, and speculate on global futures. Mitchell describes himself as a 'slow-time political writer' (Hopf 2019: 193), one who is deeply influenced by politics but reluctant to offer opinions in the explicit ways that a politically engaged author such as Hari Kunzru might do (Hopf 2019: 193). Nonetheless, both authors share a commitment to the art and politics of storytelling – the very exercise of creative freedoms – as a socially committed intervention in the world and its narrative traditions. Such a radical world literature acknowledges the formative influence of the capitalist world-system as it exerts pressure on life and literature, but it also seeks to challenge such inequities by circulating an alternative, pluralistic, vision of transformation.

David Mitchell's politics can perhaps best be understood though his approach to building an imaginary world – a literary universe – that uneasily resembles our own and critically engages with our own realities, yet freely challenges known history to inscribe alternative realities. Cosmological warfare lies at the heart of an epic oeuvre that chronicles recurring battles and conflicts over the fate of humanity and the planet. Cannibalistic and vampiric presences make manifest the violent accumulative and predatory actions of empire and capitalism throughout a long history, even as the narrative speculates on the global futures and (post)apocalypse to come. Simultaneously, the transmission and recycling of stories accompanied by the transmigration and reincarnation of souls work together to construct fresh trans-narrative, cross-cultural and long historical mappings of the world. Stylistically, Mitchell mobilizes popular cultural genres of the global literary marketplace – such as the thriller, crime fiction, science fiction, fantasy and the (neo)Gothic novel – to represent and interrogate the global order. Equally, his fictions reclaim and disseminate peripheral perspectives, folk culture, cosmological forms and narratives of dispossession to constitute a vision of the world that challenges dispossession and cultural erasure. As an imaginary world-builder, David Mitchell disseminates a story of the world that engages readers as participants and co-creators in world-making struggles over social transformation.

Overview of collection

This special collection considers the ethics and politics of Mitchell's world-making aesthetic as well as the scope and scale of his literary universe. His multi-scalar fictions interrogate the relationship between the personal and the planetary, investigating the relationship between systemic change and subjective development. In this collection, the chapters are presented largely in chronological order, following the date of publication for both novels and operatic works. Such an approach allows the reader to track the course of the author's shifting aesthetic throughout his career. To offer another pathway through the collection, we would like to introduce the chapters in terms of the relationships between arguments and themes, pointing out the kinds of critical perspectives that emerge through recurring styles or formal strategies in Mitchell's fictional universe.

Globalization is a central concern in Mitchell's work, informing both the content and the form of his novels, and a key focus in the essays by Hugh O'Connell and William Stephenson. O'Connell's reading of *Ghostwritten: A Novel in Nine Parts* focuses on issues of narrative construction, particularly the tensions between the novel's titular claim that it consists of nine parts and the fact that the novel actually includes a tenth part, entitled 'Underground.' For O'Connell, this is one of the many reality gaps that structure a novel that maps and resists the totalizing operations of the capitalist world-system, thus fulfilling a utopian function. William Stephenson considers how *The Thousand Autumns of Jacob de Zoet* confronts the historical past, even as it discloses fresh ways of negotiating past–present relations in global contexts. His analysis highlights the challenges posed by cross-cultural barriers to understanding, both as figured within the chronicle of history as well as through oblique allusions to contemporary events where similar difficulties persist. Uncanny feelings and ghostly apparitions create a non-linear understanding of temporality that disrupts and complicates the world-historical chronicle.

Personal and collective trauma are the subjects of the chapters by Rose Harris-Birtill and Jason Howard Mezey. Harris-Birtill examines the two operas for which Mitchell has written libretti, *Wake* (2010) and *Sunken Garden* (2013) to assess how they contribute to his 'biblioverse', both through their thematic concerns and via characters who appear in the novels. Approaching the two operas as *Gesamtkunstwerke*, or total works of art, Harris-Birtill explores how each opera invokes the Buddhist concept of samsara, or the cycle of life and death, and asserts that this approach highlights the ethical concerns of Mitchell's writing. Reflecting on the relationship between individual and collective trauma, Harris-Birtill claims that Mitchell's libretti move beyond a subjective focus on individual trauma to evoke a world of collective adaptation, recovery and survival. Mezey considers *Cloud Atlas* in connection with debates about postcolonial trauma and social transformation. His readings of 'The Pacific Journey of Adam Ewing' and 'Sloosha's Crossin' an' Ev'rythin' After' demonstrate how the novel's form acts uniquely on the reader to produce effects that both mimic traumatic experience and insist upon the importance of recognizing the trauma of others. As each narrative breaks off, it enters a period of latency as the reader continues through the text only to return to it much later, such that the reader becomes actively involved in the traumatic processes of working through the aftermath and consequences of historical violence. With Adam Ewing's journey towards the abolitionist cause, Mezey argues that *Cloud Atlas* shows how the acknowledgement of others' trauma can serve as a precondition for ethical action.

Martin Paul Eve and Treasa De Loughry consider the intersections of power, technology and ecology. In his reading of *Cloud Atlas*, Eve draws on the concept of technology as *pharmakon*, that which is both remedy and poison, to trace how Mitchell's representations of technology negotiate a conflicted understanding of temporality in terms of oscillations between progress and regression. Eve considers the Janus-faced nature of technological progress through each of the novel's sections, including communication technologies, nuclear power, train travel, human cloning and the ultimate regression from technological advancement in 'Sloosha's Crossin' an' Everythin' After'. Treasa De Loughry traces Mitchell's engagement with eco-crisis and civilizational collapse across *Ghostwritten*, *Cloud Atlas*, *The Bone Clocks*, and Mitchell's short story 'The Siphoners'. This world-ecological critique examines how Mitchell's works negotiate dual constructions of power, understood both as a form of social behaviour and scarce energy resource. De Loughry traces Mitchell's sharp critique of history, noting the tensions between deterministic and transformative perspectives about human agency in Mitchell's oeuvre. Like O'Connell (2015), she argues that the novel's pessimistic view of history is countered by utopianism via the seeding of political resistance through individual actions and narrative acts of resistance.

Tales of young characters in crisis often feature in Mitchell's work, and his critics are quick to apply the *Bildungsroman* label to certain novels. Focusing on thirteen-year-old protagonist Jason Taylor, Courtney Hopf's chapter on *Black Swan Green* explores how the novel addresses the relationship between disability and creative expression. Hopf argues that disability is a prism through which Mitchell can refract his humanist interest in the intersections of power, language and identity, and demonstrates that the novel's formal construction replicates the stammer experienced by its protagonist. Even as the novel maps the challenges presented by a disability, it also attests to the ways in which disability serves as a form of capability, particularly as a mode of resistance. In this novel, the stammering pauses and hesitations enable the creation of meaning, both for the disabled person, Jason as a budding writer, and the reader who engages with the text. Nick Bentley's reading of *number9dream* considers Mitchell's innovative coming-of-age story as a quest narrative. As a struggling teenager in search of his father, protagonist Eiji Miyake fits the *Bildungsroman* label, yet Bentley argues that it is the novel itself that is on a quest: one that seeks to express the post-postmodern condition by moving beyond postmodern irony towards an affirmation of alternatives that may well lie beyond the power of language to describe. In his reading of the nonsensical phrases, meaning across cultures and the open space of dreaming, Bentley insists on the social hope intrinsic to Mitchell's characteristic gesture towards a plurality of meanings and the alternatives that lie beyond the constraints of the prevailing narrative. For Chris Koenig-Woodyard, *The Bone Clocks* should be understood as an Anthropocene Bildungsroman: one in which the individual's coming-of-age story raises questions about the full scale of human development. His analysis considers the relationship between the longue durée of human existence as well as shorter scale of biological life, with the claim that Mitchell's fiction represents a *Bildungsroman* of *Bildungsromane*. The chapter ends with a deft analysis of the cultural geographies and geologies that emerge in Mitchell's work, showing how the realistic and fantastical converge to imagine alternatives to prevailing configurations of time and space.

Finally, the collection considers Mitchell as a world-builder whose fictions seek to pluralize the field of world literature and by extension democratize the world imaginary. Wendy Knepper's analysis considers the politics of Mitchell's world-building activities as an Über-novelist, particularly through the critical irrealism of *The Bone Clocks* and *Slade House*. Across these works, a thematic emphasis on cosmological warfare and animacide highlights the violence inherent in global economic life, even as Mitchell's world-making fantasy seeds dissent and re-articulates freedom as an ongoing collective struggle. Mitchell's radical poetics challenge inequality by seeking to reincorporate the histories, cultures and narratives that have been stifled or extinguished through a long global history of underdevelopment and violent transformation. This final chapter leads nicely to Courtney Hopf's exclusive interview with David Mitchell, which provides readers with a clear overview of the author's fictional universe in his own words, while also delving into new ideas and concepts of world-building. The interview ranges from discussions of the Über-novel to the role of genre and the influence of comics on Mitchell's understanding of narrative. It also addresses the direction and future his novels may travel in time and space. This interview offers a fascinating insight into Mitchell's own understanding of his role as a writer committed to the critique of power (and its abuses) as well as to the optimistic hope of social transformation.

Overall, this collection addresses the vast scale and ambitious creative vision of David Mitchell's work, seeking to shed fresh light on the politics and ethics of his world-building oeuvre. Through a sustained emphasis on the author's creative strategies, this collection considers how the author maps and challenges inequality, even as he explores the possibilities for agency and collective transformation along more affirmative lines. We position Mitchell as an author concerned with fictional world-making in the most profound sense as he seeks to understand the world in which we live as well as to explore the alternative horizons immanent within history or possible in a projected future. His cosmological and fantastical fictional universe confronts the realities of our world, even as it departs freely to consider the alternative story humanity might construct through more equitable and sustainable relations with others and the planet. By offering fresh critical perspectives on Mitchell's creative processes, we encourage students and academics alike to investigate how this oeuvre sparks critique and dissent, perhaps even ignites change, in our era of global capitalist crisis and transition.

Works cited

Bayer, G. (2015), 'Perpetual Apocalypses: David Mitchell's *Cloud Atlas* and the Absence of Time', *Critique: Studies in Contemporary Fiction*, 56(4), 345–54.

Begley, A. (2010), 'David Mitchell, The Art of Fiction no. 204', *The Paris Review*, 52, 169–200. Available online: https://www.the paris review.org/interviews/6034/david-mitchell-the-art-of-fiction-no-204-david-mitchell (accessed 1 October 2016).

Birnbaum, R. (2006), 'David Mitchell', *The Morning News*, 11 May. Available online: http://www.themorningnews.org/article/david-mitchell (accessed 8 March 2016).

Boddy, K. (2010), '*The Thousand Autumns of Jacob de Zoet* by David Mitchell: Review', *The Daily Telegraph*, 3 July. Available online: http://www.telegraph.co.uk/culture/books/bookreviews/7865861/The-Thousand-Autumns-of-Jacob-de-Zoet-by-David-Mitchell-review.html (accessed 1 October 2016).

Boulter, J. (2015), 'Posthuman Temporality: Mitchell's *Ghostwritten*', *SubStance*, 44(1), 18–38.

Byatt, A. S. (1999), 'Wild Whirl of a Ghostly World', *Mail on Sunday*, 26 September, 7.

Byatt, A. S. (2004), 'Overlapping Lives', *The Guardian*, 6 March. Available online: https://www.theguardian.com/books/2004/mar/06/fiction.asbyatt (accessed 27 August 2016).

Childs, P. and J. Green (2011), 'The Novels in Nine Parts', in S. Dillon (ed.), *David Mitchell: Critical Essays*, Canterbury: Gylphi, 25–47.

Coupland, D. (2012), 'Convergences', *The New York Times*, 8 March. Available online: http://www.nytimes.com/2012/03/11/books/review/gods-without-men-by-hari-kunzru.html?pagewanted=all&_r=0 (accessed 28 September 2016).

'David Mitchell' (2015), 'The Stuttering Foundation', 27 May. Available online: https://www.stutteringhelp.org/content/david-mitchell (accessed 29 September 2016).

'David Mitchell: By the Book' (2012), *The New York Times, Sunday Book Review*, 18 October. Available online: http://www.nytimes.com/2012/10/21/books/review/david-mitchell-by-the-book.html?_r=0 (accessed 29 September 2016).

De Cristofaro, D. (2018), '"Time, No Arrow, No Boomerang, but a Concertina": *Cloud Atlas* and the Anti-apocalyptic Critical Temporalities of the Contemporary Post-apocalyptic Novel', *Critique: Studies in Contemporary Fiction*, 59(2), 243–57.

Dillon, S. (2011), 'Introducing David Mitchell's Universe: A Twenty-First Century House of Fiction', in S. Dillon (ed.), *David Mitchell: Critical Essays*, Canterbury: Gylphi, 3–23.

Dimovitz, S. A. (2018), 'Schrödinger's Cat Metalepsis and the Political Unwriting of the Postmodern Apocalypse in David Mitchell's Recent Works', *C21 Literature: Journal of 21st-Century Writings*, 6(3). Available online: https://doi.org/10.16995/c21.50 (accessed 22 October 2018).

Dunlop, N. (2011), 'Speculative Fiction as Postcolonial Critique in *Ghostwritten* and *Cloud Atlas*', in S. Dillon (ed.), *David Mitchell: Critical Essays*, Canterbury: Gylphi, 201–24.

Edwards, C. (2011), '"Strange Transactions": Utopia, Transmigration and Time in *Ghostwritten* and *Cloud Atlas*', in S. Dillon (ed.), *David Mitchell: Critical Essays*, Canterbury: Gylphi, 177–200.

Eve, M. P. (2016), 'You Have to Keep Track of your Changes': The Version Variants and Publishing History of David Mitchell's *Cloud Atlas*', *Open Library of Humanities*, 2(2), 1–34. Available online: http://dx.doi.org/10.16995/olh.82 (accessed 12 October 2016).

Eve, M. P. (2018), 'The Historical Imaginary of Nineteenth-Century Style in David Mitchell's *Cloud Atlas*', *C21 Literature: Journal of 21st-Century Writings*, 6(3). Available online: https://doi.org/10.16995/c21.46 (accessed 22 October 2018).

Finney, B. (2014), 'Adding to the Übernovel: Why David Mitchell Does What He Does', *LA Review of Books*, 28 September. Available online: https://larevie wofbooks.org/article/adding-ubernovel-david-mitchell/# (accessed 10 September 2016).

Harris, P. A. (2015), 'David Mitchell in the Laboratory of Time: An Interview with the Author', *SubStance*, 44(1), 8–17.

Harris P. A. (2018), 'In the Labyrinth of Slow Time: "A Perturbation in the Deep Stream" and "A Perambulation in the Deep Stream"', *C21 Literature: Journal of 21st-Century Writings*, 6(3). Available online: https://doi.org/10.16995/c21.61 (accessed 22 October 2018).

Harris-Birtill, R. (2015), '"A Row of Screaming Russian Dolls": Escaping the Panopticon in David Mitchell's *number9dream*', *SubStance*, 44(1), 55–70.

Harris-Birtill, R. (2019), *David Mitchell's Post-Secular World: Buddhism, Belief and the Urgency of Compassion*, London and New York: Bloomsbury Academic, 2019.

Hicks, H. J. (2016), '"This Time Round": David Mitchell's *Cloud Atlas* and the Apocalyptic Problem of Historicism', *The Post-Apocalyptic Novel in the Twenty-First Century: Modernity Beyond Salvage*, New York: Palgrave Macmillan, 54–76.

Hooks, S. (2015), 'Palter & Prescience: On David Mitchell's *Ghostwritten*', *SubStance*, 44(1), 39–54.

Hopf, C. (2011), 'The Stories We Tell: Discursive Identity Through Narrative Form in *Cloud Atlas*', in *David Mitchell: Critical Essays*, Canterbury: Gylphi, 105–26.

Hopf, C. (2019), 'Creating a Fictional Universe: An Interview with David Mitchell', in W. Knepper and C. Hopf (eds), *David Mitchell: Contemporary Critical Perspectives*, London and New York: Bloomsbury Academic, 183–94.

Iyer, P. (2014), 'Juggling Worlds', *The New York Times Book Review*, 28 August. Available online: http://www.nytimes.com/2014/08/31/books/review/the-bone -clocks-by-david-mitchell.html?_r=0 (accessed 10 September 2016).

Jameson, F. (2015), *The Antinomies of Realism*, London: Verso.

Keating, S. (2014), 'David Mitchell: "Who cares if a book is highbrow or lowbrow. Is it any good or not?"', *The Irish Times*, 27 October. Available online: https://www.irishtimes.com/culture/books/david-mitchell-who-cares-if-a-book-is-highbrow-or-lowbrow-is-it-any-good-or-not-1.1977387 (accessed 01 February 2018).

Kirtley, D. B. (2016), 'Interview: David Mitchell', *Nightmare Magazine*, 41, February. Available online: http://www.nightmare-magazine.com/nonfiction/interview-david-mitchell/ (accessed 10 September 2016).

Knepper, W. (2016), 'Towards a Theory of Experimental World Epic: David Mitchell's *Cloud Atlas*', *ariel: A Review of International English Literature*, 47(1–2), 93–126.

Larsonneur, C. (2015), 'Revisiting Dejima (Japan): from Recollections to Fiction in David Mitchell's *The Thousand Autumns of Jacob de Zoet (2010)*', *SubStance*, 44(1), 136–47.

Larsonneur, C. B. (2018), 'Oblique Translations in David Mitchell's Works', *C21 Literature: Journal of 21st-Century Writings*, 6(3). Available online: https://doi.org/10.16995/c21.53 (accessed 22 October 2018).

Lopez, J. (2010). 'Q&A with David Mitchell, Literary Platypus', *Vanity Fair*, 20 July. Available online: https://www.vanityfair.com/culture/2010/07/qa-with-david-mitchell-literary-platypus (accessed 01 February 2018).

MacLeod, M. (2015), 'David Mitchell: "I have created my own Middle Earth"', *The Guardian*, 17 August. Available online: https://www.theguardian.com/books/2015/aug/17/david-mitchell-i-have-created-my-own-middle-earth (accessed 10 September 2016).

Mason, W. (2010), 'David Mitchell: The Experimentalist', *The New York Times Magazine*, 25 June. Available online: http://www.nytimes.com/2010/06/27/magazine/27mitchell-t.html?_r=0 (accessed 10 September 2016).

Mendelsohn, D. (2000), 'Big Blue Marble', *New York Magazine*, 18 September. Available online: http://nymag.com/nymetro/arts/books/reviews/3773/ (accessed 10 September 2016).

Mezey, J. H. (2011), '"A Multitude of Drops": Recursion and Globalization in David Mitchell's *Cloud Atlas*', *Modern Language Studies*, 40(2), 10–37.

Mitchell, D. (1999), *Ghostwritten*, New York: Vintage.

Mitchell, D. (2001), *number9dream*, London: Sceptre.

Mitchell, D. (2004), *Cloud Atlas*, London: Sceptre.

Mitchell, D. (2004), 'Enter the Maze', *The Guardian*, 22 May. Available online: https://www.theguardian.com/books/2004/may/22/fiction.italocalvino (accessed 20 November 2017).

Mitchell, D. (2006), *Black Swan Green*, London: Sceptre.

Mitchell, D. (2010), *Wake*, Nationale Reisopera, Enschede.

Mitchell, D. (2011), 'My Hero: Kate Bush', *The Guardian*, 1 January. Available online: https://www.theguardian.com/books/2011/jan/01/kate-bush-hero-david-mitchell (accessed 10 September 2016).

Mitchell, D. (2013), 'David Mitchell: Learning to Live with My Son's Autism', *The Guardian*, 29 June. Available online: https://www.theguardian.com/society/2013/jun/29/david-mitchell-my-sons-autism (accessed 10 September 2016).

Mitchell, D. (2013), *Sunken Garden*, English National Opera, London.

Mitchell, D. (2014), 'Before the Dawn', With Kate Bush, monologue in live production.

Mitchell, D. (2014), *The Bone Clocks*, London: Sceptre.
Mitchell, D. (2014), 'Guardian Reader Event: David Mitchell', Royal Geographic Society, London.
Mitchell, D. (2015), 'David Mitchell on Earthsea – A Rival to Tolkien and George RR Martin', *The Guardian*, 23 October. Available online: https://www.theguardian.com/books/2015/oct/23/david-mitchell-wizard-of-earthsea-tolkien-george-rr-martin (accessed 10 September 2016).
Mitchell, D. (2015), *Slade House*, London: Sceptre.
Mitchell, D. (2018), 'Start with the Map: A Writer's Lessons in Imaginary Cartography', *The New Yorker*, 13 September. Available online: https://www.newyorker.com/books/page-turner/start-with-the-map (accessed 15 October 2018).
Mitchell, D. and M. Faber (2014), 'David Mitchell and Michel Faber On Apocalypse', *Canongate*, 25 November. Available online: https://www.youtube.com/watch?reload=9&v=HreyY2MH2fA (accessed 12 October 2016).
Ng, L. (2015), 'Cannibalism, Colonialism and Apocalypse in Mitchell's Global Future', *SubStance*, 44(1), 107–22.
O'Donnell, P. (2015), *A Temporary Future: The Fiction of David Mitchell*, London and New York: Bloomsbury Academic.
Parker, J. A. (2015), 'From Time's Boomerang to Pointillist Mosaic: Translating *Cloud Atlas* into Film', *SubStance*, 44(1), 123–35.
Parker, J. A. (2018), 'Mind the Gap(s): Holly Sykes's Life, the "Invisible" War, and the History of the Future in *The Bone Clocks*', *C21 Literature: Journal of 21st-Century Writings*, 6(3). Available online: https://doi.org/10.16995/c21.47 (accessed 22 October 2018).
Polanki, G. (2018), 'The Iterable Messiah: Postmodernist Mythopoeia in *Cloud Atlas*', *C21 Literature: Journal of 21st-Century Writings*, 6(3). Available online: https://doi.org/10.16995/c21.59 (accessed 22 October 2018).
Schoene, B. (2009), 'The World Begins Its Turn with You, or How David Mitchell's Novels Think', in *The Cosmopolitan Novel*, Edinburgh: Edinburgh University Press, 97–125.
Schoene, B. (2010), '"Tour du Monde": David Mitchell's *Ghostwritten* and the Cosmopolitan Imagination', *College Literature*, 37(4), 42–60.
Shaw, K. (2018), '"Some Magic is Normality": Fantastical Cosmopolitanism in David Mitchell's *The Bone Clocks*', *C21 Literature: Journal of 21st-Century Writings*, 6(3). Available online: https://doi.org/10.16995/c21.52 (accessed 22 October 2018).
Shoop, C. and D. Ryan (2015), '"Gravid with the Ancient Future": *Cloud Atlas* and the Politics of Big History', *SubStance*, 44(1), 92–106.
Stephenson, W. (2011), 'Moonlight Bright as a UFO Abduction: Science Fiction, Present-Future Alienation and Cognitive Mapping', in S. Dillon (ed.), *David Mitchell: Critical Essays*, Canterbury: Gylphi, 225–46.
Trimm, R. (2018), 'Spirits in the Material World: Spectral Worlding in David Mitchell's *Ghostwritten* and *Cloud Atlas*', *C21 Literature: Journal of 21st-Century Writings*, 6(3). Available online: https://doi.org/10.16995/c21.63 (accessed 22 October 2018).
The Wachowskis (2015, 2016–18), *Sense8*, Netflix, seasons one and two.
Walker, T. (2014), 'AS Byatt's Feud with Her Sister Margaret Drabble Goes On and On', *The Telegraph*, 11 September. Available online: http://www.telegraph.co.u

k/culture/culturenews/11087784/A-S-Byatts-feud-with-her-sister-Margaret-Dra bble-goes-on-and-on.html (accessed 29 September 2016).

Walkowitz, R. L. (2015), 'English as a Foreign Language: David Mitchell and the Born-Translated Novel', *SubStance*, 44(2), 30–46.

Wood, J. (2014), 'Soul Cycle', *The New Yorker*, 8 September. Available online: http://www.newyorker.com/magazine/2014/09/08/soul-cycle (accessed 29 September 2016).

1

Globalization in David Mitchell's *Ghostwritten*: Minding 'the reality gap'

Hugh Charles O'Connell

Chapter summary

This chapter draws on Marxist perspectives and world-systems theory to offer a fresh critical reading of the representation of globalization in David Mitchell's *Ghostwritten: A Novel in 9 Parts*. The analysis pays close attention to the various reality gaps that structure this narrative, beginning with the fact that the novel subverts its own titular claims by incorporating a supplemental tenth section, entitled 'Underground'. Elsewhere the novel foregrounds tensions and contradictions within the capitalist world-system by calling attention to the problematic relationship between the narrative whole and its parts, such as through the interplay of genres within a single work or its thematic emphasis on struggles to position the self in the global order. Altogether, Mitchell's *Ghostwritten* maps and renders perceptible the totalizing dimensions of late capitalism, and in so doing, the novel fulfils a utopian function by rendering globalizing processes open to critique.

Introduction

Ghostwritten: A Novel in 9 Parts is comprised of nine discrete, first-person narratives, set in nine different locations that move from the East to the West (Okinawa, Tokyo, Hong Kong, Holy Mountain in China, Mongolia, St. Petersburg, London, Clear Island and New York). Each section has its own distinctive first-person narrator and generic influences, such that the novel comes to mediate the ghost story, techno-thriller, science fiction, romance story (with a 'meet cute' scenario) and heist narrative. Consequently, it takes the addition of a narratively excluded tenth part, 'Underground', to act as a supplemental coda that brings the themes and locations of the nine proper chapters into relation with one another. Taken together, the novel's form and content foreground the difficulties of mapping a globalized world, particularly through its thematic emphasis on subjects struggling to understand their own position. Drawing on the work of Fredric Jameson and world-systems theory, this chapter offers a new critical perspective on the structures and themes of *Ghostwritten*, a novel that maps globalization and interrogates its inner workings. In this chapter, I argue that the novel's fragmented narrative structure replicates the totalizing expansiveness of globalization as well as its decentred and disjunctive aspects. *Ghostwritten* presents an innovative formal solution to the crises of the individual's unknowable location within the shifting matrix of global late capitalism, even as it critiques globalization as a totalizing economic force.

Global novel form: Totality, cognitive mapping and utopianism

Positioning *Ghostwritten* as a critique of globalization is not new. Caroline Edwards (2011), Nicholas Dunlop (2011) and William Stephenson (2011) have argued for the oppositional political possibilities that emerge through *Ghostwritten*'s mobilization of genre conventions to produce striking critiques of late capitalism. However, despite these important interventions, most analyses of *Ghostwritten* all too hastily reject any notion of totality, whether at the formal level, as a heuristic, or as the systemic nature of capitalism. Instead, critics often provide an objective description of the decentralizing factors of globalization alongside its more positive corollary: the development of a cosmopolitan subjectivity that arises in the transition from the national to the global. Yet, as Steven Shaviro reminds us, globalization has not so much produced cosmopolitical agency, as it has furthered 'the "real subsumption" of all relations of production and consumption … of life under capital' (2012: 384). Not just labour, but all aspects of everyday life, from leisure to education, are brought under the sway of 'financial speculation, which extracts "value" from them at every turn' (2012: 384). Thus, rather than producing new historical agencies that can challenge the systemic nature of globalization, the production of systemically subjugated individuals is inextricable from late capitalism itself.

What is required, then, is a shift in emphasis away from the individual as the subject of history and towards the totality of the world-system of global capitalism. As David Cunningham argues, the novel of capitalist modernity is best understood 'not as an epic of the bourgeois "people", but as a displaced account of "the system of capitalism itself"' (2010: 14). If 'the novel is the epic form of a world which "has become infinitely *large*", ... then surely the "form-problem" of such unending richness will be constituted ... by the impossible "totality" of capital itself' (18). It is in this light that I want to restore 'totality' to the conversation about *Ghostwritten* by turning to the relationship between globalization, subjective experience and cognitive mapping. Given the abstract nature and diffuse structure of the capitalist world-system, not to mention its global scale, its representation poses what Alberto Toscano and Jeff Kinkle call an 'aesthetic problem', since 'capitalism as a totality is devoid of an easily grasped command-and-control centre' (2015: 24). Imagining and representing the post-fordist conditions of globalization becomes like trying to represent the internet: portals, nodes and pathways appear and disappear, seemingly at random, rendering its operations as paradoxically ubiquitous and invisible. The aesthetic problem, then, lies in finding 'ways of making the invisible visible' (2015: 25). This imperative to register the invisible traces of late capitalism in the form of the cultural text is what Fredric Jameson labels cognitive mapping.

Ghostwritten's cognitive mapping of globalization eschews the postmodern novel's characteristic decentring of the narrative/protagonist/reader. Instead, it employs a narrative structure that involves the discrete plots of its foundational nine chapters, suggesting that the specificity and the centeredness of closed fictional forms is central to its aesthetic. However, each chapter includes minute coincidental remainders, a certain surplus contingency whereby characters' actions leap the bounds of their own narratives and obliquely link up with others. Reflecting on this tendency, Mitchell identifies his style as the 'compounded short story' (qtd. in Dillon 2011: 4) and goes on to argue that 'short stories have a background noise that creates the illusion that the world is much bigger than the mere 10 or 15 pages, and I wanted to see if I could sync up the white noise of the background of short stories' (5). It's this emphasis on the 'background noise' that makes Mitchell's novel stand out; while each story has its own contained, subjectively and spatially organized narrative, this 'sync up' of the background noise of the larger world is an apt metaphor for cognitive mapping, for registering the imprint of the capitalist world-system in the form of the artwork.

Significantly, cognitive mapping is predicated on a recognition of its own provisional and belated abstractness: 'The project of cognitive mapping obviously stands or falls with the conception of some (unrepresentable, imaginary) global social totality that was to have been mapped' (Jameson 1988: 356). There is an affinity here between the background noise of Mitchell's novel and Jameson's 'unrepresentable, imaginary global social totality' insomuch as both register an impossible possibility, which in *Ghostwritten*'s case, is captured by the inclusion of an extratextual tenth part. In other words, the novel's utopian vocation is to raise the illegible system of connection to a brief legibility, whereby narrative chance is recast as a formal system, thus rendering the novel an impossible totality. This argument resonates with Robert Tally's assertion that the utopian impulse today aligns with cognitive mapping as a 'method by which one can attempt to apprehend the system itself ... [such that] Utopia is an attempt to construct or project a totality' (2013: ix). The utopian dream of *Ghostwritten*, then, is to expose what Mitchell refers to as the immaterial 'white noise' that connects the disparate locations, plots and protagonists across the novel's westward trajectory and thus to transform this indiscernible 'noise' into discernible 'sound'.

However, as Jameson explains, successful cognitive mapping is not necessarily grounded in 'revolutionary' victory, but 'may be equally inscribed in a narrative of defeat' that 'causes the whole architectonic of postmodern global space to rise up in ghostly profile behind itself, as some ultimate dialectical barrier or invisible limit' (1992: 415). And it is in this latter sense that *Ghostwritten* becomes both a novel *about* and *of* globalization, simultaneously charting the reduction of the subject against the expanse of the global system, *while also* affirming the necessity and specificity of difference at the cultural, political and spatial levels *and* invoking the absent present system that unites those differences in the totality of global late capitalism. It's a herculean task that can only end in failure. And, indeed, *Ghostwritten* fails to produce the capitalist world-system within its formal composition as 'a novel in nine parts'. What makes it an especially original novel of globalization, then, is its narrative failure to do so. Instead of narrative resolution, it must proffer an extra-formal mediation of the aporias of the global system through the addition of a supplemental tenth part. Consequently, the visible rendering of that very ghostly trace that global capitalism has left upon the novel's form can only be achieved through the excessive, supplemental tenth chapter of this 'novel in nine parts'.

The failure and belatedness of this project within the nine main narratives is registered by many characters' emphasis on and recourse to conspiracy, which is indelibly linked to the subjective desire to master systemic narratives. 'Conspiracy', Jameson attests, 'is the poor person's cognitive mapping in the postmodern age; it is the degraded figure of the total logic of late capital, a desperate attempt to represent the latter's system, whose failure is marked by its slippage into sheer theme and content' (1988: 356). In what follows, I will examine how *Ghostwritten* explores the problem of the constitutive 'reality gap' (Mitchell 1999: 257)[1] that forms between subjects and the capitalist world-system as seen through the novel's series of weak, paranoid conspiratorial narratives (those that reduce the complexity of globalization to a spurious and paranoid subjective mastery) and strong systemic conspiratorial narratives (those that eclipse subjective perspective in favour of revealing systemic conditions). While the former contain their mediation of globalization's totalizing violence within images of pseudo-utopian closure in the family, the latter promise immanent, perpetual and total annihilation. To reveal the irresolvable, structural oppositions of this dialectic between the subjective and the systemic and the problem of their false resolution in either pseudo-utopian escapism or anti-utopian annihilation, I'll turn to the novel's tenth part. Here the novel reveals the unifying spectre of the global capitalist system itself as simultaneously arriving too early and too late.

Weak conspiracy: The role of Quasar and the noncorpum

Conspiracy enters *Ghostwritten* as a negative aesthetic development, a false means of resolving the narrative reality gaps between subjectivity and global world-system through paranoia and illusion. While the majority of *Ghostwritten*'s nine parts are not conspiracy narratives in the traditional sense, they represent the way that conspiracy has transcended its generic borders to become a cultural dominant, where globalization's penetration of the remotest corners of the world and the psyche feel like conspiracy in their unfathomable state. Thus, one of the central aspects of Mitchell's novel concerns the domestication of conspiracy in the global narrative itself. This can be seen immediately in the opening chapter, 'Okinawa', which narrates the escape of 'Quasar, the harbinger' (5) from Tokyo to Naha following his involvement in the Subway Sarin Incident. 'Okinawa' notably foregrounds the relationship between paranoia, conspiracy and the violent desire to reconcile the global system with the individual's phenomenological and epistemological experience of the reality gap by eradicating the distinction between subject and system.

---

[1] In *Ghostwritten*, a character experiences a 'reality gap' when he or she fundamentally misunderstands who exercises actual power in a given situation (257). As Jo Alyson Parker asserts in her incisive analysis of Mitchell's *The Bone Clocks*, gaps are an essential formal aesthetic component of world-building for Mitchell's larger 'macroverse' (2018: 2). As such, she examines how the temporal gaps that structure *The Bone Clocks* are an integral aspect for obliquely figuring the ongoing class war and the destructive global climate change that it precipitates. While such temporal gaps are of a slightly different order than the epistemological reality gaps between subject and global capitalist world-system that I analyse here, both approaches demand that we 'pay attention to what is unnarrated, maybe even unnarratable' (Parker 2018: 7).

The opening description of Naha, one of Okinawa's oldest commercial ports, combines aspects of globalization, conspiracy theory and sci-fi elements in a grand paranoid mélange. Air conditioning is kept off as it 'impairs alpha waves', and curtains closed because 'you never know whose telephoto lens might be looking in' (4). Moving from the description of his room to the surrounding landscape, Quasar notes elements of modern urban development (factories, department stores, fridges, etc.) that, coupled with the control mechanisms of telecommunications infrastructure and environmental blight, amount to a conspiracy of global proportions in which Japan colludes in its own demise. At heart, it is an alienated existence that leads to Quasar's dismissal of 'their cities', in which the genitive 'their' could equally be said to refer to the 'unclean' Japanese as well as to the American forces that conspire against the integrity of the nation (4).

Against this dark backdrop of a thoroughly degraded Japan, Quasar's cult promises a transcendental negation through an occult nationalism that intermixes quasi-sci-fi trappings, including telekinesis, telepathy and astral projection, with a counter-totalizing vision. In this, it neatly reproduces within a Japanese context what Emily Apter refers to as the paranoid, totalizing subjectivity of 'oneworldedness'. Rather than cognitive mapping, which seeks to raise the system that structures individual experience, 'oneworldedness ... envisages the planet as an extension of paranoid subjectivity vulnerable to persecutory fantasy, catastrophism and monomania, ... [and produces] a delusional model of subjective recognition that apprehends itself in global schemata' (2006: 366, 371). It's an operation that, in *Ghostwritten*, recursively individualizes the totalizing violence of globalization's real processes of subsumption by placing the cult's spurious sci-fi elements in opposition to existing technoscientific regimes that are the driving force behind the totalizing aspects of globalization. Thus, Quasar believes the individualization of these quasi-transcendental sci-fi powers that reproduce the penetrating immediacy of systemic globalization will vanquish the purveyors of economic globalization, which he envisions as: 'The Americans from the military bases, ... [the] Okinawan males [that] ape the foreigners, ... [and the] businessmen, buying and selling what wasn't theirs' (11). Here, the totalizing pretensions of Quasar's nationalism merely provide an inversion of the inimically totalizing practices of globalization that he associates with the Americans and their Japanese imitators in that both desire to remake the world in their own destructive image.

This counter-totalizing reaches its fullest universalizing apotheosis in His Serendipity's words to Quasar during his initiation into the nationalist cult: '"You have transcended your old family of the skin, and you have joined a new family of the spirit. ... Our family will grow until the world without is the world within. This is not a prophecy. This is inevitable, future reality. How do you feel, newest child of our nation without borders, without suffering?"' (9). This vision takes on the most regressive totalizing aspects of global capitalism by annihilating all borders and difference. It imagines a world in which subject and object are united in the most stultifying regressive pseudo-utopian closure[2] of the purified, national family that expands to annihilate all difference that it encounters. In this paranoid oneworldedness, systemic totality – that of global capitalism – is replaced by a cultural, subjective totality in the image of a new national family, in which the desires of self and system are one and the same. In other words, it reveals that the desire to close the reality gap between globalization and subjectivity necessitates an equal and opposite violence.

Although confronting a different set of historical parameters than Quasar's narrative, the protagonist of 'Mongolia' similarly seeks to align subjectivity and system. In this chapter, we're introduced to one of Mitchell's most compelling characters, the noncorpum. Quite literally, noncorpums are disembodied spirits, peripatetic entities adrift in the world that can only subsist by invading host bodies. 'Mongolia's' noncorpum flirts with the paranoiac conspiracy narrative by positing its own search for identity as being at one with discovering the story of the 'fate of the world' (157). Although critics often portray the noncorpum as representing the diasporic subjectivity of globalization, operating through a progressive, cosmopolitan comingling, *Ghostwritten* describes the presence of the noncorpum as a violent yoking of the other to itself. It circumscribes the host's particular desires as well as physical and mental autonomy. In this way, the noncorpum highlights the violent neo-imperial logic of capitalist subsumption in an unlikely and highly mediated manner.

For the noncorpum, the host provides the means for knowledge of the new environment and the vehicle in which to traverse it, but the host's agency is radically subsumed by the noncorpum's whim. When the noncorpum describes its first encounter with a human host, its initial development evinces the sheer violence of the capitalist world-system. The noncorpum observes:

> My host tried to scream but I would not let him wake. Instinctively, his mind made itself rigid and tight. I prised my way though, clumsily, not knowing how strong I had become, ripping my way through memories

---

[2]Given the conditions of what Mark Fisher refers to as 'capitalist realism' (2009) – the widespread belief that capitalism represents the end of history, a closed system with no outside such that there can never be a more progressive replacement for capitalism as a socio-economic world-system – a politics that imagines closure and finality is aligned with the very structures of global late capitalism, and hence a pseudo-utopianism. Instead, the radical function of utopianism is conversely to imagine just such an oppositional opening up of history and the possibility of alternatives to the capitalist world-system, for example, the World Social Forum's slogan that 'Another World Is Possible'. For more on radical utopianism in Mitchell's works, see Caroline Edwards.

and neural control, gouging out great chunks. Fear of losing the fight
made me more violent than I ever intended. (162)

Here the violence of capitalist globalization is shown as 'the ultimate form of biopower insofar as it is the absolute inversion of the power of life' (Hardt and Negri 2001: 346). While the noncorpum recounts a series of lessons and ethical responses in relation to this primary, unintentional murder, the 'guilt' it feels is initially connected to 'relief' and 'power' (163). Any ethical compunction is then further undercut by the development of its biopolitical powers: 'I stayed in [my second host] for two years, learning about humans and inhumanity. I learned how to read my hosts' memories, to erase them, and replace them. I learned how to control my hosts. Humanity was my toy' (163). Ultimately, for the noncorpum, the goal is less cosmopolitan comingling and more a search for its own founding narrative. By seeking to overcome its own narrative reality gaps – to breach the opposition between the systemic conditions of its own creation and its alienated experience of a rootless homelessness – it reproduces the same founding violence upon its host bodies.

If both Quasar's and the noncorpum's actions are deplorable, the desire for such totalizing narratives of subject–object identity reveals, on one hand, the violence of such conscripting narratives of global late capitalism in their actuality and, on the other, the impossibility of such subject–system identity, whereby the individual could both fully comprehend the system they are cast into and redirect it towards their own goals without falling into a paranoid oneworldedness. However, what is most striking in the case of each narrative is the formal resolution that recontains each protagonist's project of subjective totalization. Rather than a cosmopolitan openness as response to or outcome of globalization, we find subjective escapes into the well-worn analogue of the nation and the nuclear family. Consequently, Quasar casts off familial desires with the Fellowship in favour of the care he receives from the family in Kumejima, and the noncorpum arrests its endless possibilities through parasitical invasions in order to be fully lodged in the body of a newborn baby that will die unless the noncorpum relents. Thus, at the narrative level, for both Quasar and the noncorpum, an inimical desire to be at one with the world is replaced with the localized suggestion of a familial homecoming long denied them. On the level of content, these pseudo-families stand as narrative reconciliation for initial motivating acts of alienation and trauma – Quasar's alienation from 'their' Japan and the political murder of the noncorpum's first self as boy. On the formal level, they provide strategies of narrative containment, that is, formal acts of closure that compensate for the structural violence of global capitalism and the impossibility of locating oneself at home in this world. They create the appearance of safe enclaves that seem to ameliorate the more corrosive effects of globalization. In both cases, they offer specious solutions to the original animating problems by failing to substantially address them.

Strong conspiracy: Towards a systemic critique

Whereas 'Okinawa' and 'Mongolia' present the recursive violence of the attempt to reconcile self to system, the last two proper chapters, 'Clear Island' and 'Night Train' in conjunction with the supplemental tenth part, 'Underground', work as a surprising dialectical 'resolution' to the novel and the attendant problems of cognitive mapping, totality and paranoid oneworldedness. However, the supplemental nature of the coda means that the resolution is less a determinate end to the novel than a surprising loopback, a reversal of the westward and temporal drive of the narrative and the ends of global capitalism that cannot be neatly expunged by the false resolution of subject and system, and the individual narrative conclusions of each of the discrete nine parts. Ultimately, the strong conspiratorial narrative of 'Clear Island' and 'Night Train' shifts attention from the subjective to the systemic, leading to the extra-formal admission of formal impossibility in 'Underground'.

If *Ghostwritten*'s earlier chapters utilize coincidence to intimate the chance connections that our increasingly connected global world fosters, then 'Clear Island' begins to engulf and systematize the rest of the preceding narratives through first reversing and then replaying the novel's steady westward trajectory across its locations. The chapter is narrated from the perspective of a scientist, Mo Muntervary, who had been employed by a US think tank, with connections to the CIA, to develop artificial intelligence. After realizing the militaristic implications of this research, Mo goes on the run, attempting to evade the CIA and keep her research from falling into their hands. As her journey reverses and then replicates the movement of the novel, Mo comes into greater contact with a number of previous characters. Mo's chapter thus yokes the preceding narratives to the systemic drive of globalization as the techno-militaristic development and refinement of the communications infrastructure that enables the capitalist world-system and alternately sustains paranoid oneworldedness. However, 'Clear Island' contravenes the paranoid oneworldedness of 'Okinawa' and 'Mongolia' that seeks to unite a singular subjective experience with the totalizing objective structure. Instead, it maps late-twentieth-century political machinations through the subsequent development of an abstract totalizing consciousness born of and existent in the global communication infrastructure – the AI born of Mo's research that becomes known as the Zookeeper.

Extrapolating from Heisenberg's uncertainty principle, and reproducing both the need for cognitive mapping and the impossibility of producing a final image, Mo comes up with a theory of electron agency that outstrips the reductive paranoid oneworldedness evinced by Quasar:

> Electrons in my brain are moving forwards and backwards in time, changing atoms, changing electrical charge, changing molecules, changing chemicals, carrying impulses, changing thoughts, deciding to have a baby, changing ideas, deciding to leave Light Box, changing theory, changing

technology, changing computer circuitry, changing artificial intelligence, changing the projections of missiles whole segments of the globe away, and collapsing buildings onto people who have never heard of Ireland. Electrons, electrons, electrons. What laws are you following? (360)

We see here the radicality of constant differentiation *as* systematicity that gestures towards the ghostly undergirding logic of both late capitalism and the novel's very structure. This insight provokes a number of new thoughts that drive Mo forward towards her theory of quantum cognition ('Quancog') as a form of cognitive mapping that unites the synthetic with the natural, the immaterial with the material, and the micro with the macro, under a recognition of totality: 'Nowhere does the microscopic world stop and the macroscopic world begin' (373).

Building on this scalar metaphor, Mo describes the power of Quancog as that which makes unfathomable connection visible: 'Phenomena are interconnected regardless of distance, in a holistic ocean more voodoo than Newton ... [and Quancog represents] "The simultaneity of th[is] ocean"' (375). Mo realizes that she is on the cusp of a new global technological ontology, and, as such, she sees Quancog and its instantiation in the Zookeeper AI not only as 'New Earth's computer' (372) but as the operative conscience of this system: 'Technology has outstripped our capacity to look after it. But, suppose I – suppose Quancog could ensure that technology looked after itself' (374). The interruption and change in her thought from 'I' to 'Quancog' most radically represents the difference between Mo, Quasar and even the noncorpum, and the forms of systemic mapping that they aspire to; it's an admission of subjective human impossibility, yet the utter need for just such a project. As such, the AI, like the noncorpum, is bodiless; however, unlike the noncorpum which is limited by its parasitic relation to the human body and the dataspace of a human mind, the AI inhabits all networked dataspaces simultaneously: it is the seamless ocean of globalized communications technology.

Chapter nine, 'Night Train', presents the immaterial realization of this project. As with 'Okinawa' and 'Mongolia', Mo's narrative is ultimately grounded in the subjective experience of the body and individualism, likewise ending with a spurious utopian resolution where a localized homecoming is equated with the familial (Mo, like Quasar and the noncorpum, chooses a substitute and compensatory home that allows her to maintain a sense of family rather than a global life on the run). The inefficacy of this 'individualist escapism' (Edwards 2011: 189) is marked by the destruction of this new pseudo-home by the very AI that is developed there. The Zookeeper's narrative breaks with this rooted, subjective focus by taking on the formal properties of the immaterial spaces of globalization. 'Night Train' thereby shifts the emphasis to the techno-immaterial: if human subjectivity fails to cognitively map the contours of globalization, the Zookeeper figures as the realization of this failed desire through recourse to the immaterial ones and zeroes that comprise the global communications infrastructure. As such, the Zookeeper becomes less a ghost in the machine and more the immanence of the global communications system itself.

From white noise to sound

The ninth part, 'Night Train' – the first of the official nine parts to lack a concrete setting as its name – finally cancels out the particular national grounding of each preceding chapter by turning to the inner workings of the unhomed material aspects (satellites), rhizomatic[3] networked paths and immaterial productions of the global communications networks that encapsulate the earth and drive the processes of globalization. By turning to the globalizing structures of the communications, information and finance grid in this way, 'Night Train' levels the constraints of space and time that localize each of the preceding chapters in order to present the novel's final official figure of cognitive mapping as that of global immediacy. Consequently, the chapter switches from first-person narration to a series of real-time transmissions from a radio talk show hosted by Bat Segundo. In this way, the narrative seemingly takes the reader inside the fibre optics and satellite relays of the global communications grid, suggesting that this totalizing idea can only be presented through the immaterial data stream.

The Zookeeper, the escaped AI developed by Mo in conjunction with the CIA, becomes the immanence of Hardt and Negri's Empire itself: 'The deterritorializing capacities of communications are unique: communication is not satisfied by limiting or weakening modern territorial sovereignty; rather it attacks the very possibility of an order to a space' (2001: 346–7). As new technological ontology and the literal instantiation of what could previously only be rendered as paranoid oneworldedness, the Zookeeper gives itself an untraceable origin and subsumes all of the other conspiracy theories by destroying the noncorpum that presents itself in terms of the Aum Shinrikyo cult (424) and killing the publisher of the popular conspiracies *The Invisible Cyberhand* and *Earthbound Comet* (400–1). Moreover, the Zookeeper becomes the arbiter of knowledge; as the controller of information systems, what the Zookeeper desires become inseparable from the information accessible to humans about their world (423).

---

[3]As Deleuze and Guattari note, rhizomatic structures are those without clearly defined borders or hierarchies and that are constantly forming, dissembling and reforming. In a passage that corresponds with cognitive mapping, they assert that 'Unlike the graphic arts, drawing or photography, unlike tracings, the rhizome pertains to a map that must be produced, constructed, a map that is always detachable, connectable, reversible, modifiable, and has multiple entrance ways and exits and its own lines of flight' (Deleuze and Guattari 2004: 23).

As Tally reminds us, the desire to 'construct or project a totality' is itself utopian (2013: ix). However, even with access to the totality of the systemic structures of globalization, the utopian desire for a subject–system identity that resolves the reality gap by mapping and controlling the vicissitudes of globalization begins to fall apart. In an equally humorous and desperately human touch, the Zookeeper resorts to talk radio in order to facilitate its search for the metaphysical law of all laws (387). There's an echo of the noncorpum's search for the origins of stories here; however, instead of the pseudo-utopian closure of the earlier sections in the form of the body and family, this moment pushes towards the dystopian totalizing closure of annihilation. Despite all the Zookeeper's abilities, the liberal stabilizing of capitalism as the goal of Empire produces even worse results, and the biopolitically derived four laws for AI that it has been instilled with, instead of stemming crisis, produce new ones. By the end of 'Night Train', on the one-year anniversary of Brink Day when it prevented the launch of World War III, Zookeeper calls back, still struggling with its initial question about the law of laws:

> 'Is peace of mind the co-workability of your laws?'
> 'Uh-huh ... I guess it is.'
> 'I wish to know peace of mind, Bat.'
> 'Then ditch this "ethical variable" jargon. Drop whatever is getting in the way.'
> 'The fourth law ["preserve visitors' lives"]. The visitors I safeguard are wrecking my zoo.' (428)

In a final irony, then, the movement from the subjective to the immanent falls back into the terms of 'peace of mind' and 'closure' over the openness of the presence of 'ethical variables', leading to the suggestion of the total annihilation of the world by its 'freelance zookeeper' (386). The production of consciousness, of subjectivity, that is at one with global late capitalism does nothing to alter its continually predacious, destructive tendencies. The so-called 'End of History' really is just that.

Coda

The nine stories that comprise *Ghostwritten* represent an impossible desire for a totalizing vision. This desire ultimately turns destructive when predicated on the outmoded liberal residue of individualism as it seeks to replace the totalizing aspects of the system with a totalizing and authoritarian subjectivity. This seems to reaffirm Toscano and Kinkle's conclusion concerning the problem of a fixed, totalizing viewpoint, which 'especially when it comes to capital, is a fantasy – if a very effective, and often destructive, one, ... [because] there is in the end something reactionary about the notion of a metalanguage ... that could represent, capitalism as such' (2015: 241–2). This impossible position within the narrative(s) proper, however, is ultimately what leads to the utopian surplus of the tenth part and its figuration of the impossible. Rather than subjectivity, it posits the raising of the system itself, the 'aesthetic problem' of making the 'invisible visible' (Toscano and Kinkle 2015: 24).

Turning to the coda means, among other possibilities, considering *Ghostwritten* as taking place between two sections focused on Quasar. The first sets up the paranoia that ripples throughout the novel in a less immediate, but perceptible manner. Indeed, much of the reading experience begins to feel paranoid as coincidence trips over to a systemic patterning that culminates in the novel's official conclusion, providing a quantitatively ramped up apocalyptic vision that is qualitatively comparable to where we began with Quasar; only this time recasting the annihilation of alterity offered by Quasar's nationalist cult with the totalizing death of everyone through the destruction of the earth that is intimated by the Zookeeper. However, in the final, narratively non-concluding, excluded tenth part of the novel, the paranoid oneworldism that drives Quasar's first section is dialectically recast as an oddly demystifying coda. The final coda, as a textual supplement, thus intervenes between these two apocalyptic moments and supplies a different narrative drive that, as Patrick O'Donnell illustrates, 'is both recursive and continuative' (2015: 43). This narrative shift registers a skeletal economy, replicating the narrative's westward drive through a set of reified and commodified images whereby the previous social relations between narrator and history sketched in each individual chapter are replaced by a series of commodified images and sounds.

In this sense, the train car functions as a new kind of 'time-image' for globalization (Jameson 2013: 301). It shuttles across the various geo-temporal stations of the novel, bringing the individual narratives into relation with one another in a series of juxtapositions contained in the singular moving space of the train car, such that 'we might then see the "accordianising" or "telescoping" function of combined and uneven development as a form of time travel within the same space' (Warwick 2015: 17). At the end of the novel, we see Quasar for the first time exiting the train car. While fighting his way out, he unconsciously notes objects from the different locations in the novel, before finally looping back to the start with a near repetition of the first line of the novel, 'Who was blowing on the nape of my neck?' (3). This repetition suggests the knowledge that is permanently withheld from Quasar who can only perform a model of paranoid oneworldedness that mistakes the subject for the system.

By contrast, the reader, after having read the individual narratives, is able to perform an operation of cognitive mapping, whereby the immensity of the novel's narratives and locations are brought into sharp relief. The experience of reading the novel in conjunction with the coda allows for the utopian impossibility of a cognitive mapping of the world-system: the connections between the various global objects in the train car are now fundamentally relatable to the seemingly disconnected subjectivities spread throughout the world and the global late-capitalist system that unites their disparate beings. Moreover, the connections between credit card debt, Chinese socialist entrepreneurism, first world global backpackers, terrorism, global communications and advanced weapons development begin to productively map onto one another, raising the spectral, global late-capitalist system into legibility, but now as the temporal start of the novel, as the totality that the separate narratives exist within. Thus, if the novel's *content* promises destruction twice over, then the novel's speculative *form* offers the figure of collective impossibility predicated on the ghostly fetish of the global late-capitalist market that is ultimately the subject of this entire narrative. It briefly decodes as 'sound' the 'white noise' that has connected these compacted short stories. As such, the novel as an aesthetic whole functions as a utopian evocation, forming an eidetic no place/good place through this occluded tenth part in order to reveal the impossible totality that is global late capitalism.

The new time-image of the novel's final line, 'the back of the train, accelerating into the darkness' (436), thus represents the fleeting moment of cognitive mapping where the system of global capitalism that operates as the noise undergirding the previous disparate nine narratives is brought into spectral relief by the reader who is then tasked with making the links before it disappears. The coda exposes the paradox of mapping the whole; in the sense of cognitive mapping, it always comes too late and dissipates too soon. This paradox reveals that totality *is* the open whole, unassimilable to subjective consciousness and thus in need of an impossible utopian external form. In other words, it performs the operation of the dialectic applied to the late-capitalist world-system: 'Marxism views the world not as a closed totality but an "open, structured whole, with irreducible differences" comprehended dialectically, mindful of the play of contradictions' (San Juan Jr. 2002: 228).

This utopian formal cognitive mapping of globalization, with its discrete locales connected initially by chance and then later through communications technologies, finally gets linked to the commodity chains of global capitalism. While globalization cannot simply be reduced to these elements, it is perhaps only through these reified and commodified images that we can glimpse the system of abstraction that undergirds the real process of subsumption. As such, globalization is revealed as an incommensurate experience of the complex histories of the twentieth century and their reconciliation in the contemporary commodified world-system. In other words, the coda collapses these competing, seemingly heterogeneous historical moments into the spatial time-image of the global present such that these differences are now dialectically recast as instances of the combined and uneven development of late capitalism. Consequently, our only way of mapping this through our own experience is to realize that our experience is itself conditioned by the totalizing processes of commodification and subsumption that are the global capitalist world-system.

If there is any lesson about resistance in *Ghostwritten*, it is that there is no place outside of the operations of global late capitalism. There is no sanctuary, no liminal space to retreat to in capitalist modernity's past, present or future not already colonized or where the social relationships of everyday living have not already been exploited and reconstituted by the very logic of exchange. Thus, any 'microtopian' (Edwards 2011) or cultural form of resistance (Dunlop 2011: 207–8) must begin with and wrestle against this notion of totality by organizing in and through its logic. The lack 'of a coherent whole' (Vermeulen 2012: 382) cited in one form or another by so many critics as one of the novel's constitutive strengths is, then, perhaps a symptom of the culturalist approach to Mitchell's novel itself and its attendant focus on the subject. This non-totalizing trend and concomitant emphasis on the subject continues even in the most recent Mitchell scholarship. In this vein, O'Donnell argues that the non-totalizing aspects of Mitchell's 'planetary' novels 'understand the "global" not as totality, but as a series of shifting planes and contingent zones crossed by individuals whose itineraries are often a matter of circumstance' (2015: 12). Yet, as Shaviro reminds us, while there is no singular capitalist culture, all individuals suffer under the weight of capital's totalizing penetration of every aspect of core social relations, and this is what is lost at the expense of totality. The utopian impossibility – the desire but failure to grasp the totality of late capitalism in its systemic entirety due to the local divisions and specificities of each of *Ghostwritten*'s protagonists in their own determinant cultures of capital – may be no cause for celebration after all. Instead, it represents a stark reminder of the limits of our situated imagination, which is then projected upon the continually sutured subject of capitalist realism. That Mitchell's fiction continues the desire for resistance and the need to totalize and create systemic cognitive mappings despite their failure remains its signal strength as a utopian novel both *about* and *of* globalization.

Works cited

Apter, E. (2006), 'On Oneworldedness, or Paranoia as a World System', *American Literary History*, 18(2), 365–89.

Cunningham, D. (2010), 'Capitalist Epic', *Radical Philosophy*, 163, 11–23.

Deleuze, G. and F. Guattari (2004), *A Thousand Plateaus: Capitalism and Schizophrenia*, trans. Brian Massumi, London: Continuum.

Dillon, S. (2011), 'Introducing David Mitchell's Universe', in S. Dillon (ed.), *David Mitchell: Critical Essays*, Cambridge: Gylphi, 3–23.

Dunlop, N. (2011), 'Speculative Fiction as Postcolonial Critique in *Ghostwritten* and *Cloud Atlas*', in S. Dillon (ed.), *David Mitchell: Critical Essays*, Cambridge: Gylphi, 201–23.

Edwards, C. (2011), '"Strange Transactions": Utopia, Transmigration and Time in *Ghostwritten* and *Cloud Atlas*', in S. Dillon (ed.), *David Mitchell: Critical Essays*, Cambridge: Gylphi, 177–200.

Fisher, M. (2009), *Capitalist Realism: Is there No Alternative?* Winchester: Zero Books.

Hardt, M. and A. Negri (2001), *Empire*, Cambridge: Harvard University Press.

Jameson, F. (1988), 'Cognitive Mapping', in C. Nelson and L. Grossberg (eds), *Marxism and the Interpretation of Culture*, Urbana-Champaign: University of Illinois Press, 347–57.

Jameson, F. (1992), *Postmodernism; Or, The Cultural Logic of Late Capitalism*, Durham: Duke University Press.

Jameson, F. (2013), *The Antimonies of Realism*, London: Verso.

Mitchell, D. (1999), *Ghostwritten: A Novel in Nine Parts*, London: Sceptre.

O'Donnell, P. (2015), *A Temporary Future: The Fiction of David Mitchell*, London: Bloomsbury Academic Press.

Parker, J. A. (2018), 'Mind the Gap(s): Holly Sykes's Life, the "Invisible" War, and the History of the Future in *The Bone Clocks*', *C21 Literature: Journal of 21st-Century Writings*, 6(3). Available online: https://c21.openlibhums.org/article/doi/10.16995/c21.47/ (accessed 25 October 2018).

San, J. E. Jr (2002), 'Postcolonialism and the Problematic of Uneven Development', in C. Bartolovich and N. Lazarus (eds), *Marxism, Modernity and Postcolonial Studies*, Cambridge: Cambridge University Press, 221–39.

Shaviro, S. (2012), 'Symposium on Science Fiction and Globalization', *Science Fiction Studies*, 39(3), 374–84.

Stephenson, W. (2011), '"Moonlight Bright as a UFO Abduction": Science Fiction, Present-Future Alienation and Cognitive Mapping', in S. Dillon (ed.), *David Mitchell: Critical Essays*, Cambridge: Gylphi, 225–46.

Tally, R. T. Jr (2013), *Utopia in the Age of Globalization: Space, Representation, and the World-System*, London: Palgrave MacMillan.

Toscano, A. and J. Kinkle (2015), *Geographies of the Absolute*, Winchester: Zero Books.

Vermeulen, P. (2012), 'David Mitchell's *Ghostwritten* and the "Novel of Globalization": Biopower and the Secret History of the Novel', *Critique*, 53(4), 381–92.

Warwick Research Collective (2015), *World Literature in the Context of Combined and Uneven Development*, Liverpool: Liverpool University Press.

2

Questing for the post-postmodern: David Mitchell's *number9dream*

Nick Bentley

Chapter summary

This chapter argues that *number9dream* represents a quest narrative in terms of both content and form. The novel begins by inhabiting the postmodernity of late-twentieth-century Tokyo, a setting in which the main character, Eiji Miyake, searches for a lost father and for meaning to his life and the world in which he finds himself. Alongside Eiji's *Bildungsroman* narrative, the novel itself is on its own search for a literary form that extends beyond the scepticism, ethical relativism and cynical irony associated with postmodernism. The novel is structured in such a way that it rehearses and develops a number of differing forms of narrative in order to pursue a means of articulating this post-postmodernism, including popular narrative genres, intertextual frames, journals and dream narratives. In analysing Mitchell's novel, the chapter engages with several theoretical perspectives, including Fredric Jameson's definition of postmodernism as a late-capitalist form, Timotheus Vermeulen and Robin van den Akker's identification of a metamodernism in recent aesthetic practice and Richard Rorty's concept of the ironist.

Introduction

David Mitchell's second novel, *number9dream* (2001), takes its title from the John Lennon song whose chorus lyric, 'Ah! böwakawa, poussé poussé', represents a phrase that the songwriter explained came to him in a dream (Sheff 2000). The words are nonsensical, but act as a fitting motif for a novel that explores the relationship between meaning and meaninglessness. In this chapter, I argue that the novel configures this relationship as a quest narrative with the main character Eiji Miyake's search for a lost father and return to an estranged mother a conceit for the attempt to find meaning in a world that is saturated with postmodern surfaces, images and simulacra. The novel is initially set in contemporary Tokyo, a city that is presented as existing in the interstices of the real and the fictional. Indeed, Eiji constructs the city around him by adopting a succession of popular narrative genres – espionage thriller, war movie, science-fiction adventure, Japanese Yakuza gangster film – which act as a series of frames through which he tries to make sense of his place in the world. I will argue, however, that despite its fractured structure and its examination of a consumerist and mediated Tokyo, the novel extends beyond a stultifying indeterminacy and relativism in its attempt to relocate meaning in an alternative system of signification that gestures beyond the limits of the postmodern. As Eiji is questing for some sense of meaning to frame his adult life, I intend to show that the novel itself is questing for a form of writing that extends beyond the radical scepticism, enclosed self-reflexivity and compromised ethics of postmodernism. In this context, I will identify some of the possibilities the novel puts forward to circumvent postmodernism's debilitating relativism and offer a reading of the novel that chimes with Richard Rorty's notions of a pragmatic contingency and the critical outlook of what he calls the 'ironist'.

As many critics and cultural commentators have noted, postmodernism reached its high point in the last quarter of the twentieth century, with the turn of the millennium attracting increasing speculation about the nature of a new set of aesthetic and literary practices that in differing ways rejected, interrogated or developed its radical scepticism. Various literary critics, cultural commentators and creative practitioners have been keen to offer a twenty-first-century response to (post)modernity, including Nicolas Bourriaud's altermodernism (2009), Alan Kirby's digimodernism (2001), Jose Lopez and Garry Potter's critical realism (2001), Gilles Lipovetsky's hypermodernism (2005), Vermeulen and van den Akker's metamodernism (2010) and David Foster Wallace's new sincerity (1993). The publication of *number9dream* in 2001 fits well with this sense of moving beyond the postmodern. As Adam Kelly (2011) has noted, several novelists who emerged in the late 1990s and early 2000s had grown up during a period in which postmodernism had become the dominant literary mode. In terms of literary influence, Kelly notes that novelists such as Jennifer Egan, Jonathan Frantzen, Richard Powers, David Foster Wallace and Colson Whitehead challenged the dominant paradigm in order to project their work as a fresh and new response to a set of historical and cultural contexts that exceeded the postmodern moment. Published in 2001, Mitchell's novel casts a backward glance at the 1990s, the decade when postmodernism went mainstream and lost any potentially radical or countercultural edge (Bentley 2005; Chute 2011).

Mitchell's relationship to postmodernism has already generated a certain amount of critical debate. Richard Bradford, for example, places him in a category he calls the 'new postmodernists' alongside writers such as Nicola Barker, Jonathan Coe, Toby Litt, Will Self and Ali Smith. Bradford (2007) identifies this group as sharing the experience of receiving a higher education during a period in which postmodernist aesthetic practices were studied alongside poststructuralist critical theory, forming a 'mutually supportive symbiotic relationship' (64). With this background, these authors 'execute a calculated and premeditated shift away from an implied mindset, outside the novel, that involves the plausible, the rational and the predictable', which he considers to be a consumer-friendly form of postmodernism that marries literary experimentation with a commercial nous (67). Alternatively, Peter Childs and James Green (2011) reject the claim that Mitchell is a 'new postmodernist', arguing that his 'novels do not merely rehearse the stylistic inflections of a domesticated postmodernism, as Bradford terms it, but rather articulate a complex response to the current material conditions of the world' (26). They go on to identify postmodernism as 'increasingly unsatisfactory to describe the flows of mediated identity, the global reach of capital, the possibilities of new political paradigms, and the modulating networks of the world market' (24). Like Childs and Green, I am more inclined to see Mitchell as moving beyond a postmodern nexus in his interrogation of postmodernism as an exhausted critical frame, while continuing to examine, rehearse and play with some of its common tropes in order to explore the possibilities of new forms of critique of contemporary neo-liberal and globalized practices.

Mitchell incorporates knowledge of late-twentieth-century theories of culture and aesthetic practice into his fiction, but he does so with a certain level of critical distance. An experimental novelist, of course, is obliged to interrogate the dominant and prevailing forms of aesthetic practice, and in contrast with Bradford's suggestion that Mitchell is one of a group of writers who have merely exploited a recognizable and saleable trend, this chapter contends that *number9dream* pushes the experimentalism associated with postmodernism towards its limits. In this sense, rather than being a late postmodernist, Mitchell fits well with a number of American novelists who emerged in the 1990s, such as David Foster Wallace, Mark Danielewski, Jonathan Safran Foer and Steve Tomasula, a group of writers that Mary K. Holland (2013) has described as producing fiction that 'absorbs poststructuralist assumptions about language, wrestles with the problems inherent in those assumptions, and proposes methods of solving those problems from within poststructuralism itself' (3).

This recognition that solutions can potentially be found by interrogating some of the apparently paradoxical aspects of poststructuralist theory and postmodern aesthetics has many characteristics of what Timotheus Vermeulen and Robin van den Akker (2010) have identified as metamodernism, a predominantly twenty-first-century coalescing of aesthetic practices that demonstrates knowledge about postmodernism but rejects the implications of its ethically debilitating relativism. They describe metamodernism as 'oscillating between a modern enthusiasm and postmodern irony' (1) and an 'oscillation between a typical modern commitment and a markedly postmodern detachment' (2). They go on to define this in temporal, spatial and structural terms: 'metamodernism should be situated epistemologically *with* (post) modernism, ontologically *between* (post) modernism, and historically *beyond* (post) modernism' (2). The idea of oscillation is important here, in that it suggests a movement back and forth between the two contradictory but dependent concepts of the modern and the postmodern. Similarly, the artist Luke Turner suggests in his *Metamodernism // Manifesto* that 'movement shall henceforth be enabled by way of an oscillation between positions' (2011). However, 'oscillation' suggests a particular kind of framed movement – a machine in oscillation paradoxically combines both movement and stasis, as the object that moves between opposite poles does so within a framework that actually goes nowhere.

Mitchell's novel elicits this sense of paradox, most notably in its binary opposition of dreams and reality as well as through its very title, *number9dream*. On the one hand, 'number' suggests a system of logical ordering that accepts the ability to count objects and therefore presupposes a rational, materialist conception of the world. The ordering of Mitchell's novel adheres to this logical numbering, as there are eight chapters preceding the final Chapter Nine, which is exceptional due to its lack of content. (I will return later to the nothingness contained in the final chapter.) On the other hand, alongside the numerical system, the very dreams that are being enumerated effectively eschew a rational and logical framework, suggesting the opposite swing of the oscillating pendulum towards the irrational, surreal and illogical.

Despite its attractiveness and its valuable application to some of the examples of twentieth-first-century artists and film-makers cited by Vermeulen and van den Akker, their model of oscillation does not fit altogether well with one important sense of movement *number9dream* presents – that of the quest.[1] Unlike an oscillating system, the Western quest narrative traditionally represents a movement forward temporally, spatially and in terms of the experience and self-knowledge of the questing individual. The logic of the quest as it develops, for example, in the modern European

---

[1] Vermeulen and van den Akker cite Armin Boehm, Tacita Dean, Michel Gondry, Mona Hatoum and David Thorpe as exemplars of metamodernism.

Bildungsroman parallels that of modernity and the Enlightenment project, being inherently teleological; even if the quest is frustrated or the object of the quest is initially unspecified, a quest narrative is usually instigated on the basis that the journey will disclose some attainable goal. As Franco Moretti (1987) has noted, the heroic quest narrative as it manifests in modernity is the *Bildungsroman*, in which the old romance notion of questing for an object or outcome is turned into an individual search for a central character's placement within a secure and stable position within society, from which they have previously been excluded, as they move from adolescence into adulthood. This pattern is followed by *number9dream* to a certain extent in that it is centred on the classic figure of the orphan or abandoned child, who searches for knowledge about his or her family heritage, and in Eiji's case, a desire to meet with his lost father. In that sense, the search for a rightful position in society is bound up with the search for meaning, both in terms of identifying what is important in the individual's relationship with the society in which they are placed and, more broadly, in terms of understanding the meaning of life as a belief system, generating certain codes of practice which the individual comes to advocate willingly.

Mitchell's narrative is placed within this tradition of the youthful figure trying to locate the meaning of his/her life; however, Eiji's search is presented in a cognitive landscape that interrogates the concept of meaning as something that can be located and defined. In this way, Mitchell's novel has a self-reflexive relationship with the traditional *Bildungsroman* narrative and, as Kathryn Simpson argues, could be described as a postmodern *Bildungsroman*, in which 'the knowingly postmodern qualities of the novel are held in productive tension with the more humanist and ethically focussed aspects of Eiji's quest' (2011: 51). This tension between the postmodern and the humanist is convincing, but the novel's awareness of its form goes one stage further in that it contains a self-reflexive, often parodic stance towards postmodernism itself as an outmoded style: a form of postmodernism turned in on itself, as it becomes the target for its own critical interrogation. As Simpson later suggests, 'The novel plays with the reader's expectations of postmodern fiction ... as it simultaneously plays with the expectation of what should be included in a coming-of-age narrative for boys' (59). This is closer to Adam Kelly's identification of the writer as part of a generation for which postmodernism has become the dominant mode.

I would argue that this tension between the fluid, postmodern landscape Eiji moves through and the quest for fixity implied in the *Bildungsroman* narrative frame can be reconfigured as dramatizing a journey motif of literary form itself. Formally, then, the novel begins in the postmodern moment with a suitably imagined fantasy in a hyperreal space, but it quests beyond that cultural paradigm. Eiji's coming-of-age narrative could then be said to parallel a modal shift from the postmodern to the post-postmodern, a narrative that brings a new maturity and a knowing critique of a previous and younger self's desire to search for fixed meaning and identity through a framework of postmodernist irony and scepticism. In this sense, alongside the *Bildungsroman* quest narrative of the search for a lost father and the reestablishment of the orphan Eiji back into a secure societal position, the trajectory of the novel represents a quest for an adequate narrative form to express the experience of living at the beginning of the twenty-first century. This quest involves the movement away from postmodern contingency and relativism to a tentative set of positionings from which can develop the establishment of some kind of crystallized identity with its own set of positive ethical codes.

One of the reasons for the appropriateness of associating the term 'postmodernism' with *number9dream* is the fact that it is largely set in contemporary Tokyo. Although many of the spaces of postmodernism have been located by Western theorists in North America – Disneyland (and America generally) for Jean Baudrillard (1981), the Bonaventura Hotel for Frederic Jameson (1983), Los Angeles for Edward Soja (1989) – Tokyo is also an urban environment that readily displays characteristics of the postmodern city. In his book on Japan, *Empire of Signs*, Roland Barthes describes Japan as a country in which 'the empire of signifiers is so immense, so in excess of speech, that the exchange of signs remains of fascinating richness, mobility, and subtlety' (1982: 9). The apotheosis of this abundance of meaning is Tokyo; however, the city for Barthes offers a paradoxical tension between meaning and emptiness. Unlike most Western cities, he suggests, Tokyo has at its heart an 'emperor who is never seen. ... In this manner, we are told, the system of the imaginary is spread circularly, by detours and returns the length of an empty space' (30–1).

The model offered by Barthes of an excess of signifiers without a fixed central meaning fits well with Mitchell's description of Tokyo, or rather with Eiji's perception of the hyperreal, super-consumerized urban landscape he navigates: 'Under its tight-fitting lid Tokyo steams – 34°C with 86% humidity. A big Panasonic display says so. Tokyo is so close up you cannot always see it. No distances' (3). This early description identifies the way in which the postmodern urban landscape feeds messages through visual signifiers that claim to offer a description of reality, but are filtered through modern technologies. The fact that Tokyo is so close that 'you cannot always see it' also suggests that Eiji is initially immersed in this culture to the extent that there is no external point of observation from which he can verify its truth claims. The arbiters of knowledge in this setting are multinational companies in charge of setting both the time and the climate. This passage, however, is complicated by the framing device with which Mitchell opens the novel, as Eiji's narration of his situation is filtered through filmic, literary and gaming genres and, in particular, a combination of cyberpunk action movie and espionage thriller – at one point in his fantasy, for example, Eiji uses a 'witty pun in the manner of James Bond' (9). It becomes clear that Eiji casts himself in the role of the action hero as compensation for his lack of agency in the face of the dominant, capitalist world to which (he assumes) his father belongs, hidden, as the latter is, in the PanOpticon tower block in the financial district of the city. The naming of this block, of course, refers to Michel Foucault's use of the panopticon prison concept (designed by Jeremy Bentham) as an appropriate metaphor for the all-pervasive gaze of late-capitalist power. As Rose Harris-Birtill has identified, the 'panoptic paradigm becomes an insidious presence' in Mitchell's novel as 'multiple overlapping panopticons are created and internalized by ... Eiji' (2015: 56).

The PanOpticon building operates as a synecdoche for Tokyo, whose hyperreal surfaces affect the socio-economic identities of those that inhabit its streets: 'Tokyo turns you into a bank account balance with carcass in tow. The size of this single number dictates where the carcass may live, what it drives, how it dresses, who it sucks up to, who it may date and marry, whether it cleans itself in a Jacuzzi or a gutter' (16). The combination of late-capitalist practices and postmodern urban landscape in *number9dream* chimes in particular with Fredric Jameson's description of postmodernism as 'closely related to the emergence of ... late, consumer or multinational capitalism' in which its 'formal features in many ways express the deeper logic of that particular social system' (1983: 143). The way in which Eiji renders the Tokyo landscape corroborates Jameson's identification. However, it must be remembered that the positional observation of this late-capitalist culture is filtered through Eiji's recourse to those recognized popular cultural forms noted earlier. Jameson goes on to write, 'Postmodernism replicates or reproduces – reinforces – the logic of consumer capitalism' (144). This is worth pursuing in Mitchell's case. Firstly, the relationship between a parodic text and its object is problematized in terms of levels of irony. To describe, in fiction, a culture that is saturated in consumerist practices is hardly a corroboration of those practices. Eiji's initial attraction to the hypermodern spaces of Tokyo is driven not by a reinforcing logic of its ethical and ideological outlooks, but is rather a pragmatic way of expressing a feeling of insufficiency in the face of that environment. The analysis may appear ambivalent, but behind Eiji's perspective lies an implicit critique of capitalist patriarchy, from which emerges the desire for an alternative understanding of the world that extends beyond the consumerist dimensions of late capitalism and neo-liberal globalization.

Similarly, the novel could be accused of reproducing dominant, media-constructed images of Japan (and Tokyo in particular) as a paradigmatic postmodern culture, a form of contemporary orientalizing that Toshiya Ueno (2002) has described as 'techno-Orientalism' in which 'Western or other people misunderstand and fail to recognize an always illusory Japanese culture' (228). Baryon Tensor Posadas (2011) has perceptively noted how in Mitchell's novel, the idea of 'Japan' as a mediated, Westernized construct is re-mediated back in a number of cultural icons and images, most notably in the genre of cyberpunk. This process produces what he calls (following Takayuki Tatsumi [2002]) a Japanoid figure, a cultural construct that places the Japanese individual as an exoticized cyborg. However, as

Posadas argues, 'what these narrative strategies suggest is that this is a novel that does not simply make a naïve attempt at representing an imagined truth or essence of "Japan"' (80–1). He goes on to argue that because of its self-reflexive nature, *number9dream* interrogates and deconstructs such mediatized constructions: '*number9dream* partakes of and reproduces the techno-Orientalizing logic of the Japanoid, as any contemporary text that engages with the category "Japan" unavoidably does. However, in its self-referentiality to this logic, *number9dream* puts it under erasure' (97). This process of rehearsing a set of cultural aesthetics in order to create a critical distance from them is, of course, one of the benchmarks of parody and relates to the way in which Mitchell's novel exceeds the well-tested characteristic of postmodernism to engage in pastiche. Jameson identifies pastiche as the 'blank parody' of postmodernism 'without parody's ulterior motive, without the satirical impulse, without laughter, without that still latent feeling that there exists something normal compared to which what is being imitated is rather comic' (167). Linda Hutcheon (1988) famously takes issue with Jameson's reading of postmodernism as a pastiche-saturated, non-critical, ahistorical mode. However, if we accept the blank parody accusation as a mark of the postmodern aesthetic, then where might we place Mitchell's novel? If *number9dream* is, as I am claiming, a work that gestures towards the post-postmodern, then what does it offer as a set of beliefs that can act as an antidote to, or oscillation away from, postmodernism's blithe scepticism towards (ethical) grand narratives?

We can approach this question by way of Eiji's relationship to his grandfather's generation and the Second World War as related in Chapter Six of the novel, 'Kai Ten'. This chapter intersperses Eiji's narrative with journal entries from his great-uncle's experiences of training as a suicide submarine pilot. After Eiji is contacted by his grandfather Takara Tsukiyama (whom he has never seen), a meeting is arranged with a Mr (formerly Admiral) Raizo, who claims to be his grandfather's old friend and who gives him the war journal of his great-uncle, Subaru Tsukiyama. As Raizo tells Eiji, his grandfather 'wants what you want ... Meaning', which is especially important in the contemporary moment as 'Truths mutate to whims. Faith becomes cynical transactions between liars. Sacrifices turn out to be needless excesses. ... Ethics become logos on sports clothing' (275). At a meeting a week later with his father's wife and their daughter, Eiji learns that the man calling himself Raizo was in fact Eiji's grandfather, who it turns out has died since they met. Thus, extra poignancy is given to his grandfather's final adjuration to read the journal, and it is significant that it is in the past, a specifically pre-postmodernist moment, presented in the relatively 'transparent' confessional form of the journal, that Eiji is directed to find meaning to his life in the present.

This episode raises potential generational tensions; however, when reading through the entries in the journal, Eiji is impressed by the absolute surety with which his great-uncle approached his duty towards the emperor of Japan and his people. As a master signifier, the nation, with the emperor at its head, becomes a grand narrative to which Subaru dedicated his energies, ethical outlook and ultimately his life. This world view is not in itself challenged by Eiji, but it *is* historically contextualized: 'What would Subaru say about Japan today? Was it worth dying for? Maybe he would reply that *this* Japan is not the Japan he did die for. It was the possible future, auditioned by the present but rejected with other dreams' (310). The text thus defends the value of his great-uncle's actions and beliefs, while accepting that neither can be extrapolated to form the basis of Eiji's, or indeed anyone else's, value systems in the present. In an echo of Sartrean existentialism, the search for the meaning of one's life remains valuable, but judged with respect to the individual's conscience rather than against an external and inherited philosophy. This qualified relativism has been introduced earlier by one of the characters high on the novel's hierarchy of discourses, Ai; when Eiji tells her that he 'always wanted to know the meaning of life' she replies that his question is misguided and that it should be '"What is *your* meaning of life?" Take Bach's *Well-Tempered Clavier*. To me, it means molecular harmony. To my father, it means a broken sewing machine. To Bach, it means money to pay the candlestickmaker. Who is right? Individually, we all are. Generally, none of us is' (288). Meaning is thus partly subjectivized and contextualized, but the search for it is not completely disregarded as worthless endeavour. In this way, the novel advocates openness to a plurality of perspectives including potentially dissenting views.

The sixth chapter paves the way for Eiji to meet his father in the seventh, and indeed, the structuring of the novel itself begins to exemplify a plural perspectivism in its series of chapters that attempt to identify meaning through differing forms and genres, including the cyberpunk action movie, gaming, fantasy fiction, the Yakuza gangster narrative and the war journal, each of which offers a particular ethical and behavioural world view. However, although each is given respect in its own right, none of these forms and systems are found to be fully adequate to fulfil the son's quest for his father, and consequently to reveal guidance for a meaningful life. When Eiji finally meets his father, he discovers him to be more interested in women and fast food than in offering any profound guidance or inspiration, so much so that when Eiji delivers him a pizza he elects not to disclose his identity. The reality of the father is thus revealed as a hollow absence inside the PanOpticon building, much like the empty signification of Tokyo itself, suggesting the lack of meaning behind the shiny surfaces of contemporary postmodern consumer culture. For Patrick O'Donnell (2015), the discovery of the father as an empty signifier parallels the deconstruction of the postmodern image of the city: 'The protagonist of this failed or fractured *bildungsroman* is not Eiji Miyake, but the metropolis itself that, beneath its shiny corporate surfaces, chronologies and organizational systems underlying everything form pizza delivery schedules to gang hierarchies, encrypts the secret of a labyrinthine and chaotic reality' (59). This disappointment forces Eiji to reassess his whole quest up to this point, and he decides to leave Tokyo and go on an alternative search for his mother in rural Japan. In this context, Harris-Birtill (2015) reads Eiji's obsessive search for his father as 'another panoptic model constructed around a powerful controlling center' and his decision to throw up the search at this point in the novel as 'one of the textual acts of resistance that provide a form of escape from the viral panoptic structures that surround him' (56). The spatio-cultural geographies of the text suggest that this move is also a rejection of the postmodern fragmentation and depthlessness of contemporary consumer society in an attempt to locate meaning in a more traditional locale. This alternative location promises a fixed set of beliefs aligned with a national and personal past that may compensate for the failure to locate meaning in the postmodern metropolis.

Alongside this return to the mother, however, the novel continues to offer suggestions for alternative father figures, including one who has been hovering in Eiji's dream consciousness, John Lennon.[2] The text makes this clear, for example, when Eiji's friend Suga, upon seeing a poster of Lennon, asks if the 'man in the funny sunglasses' is his father (302); and in one of the dream sequences in which Eiji meets Lennon and Yoko Ono, the latter refers to Eiji as 'Sean', the name of Lennon and Ono's son (397). Of course, the existential status of this surrogate father is different from the others on offer for Eiji – Buntaro, Kozue Yamaya, Mr Morino, Subaro Tsukiyama – as Lennon represents an unattainable fantasy father. Nevertheless, it is within this dream landscape that the relevance of the novel's title is developed, especially, as noted earlier, in its paradoxical combination of the logical and the non-logical. For Patrick O'Donnell, the novel erases the barrier between reality and dream, effectively placing them in a relationship of equal significance to Eiji's understanding of the world and his place in it. As he argues, 'In *Number9Dream*, "dream" and "reality" are not merely paired off against each other, the dividing line between them erased as Eiji experiences the temporal and spatial disruptions of the metropolis' (67). In this context, O'Donnell cites the novel's epigram, taken from Don DeLillo's *Americana* – 'It is so much simpler to bury reality than it is to dispose of dreams' – as misleading in its apparent privileging of dream knowledge over real experience. O'Donnell's point holds up best with respect to Eiji's experience of Tokyo; however, Chapter Eight, in which he leaves the city, is more attuned to the sentiment in the DeLillo quotation, namely that dreams convey more opaque but nevertheless profound truths.

The emphasis on the importance of dreams is foregrounded in the fourth dream section of Chapter Eight, in which Lennon describes his song '#9

---

[2] Both Simpson (2011) and Posadas (2011) have noted the number of surrogate fathers that Eiji encounters on his journey, including the Yakuza figures Mr Morino and Kozue Yamaya, Eiji's landlord Buntaro and his great-uncle Tsukiyama; however, neither mentions John Lennon.

Dream' as a dream echo of 'Norwegian Wood'.³ The former song carries the chorus 'Ah! böwakawa, poussé poussé', which, as noted earlier, were words that came to Lennon in a dream. The end of this section is worth analysing closely:

'What does the title mean?'
'The ninth dream begins after every ending.'
A guru is furious. 'Why are you quitting your search for enlightenment?'
'If you're so bloody cosmic', scoffs John, 'you'll know why!'
I am laughing so hard that I— (398–9)

This passage reveals a number of important aspects of the novel. It provides a basis for the structure of the eighth chapter, which includes eight dream sequences interspersed with Eiji's waking actions, and the novel as a whole – which has eight main chapters, followed by a ninth, which consists of just a title without any content. The fact that the guru figure questions the abandonment of searching for enlightenment suggests a rejection of the teleological quest for understanding and resonates with Lennon and the Beatles' flirtation with Eastern religions (or rather Western constructions of Eastern religions) in the mid-1960s. The word 'enlightenment' evokes the eighteenth-century, Western European concept of the rational, material and teleological search for meaning, a system that is clearly compromised by allotting importance to the nonsensical phrase taken from the dream – 'Ah! böwakawa, poussé poussé'. These words are meaningless; or rather, they only gain meaning at the moment they are expressed. They come to signify an expression gesturing towards a kind of knowledge beyond recognized systems of meaning. Their meaning therefore exists beyond the capacity for a material and logical understanding. Paradoxically, however, the words then come to mean 'an expression beyond meaning', cryptically suggested by the aphorism Mitchell gives to Lennon in the novel: 'The ninth dream begins after every ending' (398). Emphasis, here, is given to the unfinished sentence, to a gesturing towards a significance that is beyond the power of language to describe. Eiji's response, 'I am laughing so hard that I—' anticipates (but frustrates) closure and suggests the power of bodily rather than intellectual responses. In the ontological dream world, the epistemological point of arrival remains out of reach for the rational mind.

---

³Although not mentioned directly, another significant intertextual reference here is the Japanese novelist Haruki Murakami (2000), who took 'Norwegian Wood' as the title of one of his novels. Murakami's postmodernist novel explores contemporary experience in Japan with respect to a range of historical narratives of the nation. Mitchell has cited Murakami as an influence on *number9dream* and his writing generally (Begley 2010), and several critics discuss this connection (for example, Posadas 2011; O'Donnell 2015).

In this context, we might discuss Mitchell with respect to Richard Rorty (a theorist often, although erroneously, associated with postmodern relativism) and his description of the attitude adopted towards world-systems by what he calls the 'ironist'. In his 1989 book, *Contingency, Irony, and Solidarity*, Rorty suggests that all human beings have a 'final vocabulary' with which they try to articulate their sense of the world; however, ironists are aware of the limitations of that vocabulary when they encounter other plausible vocabularies. The ironist is thus defined as having 'continuing doubts about the final vocabulary she currently uses' and 'realizes that arguments phrased in her present vocabulary can neither underwrite nor dissolve these doubts' (73). This description fits well with Eiji's outlook as it develops in the novel and, I would argue, Mitchell's position as represented by the novel as a whole. The nothingness, for example, that is represented by the empty ninth chapter suggests an alternative beyond any final vocabulary; indeed, the structure of the novel with its division into eight chapters, each with its own genre or vocabulary, suggests that a series of articulations is justifiable in the novel's quest for meaning, but none represent the last word. Within the context represented by the Rortean ironist's attitude to language, it is possible to search for a meaning to one's life, but always with openness to alternative perspectives and worldviews, and without the desire to impose your own beliefs on others. As with Eiji, this results in a tentative recognition that one's own perspective, although having value, does not outweigh the alternative and potentially oppositional values of others. This produces a kind of positive doubt, whereby an ethics can be developed from a position of acceptance and respect for alternative systems of thought.

Rorty's position in itself can be seen as a form of metamodernism (as Vermeulen and van den Akker define it), rather than the postmodernism with which it is most often associated, in that it accepts an oscillation between the certainties of one's own outlook and the inevitable, perpetual and welcome challenge that alternative and potentially oppositional systems offer. In Mitchell's novel, this kind of understanding of meaning results in a resting place, a negative capability represented by the empty ninth chapter. This position can simultaneously accept the radical subjectivism with which postmodernism is associated, but also maintains a sincere belief in an authentic teleological drive in that we each might discover our own system of meaning. In this way, a suturing of a modernist teleology with a postmodern subjectivism appears to be the arrival point of the novel. Ultimately, Mitchell's post-postmodernism is a combination of a Sartrean existentialism with a Rortean irony, in which the individual is under obligation to find their own ethical system, while recognizing the contingency of one's currently accepted beliefs. The arrival at this position is presented as a journey for Eiji, and in that sense the novel represents not only Eiji's postmodern *Bildungsroman* but a journey from one formal and philosophical paradigm to another, from postmodernism to some tentative configuration of a post-postmodernism.

Given the ahistorical trajectories herein involved, the arrival point might very well be a return to a pre-postmodernist existentialism or the indication of a new, as yet unformed, ethical system as represented by the empty (or silent) ninth chapter.

Works cited

Barthes, R. (1982), *Empire of Signs*, trans. Richard Howard. London: Jonathan Cape.
Baudrillard, J. (1981), *Simulacra and Simulation*, trans. Sheila Glaser. Ann Arbor: University of Michigan Press.
Begley, A. (2010), 'David Mitchell, The Art of Fiction No. 204', *The Paris Review*, 193, n.p.
Bentley, N. (2005), 'Introduction: Mapping the Millennium', in N. Bentley (ed.), *British Fiction of the 1990s*, London and New York: Routledge, 1–18.
Bourriaud, N. (2009), *Altermodern*, London: Tate Publishing.
Bradford, R. (2007), *The Novel Now: Contemporary British Fiction*, Malden and Oxford: Blackwell.
Childs, P. and J. Green (2011), 'The Novels in Nine Parts', in Sarah Dillon (ed.), *David Mitchell*, Canterbury: Gylphi, 25–47.
Chute, H. (2011), 'The Popularity of Postmodernism', *Twentieth-Century Literature*, 57(3 & 4), 354–63.
Harris-Birtill, R. (2015), '"A Row of Screaming Russian Dolls": Escaping the Panopticon in David Mitchell's *number9dream*', *SubStance*, 44(1), 55–70.
Holland, M. K. (2013), *Succeeding Postmodernism: Language and Humanism in Contemporary American Fiction*, New York: Bloomsbury.
Hutcheon, L. (1988), 'Modelling the Postmodern: Parody and Politics', in *A Politics of Postmodernism*, London and New York: Routledge, 22–36.
Jameson, F. (1983), 'Postmodernism and Consumer Society', in Hal Foster (ed.), *The Anti-Aesthetic: Essays on Postmodern Culture*, Seattle: Bay Press, 127–44.
Kirby, A. (2001), *Digimodernism: How New Technologies Dismantle the Postmodern and Reconfigure Our Culture*, London: Continuum.
Kelly, A. (2011), 'Beginning with Postmodernism', *Twentieth-Century Literature*, 57(3 & 4), 391–422.
Lipovetsky, G. (2005), *Hypermodern Times*, Cambridge: Polity.
López, J. and G. Potter (eds) (2001), *After Postmodernism: An Introduction to Critical Realism*, London and New York: The Athlone Press.
Mitchell, D. (2001), *number9dream*, London: Hodder and Stoughton.
Moretti, F. (1987), *The Way of the World: The Bildungsroman in European Culture*, London: Verso.
Murakami, H. (2000), *Norwegian Wood*, trans. J. Rubin, London: Vintage.
O'Donnell, P. (2015), *A Temporary Future: The Fiction of David Mitchell*, London and New York: Bloomsbury.
Posadas, B. T. (2011), 'Remediations of "Japan" in *number9dream*', in Sarah Dillon (ed.), *David Mitchell: Critical Essays*, Canterbury: Gylphi, 77–103.
Rorty, R. (1989), *Contingency, Irony, and Solidarity*, Cambridge: Cambridge University Press.

Sheff, D. (2000), *All We Are Saying: The Last Major Interview with John Lennon and Yoko Ono*, New York: St. Martin's Griffin.

Simpson, K. (2011), '"Or Something Like That": Coming of Age in *number9dream*', in Sarah Dillon (ed.), *David Mitchell: Critical Essays*, Canterbury: Gylphi, 49–76.

Soja, E. (1989), *Postmodern Geographies: The Reassertion of Space in Critical Social Theory*, London: Verso Press.

Tatsumi, T. (2002), 'The Japanoid Manifesto: Towards a New Poetics of Invisible Culture', *New Japanese Fiction, Special Issue of Review of Contemporary Fiction*, 22(2), 12–18.

Turner, L. (2011), *Metamodernism // Manifesto*. Available online: http://www.metamodernism.org/ (accessed 8 June 2016).

Ueno, T. (2002), 'Japanimation and Techo-Orientalism', in Bruce Grenville (ed.), *The Uncanny: Experiments in Cyborg Culture*, Vancouver: Arsenal Pulp Press, 223–36.

Vermeulen, T. and R. van den Akker (2010), 'Notes on Metamodernism', *Journal of Aesthetics & Culture*, 2, 1–14.

Wallace, D. F. (1993), 'E Unibus Pluram: Television and U.S. Fiction', *Review of Contemporary Fiction*, 13(2), 151–94.

3

'What was knowledge for, I would ask myself': Science, technology and *pharmakon* in David Mitchell's *Cloud Atlas*

Martin Paul Eve

Chapter summary

This chapter discusses science and technology in David Mitchell's *Cloud Atlas* (2004 [2008]) as a consistently double-edged phenomenon. Starting with an appraisal of the background of *techne*, I begin by drawing on recent work on technogenesis to highlight the centrality of technology to human history but also to Mitchell's text. From here, I turn to the technology of the book and the systems of remediation upon which *Cloud Atlas* draws. The chapter then works through a series of case studies, the most pronounced of which centres on the colonial technologies of medicine in the 'Pacific Diary of Adam Ewing', but which touches on every section of the novel. In conclusion, I point to the ways in which the technologies of *Cloud Atlas* can be read as reflexive statements on the novel's own cyclical temporal structures, situating its own novelistic form within a technogenetic feedback loop that is at once both remedy and poison (*pharmakon*).

Introduction

The word 'technology', as it occurs in contemporary English, is derived from the Latinized form of the Greek term τέχνη (*techne*) along with the suffix λόγια (*-logia*). While the latter part of the derivation pertains to communication and speech (and can be compared to the related form *logos*), τέχνη is concerned with art, skill and craft but also refers to methods and systems of action. Of course, in the twenty-first century, we are most accustomed to thinking of 'technology' as an electronic phenomenon. The 'latest tech' usually means consumer luxury gadgets, fuelled by that underlying animating force of electricity, the monetized output products of applied scientific research. Yet, this was not historically always the case. Prehistoric cave tools, the scroll and codex, weaving looms, pen and ink, wheelbarrows, bookshelves and plumbing are all, in their own way, technologies. They each are associated with methods and systems of doing things, with arts, crafts and making. It is only within a relatively recent time period that our notions of technology have shifted to a far narrower definition.

Indeed, technology has been key to human kind from its inception and has conditioned the development of our species within a feedback loop that N. Katherine Hayles terms 'technogenesis' (Hayles 2012). Thinkers such as Stanley Ambrose, for instance, have linked the development of 'Broca's area' in the frontal lobe of the human brain – which has a substantial function in language processing – to the motor control needed for our prehistoric use of compound-tool technologies (such as stone axes) (Ambrose 2001; Hayles 2012: 90–1). In this theory, learning to use tools might have led to the requisite neural abilities for language. Hayles also points out that, in more recent years, a woman who worked at the Bletchley Park cryptanalysis facility during the Second World War was so neurologically conditioned by her experiences of listening to encoded messages that 'she heard Morse code everywhere – in traffic noise, bird songs and other ambient sounds – with her mind automatically forming the words to which the sounds putatively corresponded' (Hayles 2012: 128). In such a system of technogenesis, neither are people conditioned purely by technology nor is technology fashioned independently by human actors – it is what might be termed a subject → technology → subject feedback loop.

The relationship between humankind and technology is, therefore, complex and reciprocal. People have always built technologies in order to accomplish necessary tasks and, *pace* Marx, to amplify their labour power (Marx 1992, chap. 7). At the same time, elements of our species' neurological, physiological and sociological aspects have all, in turn, been conditioned by the technologies that we build. Technology cannot be seen, then, as some externalized object of a one-way process of construction and mastery by people. Instead, technology is linked to specific epistemological paradigms (in our era: science) that allow their emergence and then feed into and partially condition human identity. Technology is about knowledge and it is about the self as much as it is about art, craft and systems of doing.

As one would expect then, despite this longer history, electronic technologies both real and imagined play a major role in much contemporary fiction. Whether one considers Thomas Pynchon's recent meditations on the 'deep web' in *Bleeding Edge* (2013), Jennifer Egan's parody of Facebook in *Look at Me* (2001 [2011]), Don DeLillo's work on cryogenics in *Zero K* (2016), or Tom McCarthy's examination of early wireless telegraphy in *C* (2010), it is clear that there is fertile ground in fictionalizing contemporary and historical technologies. However, few novels in the past two decades have spanned such a broad historical period as David Mitchell's monumental *Cloud Atlas* (2004); an 'experimental epic' that maps the 'violent global history of change and crisis through the longue durée', in Wendy Knepper's words (Knepper 2016: 99). Indeed, as Patrick O'Donnell has noted, '*Cloud Atlas* moves across spatial and temporal domains stretching from the islands of the South Pacific in the mid-nineteenth century to ... a distant future that foresees a return to a primitive, survivalist past in postapocalyptic Hawaii' (O'Donnell 2015: 69). Within the range of discrete time periods covered by Mitchell's work, each section of the novel presents the reader with an array of ways in which systems of knowledge and identity intersect through historically contingent sociotechnical assemblages.

In this chapter, I appraise a representative range of technologies that appear in and above Mitchell's genre-fusing work, in each case drawing out the epistemologies that facilitate their emergence but also the challenges for identity that they pose. Ultimately, I will argue that while Mitchell's novel cannot be said to be *about* technology, it *is* a text about people and societies over history (or time). Without an understanding of the technologies shaped by and that shape the societies and historical periods in Mitchell's work, however, it is not possible to grasp fully the complex interrelation of people and things that runs through *Cloud Atlas*'s vast time span, a relationship that is always double-edged. I will argue here, then, that the technologies in *Cloud Atlas* mirror the text's own conflicted temporality: at once representing progress and regression. Indeed, it is as though, for Mitchell, we erroneously seek to use technology to measure time, as though technological progression were a straight line. Yet, Mitchell is a long-standing fan of the British television show, *Doctor Who*, and so it might be more appropriate to say that although 'people assume that time is a strict progression of cause to effect', it is actually 'more like a big ball of wibbly-wobbly ... timey-wimey ... stuff' (MacDonald 2007), an interpretation with which *Cloud Atlas*'s depictions of technology seem to agree (Mitchell's love of *Doctor Who* was explored by, for example, Ishiguro and Mitchell 2016).

The technology of the book

The first and perhaps most important technology of *Cloud Atlas* for the reader is the medium within which the work is contained. For many, this is the codex; the paginated and printed editions of dead tree with which we are familiar. For others, it may be an e-reading device such as Amazon's Kindle. For still others, it may be read on a laptop or other device with a visual display unit (VDU). In the case of Mitchell's novel, the specific technology of reading within which the text is encountered holds significance for two reasons. First, the novel's radical form is presented extremely differently within each medium. Second, through a set of inadvertent errors in the publishing process, the text available in each of the editions and forms is substantially different.

To the first of these points, the specific medium within which Mitchell's novel is read matters because *Cloud Atlas*'s structure is unusual. Indeed, among Mitchell's oeuvre, *Cloud Atlas* is his 'most ambitious experiment in narrative form and the possibilities of storytelling', as Courtney Hopf puts it (Hopf 2011: 108). The novel is famous for its pyramid structure in which the narrative of each section breaks, sometimes mid-sentence, to begin the next chapter before resuming in the opposite order after the halfway point of the text. This 'intertextual microeconomy', as O'Donnell terms it, in which the sub-narratives interrupt each other, has broad implications for the novel's philosophy of interconnectedness (O'Donnell 2015: 72). However, this textual playfulness also has physical and technological implications for the reader.

To understand this, however, it is first necessary to journey briefly into the technological history of the 'book'. The codex (the printed book) evolved as the best compromise technology for reading that could provide both random and sequential access in a convenient and portable form. In other words, the codex works well for readers who wish simply to read in a linear fashion from start to end (sequential access), but also allows users to 'jump' (random access) to specific moments in the novel through that other most useful technology of reading: the bookmark. The scroll, one of the codex's predecessors, lacked the affordances of the codex with respect to portability and random access, although it was fairly competent at sequential access. Some of the codex's claimed successors, such as the Amazon Kindle, improve on the affordances of portability (allowing a reader to carry potentially hundreds of books) but once again compromise on random access (as anyone who has ever taught a seminar knows, it is ungainly and difficult to move to specific locations in a text on many digital readers).

In a novel such as *Cloud Atlas* where the textual and narrative layout is part of the work – as it is in other texts, such as Mark Z. Danielewski's *House of Leaves* (2000) or his *Only Revolutions* (2006 [2007]) – the specific technological presentation of the 'book' changes the readerly experience. Since the text relies on the reader holding the first half of Ewing's narrative in his or her working memory for almost the entire length of the book, it is likely that most readers will wish to flick back and forth through the novel in order to refresh their memories. In an electronic edition, this is substantially harder, a phenomenon also present in other works that require deliberate transversal to endnotes, such as David Foster Wallace's *Infinite Jest* (1996). Likewise, the absence of specific spatial orientations in an electronic reader changes the experience of *Cloud Atlas* (i.e. in a print version there is a known, tactile and perceivable 'location' sensation in the book that is not captured by percentage metrics in electronic editions). Readers working within the codex may experience the sensation of falling as they move down into the latter part of the novel and cascade back towards the first text. Such elements of embodied reader experience, though, are not present in other virtualized reading technologies, such as the Kindle or VDU (see Nielsen Norman Group 2006; Mangen 2008).

On the second of my points, as I have written elsewhere, the technological specificity of the edition of *Cloud Atlas* matters intensely because there are huge textual differences between published versions of the novel. Due to a combination of social and technological editorial processes, two different co-genetic versions of the novel's text have entered public circulation. The specific technological book medium chosen by the reader is important, then, because it will determine which version of *Cloud Atlas* he or she will encounter (Eve 2016). At its most abstracted levels, therefore, *Cloud Atlas* is a novel that depends upon readerly choices of the technologies of the book but is one that also conditions the reader through this technology. Indeed, so integral is this presentation of book technology that the fundamental identity of the text is changed depending on the reader's selection of edition. The novel demonstrates the technogenetic feedback loop of identity as much as any technology it depicts. Importantly, though, *Cloud Atlas* is also known for the way in which each of its narratives is passed down the narrative chain. In other words, almost every sub-narrative in *Cloud Atlas* is represented as a technological object of reading in the next narrative (for more on this, see, again, Hopf 2011). Indeed, three of the narratives within *Cloud Atlas* are presented as texts while three others are respectively encapsulated as a film, seen in a holographic device, and related through the oral storytelling tradition.

Each of these storytelling, or booklike, objects is, to some extent, a metatextual signifier. The presence of objects that tell stories within novels cannot but draw attention to the artifice of the work itself. More than this, though, in the heterogeneous forms that these technologies take (they are, after all, not all printed books), Mitchell paradoxically draws attention both to the *specificity* and *material uniqueness* of the medium in which his reader may be encountering *Cloud Atlas* but also to the *interchangeability* and *comparability* of diverse narrative mediums. In the first instance, by their *difference from* yet *repetition of* the specific form of the book encountered by the reader, the particularity of the edition of *Cloud Atlas* is foregrounded.

The fact that each of these objects retells part of the narrative enables the reader to perceive similitude between the novel and the sub-objects that it presents. That these objects are not the same in form as the 'book' held by the reader, though, encourages a focus on materiality and uniqueness. The book the reader is holding is different to the films, orisons and even books within the text. On the other hand, all of the objects perform *the same function* as the novel itself; they each tell part of Cloud Atlas's story for the next temporal setting. In this way, despite the differences of technology in the presentation of narrative, each can be recognized as a microcosmic functional substitute for the novel itself.

Technologies of knowledge and identity

Books, though, are not the only technology in Cloud Atlas. In order to draw a broader survey of technologies from Mitchell's novel, I intend to move progressively through the sections of Cloud Atlas. To begin, then, I want to turn initially to 'The Pacific Diary of Adam Ewing', Mitchell's first environment and the one upon which I will draw most extensively. This portion of the novel is set in the nineteenth century, predominantly around the Chatham Islands but also aboard a ship called the *Prophetess*. The main sources for this section of Mitchell's novel are well documented and implicitly include A. Shand's 1892 work in *The Journal of the Polynesian Society* on the Moriori genocide, but also Jared Diamond's *Germs, Guns and Steel*, which Mitchell cites as the origin of Cloud Atlas (Shand 1892; Diamond 2005: 53–7; Mitchell 2005), although Wendy Knepper also suggests a useful range of broader sources for this section (Knepper 2016: 104–5).

The dominant driver of narrative action in this portion of the text is the slow poisoning of Ewing by the sinister Dr Henry Goose. Indeed, it emerges that Goose is a robber, intent on killing Ewing in order to retrieve the 'entire estate' that he believes to be in Ewing's trunk (523). Goose almost achieves this feat by convincing the narrator that an internal worm is causing Ewing's illness. The deceit works by Goose disguising his poison as medicine, substituting in narrative the toxin for the cure, while thereby also drawing a metaphorical parallel between the supposed parasite within Ewing's body and the parasite that is Goose within Ewing's confidence. Ewing so heartily swallows the lie – even if readers can perceive the threat and dramatic irony – that he proclaims that 'Henry's powders are indeed a wondrous medicament' (37).

The technology of medicine, then, is the dominant strain that I identify in this first section of Cloud Atlas. This technology is here depicted, though, as metaphorically determined by and developed within two epistemic constructs: that of empire and that of *pharmakon*. On the first of these points, as Pratik Chakrabarti has convincingly demonstrated, 'the history of modern medicine cannot be narrated without the history of imperialism'

(Chakrabarti 2014: ix). While each permutation of empire brought with it different intersections with the development of medicine – be it the 'civilizing mission', the 'age of empire', or the 'scramble for Africa' (Chakrabarti 2014: x) – the most relevant paradigm for the Ewing section of *Cloud Atlas* is the collision of tropical colonialism with parasitology. Indeed, the contemporary discipline of 'tropical medicine', although problematic for its collapse of many heterogeneous geographies and climates into the single term 'tropical', has its genealogical roots in healthcare provision for European colonial troops and expatriate civilians (Chakrabarti 2014: 141). From there, as Michael Worboys has noted, tropical medicine became the 'main scientific expression of Western medical and health policy for the Third World' in the twentieth century (1976: 75). In particular, the epistemology of 'germ theory' around this time underwent revision as military physicians attempted to grapple with malaria. Of note, Charles Louis Alphonse Laveran's discovery of the protozoan cause of malaria in 1880, coupled with Patrick Manson's 1877 work on filarial worms, paved the way for parasitology and vector studies to combine, thus creating the discipline of tropical medicine, all within a colonial context (Manson 1878; Chakrabarti 2014: 141–63).

The requisite colonial context for an exploration of the technologies of tropical medicine, then, is given on just the first few pages of Mitchell's novel. The reader is presented with a so-called 'Indian hamlet' in the text's very first sentence, re-enforced a page or so later with mention of an 'Indian war-canoe' and the attendant colonial racism of reference to a 'sullen miss' who has a 'tinge of black blood' with a suspicion that 'her mother is not far removed from the jungle breed' (3, 5). The initial scene of the text then quickly moves to a 'public flogging' of particular violence in which a 'tattooed' throng of 'slaves' and a tribal 'chieftain' watch a 'Goliath' of a 'whip-master' work upon a 'beaten savage'. The scene is clearly supposed ironically to invoke the imperial logic of a 'civilizing' morality when the 'only two Whites present … swooned under each fall of the lash' even while raising the spectre of colonial trade and slavery when Ewing thinks that the 'pelt' of the whip-master would 'fetch a fine price' (6). From the very beginning, then, *Cloud Atlas* signals an imperial ontology and epistemology for 'The Pacific Diary of Adam Ewing', and the novel's language is highly racially charged.

It is, though, against this racist and colonizing epistemology that the core plot point for Ewing's narrative can emerge. Dr Goose's claimed knowledge of parasitical worms and their treatment – although slightly misaligned with the timescale of the actual development of parasitology – is vital for the imagined savage world of darkness, of 'blood-frenzy' (15) threat and of sights 'at once indelible, fearsome & sublime' (20) that Ewing constructs. Indeed, Ewing builds a picture throughout the narrative of the regions he is visiting as a sort of 'white man's grave' (Chakrabarti 2014: 144, 159) in which the supposed innate danger of the landscape and its climate (reflected through the blackness of its inhabitants and reported by Goose as a 'fever of the clime' (37)) poses a unique threat to the 'civilized' figure and the only solution is to find a 'specialist in tropical parasites' (22).

Yet, the falseness of this epistemology and its technological remedy (the poison/medicine) is revealed through a parallel to the stowaway episode of Ewing's tale. For, shortly into his voyage, Ewing discovers an 'uninvited cabin-mate' in his room; the very man, Autua, who was whipped in the opening scene (33). The metaphorical parallels with the 'worm inside' are clear here: the supposedly 'civilized' man has an element of the environment leeching off his body (the 'worm') and now feels he has an 'Indian' (for all non-whites are 'Indians' to him) parasitizing his living quarters. The 'cure' to the stowaway situation proposed (although not eventually administered) by the captain of the ship, however, provides the link to the second surrounding context for medicine in this part of *Cloud Atlas*: *pharmakon*. The captain proposes to shoot Autua while he is climbing the mizzen (35). The callousness of this planned murder, as a supposed 'remedy' to the situation, thereby re-highlights colonialism's toxicity by analogy. For the solutions empire gives in its spatial and cultural appropriations turn out in this novel to be as poisonous as Goose's medical approaches. The colonial 'medicines' – with their white 'cures' of cultural domination, metaphorically embodied in Goose's tropical remedies – are genocidal, toxic technologies.

Such a reading sits tightly with the second element on which I wish to draw: Jacques Derrida's (in)famous work on the φάρμακον (*pharmakon*) in his essay 'Plato's Pharmacy'. In this tract, Derrida focuses his attention on the fact that the Ancient Greek term *pharmakon* – used by Plato in his Φαῖδρος (*Phaedrus* [*Dialogue*]) – is a 'medicine ... which acts as both remedy and poison' (Derrida 2004: 75). Indeed, Derrida writes that he hopes 'to display ... the regular, ordered polysemy that has, through skewing, indetermination, or overdetermination, but without mistranslation, permitted the rendering of the same word by "remedy", "recipe", "poison", "drug", "philter" etc.' (Derrida 2004: 77). Although, then, Mitchell makes light fun of the era of Derridean stylistics with his passing reference to 'MAs in Postmodernism and Chaos Theory' (152), the overlaps between his novel and Derrida's focus on the ambiguity in the language of medicine, drugs and pharmakon cannot so easily be dismissed. Yet, there is more to this than the simple specificity of medicine. For Derrida, the pharmakon is reflected in the acts of translation and interpretation – violent destructions that must reduce the text 'to one of its simple elements' – but also in 'the eidos, truth, law, the episteme, dialectics, philosophy', all of which are 'other names for the pharmakon' (Derrida 2004: 101, 127). In Derrida's elaborate reading, 'what is at stake in this overturning [the involution of the pharmakon's bounded polysemy that creates a constant "non-identity-with-itself"] is no less than science and death' (Derrida 2004: 121).

Indeed, in *Cloud Atlas*'s first section, the scientific technology of medicine acts as a doubly functional element: at once curing and killing, engendered by a colonial epistemology, and producing a technogenetic ironic imperial identity. To understand this final link in the chain – that the technology produces an ironic imperial identity – requires a brief examination of Mitchell's stylistics. For much like Derrida's characterization of the pharmakon, the performance of Mitchell's hyperbolic enactment of colonial-style discourse contains its own knowing winks at its opposite, even when 'the charade was having its desired effect', as the text puts it (497). This is because this section of *Cloud Atlas*'s style is juxtaposed with six other distinct linguistic registers, each of which acts as a temporal locative marker for the reader. Consider, for example, the courtroom scene in Ewing's narrative contains lines of dialogue that include faux nineteenth-century redactions: 'Unhand me you sons of w—s!' (513).

There is a long literary history behind this tradition of redaction, particularly when it comes to names and expletives (Barth 1988: 73). As Lisa Gitelman notes, however, these blanks were only ever nominal since everybody knew what they masked: 'they are not really blank but only virtually so'; they are 'sites of transaction between a knowing author and a knowing reader' (Gitelman 2014: 27). In such cases, the reader is supposed to be able to infer what lies beneath. Yet, from just this single instance, we can see how Mitchell's language registers (themselves a type of τέχνη) function and, yet again, they have a metaphorical parallel to the mediating technology in this chapter. For, in examples such as this redaction, the 'sites of transaction between a knowing author and a knowing reader' are not merely concerned with decoding the text underneath the blank, but rather in correctly placing Mitchell's characters within a nineteenth-century imperial identity context. Readers can see the irony of these overblown speech patterns – as constructed by a contemporary novelist in order to critique empire – even while the speech patterns can be used by a reader to determine accurately the identity of Mitchell's characters. In this way, the treacherous double-facing technology of medicine can move from a mimetic depiction conditioned by the spatial epistemology of empire to one that acts even as a metaphor for Mitchell's stylistic play, all stemming from a linguistic root and intra-diegetic depiction of the *pharmakon* as a remedy and as a cure. It is also fair to say that Mitchell's styling is key to this metaphorical link between empire, medicine and *pharmakon*.

'How bad would an accident be?'

The doubled nature of technology as *pharmakon* is continued in the second of Mitchell's narratives, 'Letters from Zedelghem'. In this section, communication technologies, in all their forms, serve as the central mechanism for a technology that both heals and poisons: that is grounded in particular epistemological roots and that engenders subjectivity through a technogenetic feedback loop. Indeed, the very title of the chapter – invoking the history of the epistolary novel – refers to the inter-European postal service in the 1930s but, specifically, to the uniquely delayed temporality of this technology (on which, see Bray 2003).

The first crucial point to note about the technology of the postal service is that it is contrasted with the telegraph within Mitchell's novel. At one point, Augustowski sends an 'enigmatic telegram after the performance in Cracow', which reads: 'FIRST TODTENVOGEL MYSTIFIED STOP SECOND PERFORMANCE FISTICUFFS STOP THIRD ADORED STOP FOURTH TALK OF TOWN STOP' (71). What is important about the telegraph here is that it provides rapid communication in ways that were not previously possible; the telegraph comes first and the 'newspaper clippings followed' (71). In fact, the telegraph begins an age in which the two combined components of the word 'newspaper' – referring to that which is new but also that which is printed on paper – come to be oxymoronic as paper becomes too slow to contain 'the new'. In addition, it is also only too easy to draw parallels between the speed of the telegraph and the speed of the contemporary internet (see Hayles 2012: 125; Carey 1989). This contrast between the technologies of electric transmission and physical postage are all the more accentuated in *Cloud Atlas* when Frobisher at first complains of their rare speed, calling Rufus Sixsmith an '*ass*' for sending him a telegram because 'telegrams attract attention' (52), even while later in the novel he threatens that 'if you think I'll wait around for your letters to appear, I'm afraid you are much mistaken' (471).

The epistemology that roots the communication technologies in this section, then, is one of speed scarcity in a world on the cusp of a new era. Even as Frobisher acknowledges his desire for speed and accelerationism, he is unable to accept speed of communication as a mass commodity and, in one crucial way, denounces it. In fact, in one of the most temporally disorientating scenes in the text, Frobisher explicitly relies on the delayed timing/slowness of postal technologies to communicate his love and death for Sixsmith from beyond the grave. When Frobisher writes that he 'shot [him]self through the roof of [his] mouth at 5 a.m. this morning', the time is out of joint (487). Indeed, the character knows that 'time cannot permeate this sabbatical' in more ways than his belief in reincarnation (490). For not only must Frobisher have written this letter in the past tense, using the past participle before the action, but he is also aware that Sixsmith will receive the letter a fair while after his death, thus then restoring linear time, at least in part. Frobisher thereby uses the split epistemologies of slowness and accelerationism, mediated by the technologies of postal letters and the contrasting telegraph, to craft a technogenetic self-identity that can defy the linear flow of time. The technology is a form of *pharmakon* in that while Frobisher's final letter is a love letter to cure the soul – 'we both know in our hearts who is the true love of my life [Sixsmith]' – it is also a heartbreaking and poisonous suicide note (489).

As 'Letters from Zedelghem' cedes to 'Half Lives: The First Luisa Rey Mystery', however, Mitchell's technological focus point shifts once more.

The clear locus of narrative action in this chapter is the technology of nuclear power, encapsulated in Mitchell's 'Swanneke Island' fission plant, owned by the malignant 'Seaboard Corporation'. As Luisa Rey, the plucky yet reluctant journalist/detective crossover figure, uncovers ever-deepening layers of conspiracy surrounding the plant's safety, the *pharmakon*-like element of this technology is brought to the fore. This is because the background epistemological context against which nuclear power must be situated is that of global warming. Nuclear power was born as a saviour of the planet, a treasured child of the 'Environmental Protection Agency' to which *Cloud Atlas* makes reference, even if Greenpeace – the model for Mitchell's 'GreenFront' – has always been opposed (127, 131). Indeed, when it became a political and economic 'impossibility' to reduce energy consumption, nuclear energy once promised a clean and limitless source. Of course, this idea was demolished by Chernobyl and Three Mile Island, the historical scenarios that *Cloud Atlas* clearly summons when it mentions a 'hydrogen build-up, an explosion, packed hospitals, the first deaths by radiation poisoning. The official inquiry' (130). Once again, Mitchell's text presents a version of technology that is doubled against itself.

Perhaps the purest representation of this *pharmakon* phenomenon, however, is found in the *least* technologically orientated of Mitchell's narratives: 'The Ghastly Ordeal of Timothy Cavendish'. For, in this chapter, it is the quintessential symbol of modernity – the train – that bears Cavendish away and into the hands of the Foucaldian juridico-medical apparatus. In fact, the journey that Cavendish takes, primarily by train, occupies a remarkably lengthy portion of this text, at fifteen or so pages (160–75). However, this is appropriate, for, as Jani Scandura and Michael Thurston have noted, the train is 'the primary metaphor of modernity and its metonym' (2000: 25); it is the central figuration of technological modernity and entire nations' geopolitical arrangements were shaped by the assemblage of railways (Dinnerstein 2008: 207–8). Indeed, the railway is also a signifier of globalization in *Cloud Atlas* as, according to Cavendish, 'rolling stock in this country is built in Hamburg or somewhere, and when the German engineers test British-bound trains, they use imported lengths of our buggered, privatised tracks because the decently maintained European rails won't provide accurate testing conditions' (171). For the bigoted Timothy – 'I'm not a racialist, but' (172) – Cavendish, the railway harks back to an era of Empire and, with his nation's fading status in the world, through the train, he feels compelled to ask the clichéd question, 'Who really won the ruddy war?' (171).

Yet, once more, technological progression here proves itself to be a fickle friend. Despite its many trials, the breakneck pace of escape from his violent creditors, facilitated by the train, appears to Cavendish as a supernatural or theological miracle, delivering him to 'an angel incarnate' (175). However, within a few short pages he has signed a document that 'authorizes [... the staff of Aurora House] to apply compliancy' and to subject him to physical violence in the name of medical treatment (176–7). The historical and technological narrative is clear here: fleeing on the symbol of technological modernity, the train, does not save Cavendish. Instead, it delivers him into the hands of a Foucauldian institution of power, a medical institution legitimated by the juridical mechanisms of the state, represented in the self-binding contract of the signature and overseen through an objectifying gaze (Foucault 2009). For his eventual rescue, he will require a different form of technological transport: the motor car. Where this technology, with its gas-guzzling tendencies, might eventually lead is not implied to be a bright future in *Cloud Atlas*.

As *Cloud Atlas* moves beyond history and the present into the future world of Sonmi~451, the novel reaches its most technologically advanced (although not temporally progressed) stage. In both editions of the novel, the narrative here concerns the condemned clone prisoner Sonmi~451, who belongs to a race of synthetic beings called 'fabricants', whose brief lifespans are ended when they are killed in order to be fed back to other fabricants in the form of 'soap'. In fact, this chapter would not even be possible without the synthetic cloning technology that is used to create and sustain the fabricant race, even if Mitchell clearly intends his clones to be as human-like as possible. In this light, that Mitchell's text begins here to most positively signal its ambivalence towards technological progress – at the moment when we are first encountering a future world – is not surprising. What is perhaps curious is that this distrust of future positivism is indicated by a focus on the recording of history, for Sonmi remarks, in response to the archivist's provocation, that 'no other version of the truth has ever mattered' (187. In the electronic edition this is slightly different: 'TRUTH IS SINGULAR. ITS "VERSIONS" ARE MISTRUTHS.').

Although this affirmation is designed to *counter* a pluralization of historical narratives and assert the singularity of occurrence, it has the effect of suggesting that the archivist's record for the state will be perspectivized and partial, used for political purposes. In having this section open with such a remark – sceptically drawing attention to the fact that history is not an accumulation of facts but a non-linear proliferation of narratives – within a world that is supposedly technologically advanced, Mitchell draws attention to the non-linear moral progress of technology. For even as technology seems to become more powerful (perhaps like time in the text, which does nonetheless move forwards into the future), the commensurate ethical development is not linear, but regressive.

This is finally shown in an even more powerful way in Mitchell's last narrative sequence, 'Sloosha's Crossin' an' Ev'rythin' After'. Linguistically and thematically predicated on Russell Hoban's *Riddley Walker* (1980), the setting for this section is a world far in the future but one that has undergone some kind of (nuclear) catastrophe that has caused a technological regression to the Iron Ages (Eve 2014). The central question that this section seems to ask is, 'So is it better to be savage'n to be civ'lized?' (318. In the electronic edition the capitalization is different again: 'So is it better to be savage'n to be Civ'lized?'). Yet, the way that these terms are measured is diffuse, at once to do with the rule of 'laws' but also concerned with time. Indeed, the reader is told that the primary difference, at least in Meronym's explanation, is that 'the savage sat'fies his needs now' while 'the Civ'lized ... sees further' and plans for the uncertainty of the future. Most importantly, though, it is clear from Mitchell's description that these categories break down when 'progress' is measured by technological change. For the 'old'uns', those before the worldwide catastrophe, had great technology ('the Smart') but they also had viciousness and cruelty ('the savegery o' jackals') and it is this that 'tripped the Fall' (318–19. The electronic edition features different capitalization and punctuation in these quotations). Once again, technology is *pharmakon*, it can be poison or remedy depending on its use, across time, informing and conditioning but never totally determining identity.

Conclusion

In this chapter, I have appraised a range of technologies that appear in David Mitchell's novel *Cloud Atlas* in the service of a dual-pronged argument. The first part of this argument is that technology is always part of a technogenetic feedback loop in which character- and textual-identity is, in part but not totally, determined by human–machine/technique interactions. I do not here go as far as Hélène Machinal in suggesting a 'subjection of the human through technology' but instead point to frameworks of technogenesis that imply a subject → technology → subject feedback loop (Machinal 2011: 128). The second part is that technological progress is Janus-faced with a temporality that points in both directions, framed here by Derrida's reading of the *pharmakon* – technology as both cure and disease, remedy and poison. As I have also pointed out, these perspectives on technology can even be read into the overarching structure of the text's editions and the variance between them – the 'technology' of the book.

I have not, of course, exhausted the possibility for technological readings of Mitchell's novel and there is undoubtedly a great deal more to say. Indeed, I have focused primarily here on the postcolonial implications of technology rather than its embroilment with the economic incursions of neo-liberal globalization among a range of societies presented in Mitchell's novel. Yet, ultimately, what I have hoped to excavate is a framework for answering the question posed by Sonmi~451: 'What was all this knowledge for, I would ask myself, if I could not use it to better my xistence?' (233. In the electronic edition this reads: 'What was knowledge for, I would ask myself, if I could not use it to better my xistence?'). Knowledge and its translation into technology in *Cloud Atlas* brings no guarantee of bettering one's existence. Through a self-aware study of technology and technogenetic identity, though, *Cloud Atlas* hints that it may be possible to know oneself a little better and to avoid the trap of positivist thinking that might see technological progress and knowledge as a pure and sealed benchmark of the self. For, as the text tells us, 'knowledge without xperience is food without sustenance' (233. In the electronic edition this reads: 'I said something about reading not being knowledge, about knowledge without xperience being food without sustenance').

Works cited

Ambrose, S. H. (2001), 'Paleolithic Technology and Human Evolution', *Science*, 291(5509), 1748–53.
Barth, J. (1988), 'Lost in the Funhouse', in *Lost in the Funhouse: Fiction for Print, Tape, Live Voice*, The Anchor Literary Library, New York: Anchor Press, 72–97.
Bray, J. (2003), *The Epistolary Novel: Representation of Consciousness*, London and New York: Routledge.
Carey, J. W. (1989), 'Technology and Ideology: The Case of the Telegraph', in *Communication as Culture: Essays on Media and Society*, New York: Routledge, 201–30.
Chakrabarti, P. (2014), *Medicine and Empire: 1600–1960*, Basingstoke: Palgrave Macmillan.
Danielewski, M. Z. (2000), *House of Leaves*, London: Anchor.
Danielewski, M. Z. (2007), *Only Revolutions: A Novel*, Reprint edn, New York: Pantheon.
DeLillo, D. (2016), *Zero K*, New York: Picador.
Derrida, J. (2004), 'Plato's Pharmacy', in *Dissemination*, London: Continuum, 67–186.
Diamond, J. M. (2005), *Guns, Germs and Steel: A Short History of Everybody for the Last 13,000 Years*, London: Vintage.
Dinnerstein, J. (2008), 'Modernism', in K. Halttunen (ed.), *A Companion to American Cultural History*, Blackwell Companions to American History, Malden: Blackwell Pub, 198–213.
Egan, J. (2011), *Look at Me*, London: Corsair.
Eve, M. P. (2014), '"Some Kind of Thing It Aint Us but Yet Its in Us": David Mitchell, Russell Hoban, and Metafiction After the Millennium', *SAGE Open*, 4(1). Available online: http://sgo.sagepub.com/content/4/1/2158244014521636 (accessed 12 February 2014).
Eve, M. P. (2016), '"You Have to Keep Track of Your Changes": The Version Variants and Publishing History of David Mitchell's *Cloud Atlas*', *Open Library of Humanities*, 2(2). doi:http://doi.org/10.16995/olh.82.
Foucault, M. (2009), *The Birth of the Clinic: An Archaeology of Medical Perception*, London: Routledge.
Gitelman, L. (2014), *Paper Knowledge: Toward a Media History of Documents*, Durham: Duke University Press.
Hayles, N. K. (2012), *How We Think: Digital Media and Contemporary Technogenesis*, Chicago: University of Chicago Press.
Hoban, R. (1980), *Riddley Walker*, London: Jonathan Cape.

Hopf, C. (2011), 'The Stories We Tell: Discursive Identity Through Narrative Form in *Cloud Atlas*', in S. Dillon (ed.), *David Mitchell: Critical Essays*, Canterbury: Gylphi, 105–26.

Ishiguro, K. and D. Mitchell (2016), *Among Giants and Ghosts: The Southbank Centre*, London.

Knepper, W. (2016), 'Toward a Theory of Experimental World Epic: David Mitchell's *Cloud Atlas*', *ariel: A Review of International English Literature*, 47(1), 93–126.

MacDonald, H. (2007), 'Blink', in *Doctor Who* by Steven Moffat, Series 3, Episode 10.

Machinal, H. (2011), '*Cloud Atlas*: From Postmodernity to the Posthuman', in S. Dillon (ed.), *David Mitchell: Critical Essays*, Canterbury: Gylphi, 127–54.

Mangen, A. (2008), 'Hypertext Fiction Reading: Haptics and Immersion', *Journal of Research in Reading*, 31(4), 404–19.

Manson, P. (1878), 'On the Development of Filaria Sanguinis Hominis, and on the Mosquito Considered as a Nurse', *Journal of the Linnean Society of London, Zoology*, 14(75), 304–11.

Marx, K. (1992), *Capital*, London: Penguin.

McCarthy, T. (2010), *C*, London: Jonathan Cape.

Mitchell, D. (2004), *Cloud Atlas*, Kindle Edition, New York, NY: Random House/Amazon Kindle.

Mitchell, D. (2004), *Cloud Atlas*, New York, NY: Random House.

Mitchell, D. (2004), *Cloud Atlas*, London: Sceptre.

Mitchell, D. (2005), 'Genesis', *The Guardian*. Available online: https://www.theguardian.com/books/2005/apr/16/featuresreviews.guardianreview23 (accessed 27 July 2016).

Mitchell, D. (2008), *Cloud Atlas*, London: Sceptre.

Nielsen Norman Group (2006), 'How People Read on the Web: The Eyetracking Evidence'. Available online: https://www.nngroup.com/reports/how-people-read-web-eyetracking-evidence/ (accessed 14 April 2016).

O'Donnell, P. (2015), *A Temporary Future: The Fiction of David Mitchell*, New York: Bloomsbury Academic.

Pynchon, T. (2013), *Bleeding Edge*, London: Jonathan Cape.

Scandura, J. and M. Thurston (2000), *Modernism, Inc.*, New York: New York University Press. Available online: http://nyupress.org/books/9780814781371/ (accessed 19 February 2016).

Shand, A. (1892), 'The Occupation of the Chatham Islands by the Maoris in 1835: Part II, The Migration of Ngatiawa to Chatham Island', *The Journal of the Polynesian Society*, 1(3), 154–63.

Wallace, D. F. (1996), *Infinite Jest*, Boston: Little, Brown and Company.

Worboys, M. (1976), 'The Emergence of Tropical Medicine: A Study in the Establishment of a Scientific Speciality', in G. Lemaine et al. (eds), *Perspectives on the Emergence of Scientific Disciplines*, The Hague: Mouton, 75–98.

4

Witnessing transhistorical trauma in *Cloud Atlas*

Jason Howard Mezey

Chapter summary

A narrative tour de force that deploys six nested stories on a global, transhistorical scale, David Mitchell's celebrated novel *Cloud Atlas* is a meditation on trauma and the legacies of traumatic memory. Focusing on Adam Ewing's Conical Tor encounter with the Moriori dendroglyphs, I adapt Freud's concept of the primal scene to identify a specific form of traumatic witnessing Ewing is only gradually able to undertake. Through Ewing, Mitchell presents a model for readers to rewrite the fall of humankind previewed by the novel as a self-inflicted, species-wide trauma, suggesting that ethical choices may arise even from predatory environments and that acknowledging the trauma of others is not only an ethical stance but also a precondition of ethical action. To do this, Mitchell implies, we must witness, process and undertake our own custodianship of the traumas of others.

Introduction

Sunt lacrimae rerum et mentem mortalia tangunt.[1]

—VIRGIL, *The Aeneid*

Hae-Joo showered and changed. He told me he had to attend a Union cell meeting and warned me to keep the window shutter down and not to answer the door or fone unless it was him or Apis with this crypto: he wrote the words 'These are the tears of things' on a scrap of paper, which he then burned in the ashtray.

SONMI~451, *narrating her Orison*

In a direct nod to the epic genre David Mitchell reinvents in *Cloud Atlas* (Knepper 2016; Mezey 2011), Robert Frobisher's suicide letter to Rufus Sixsmith concludes with the opaque Virgilian quotation 'sunt lacrimae rerum' (Mitchell 2004: 471). Drawn from the *Aeneid*'s description of Aeneas weeping at images of the Trojan War, the closing of Frobisher's letter speaks not only to his own yearning for memorialization through his *Cloud Atlas Sextet* but also to the complex connections between trauma and its representation in narrative. Through each of their respective narratives, Aeneas (Virgil 2006: 63–4) and the main characters of *Cloud Atlas* view a series of events that simultaneously includes them (Aeneas sees himself depicted on the walls of Juno's temple amid the battle scenes) and reaches out to them across time. As both Virgil and Mitchell imply, such are the 'burdens of mortality' – to be personally implicated in and moved by the narratives of others. According to Patrick O'Donnell, the role characters and readers alike collectively play in disseminating such narratives are the key to human endurance in the inhospitable universe of *Cloud Atlas*: 'If "we" survive, Mitchell tells us, it will be because we have a hand in delivering and passing on narratives that offer alternatives to those fatal territorial stories of empire and supremacy, narcissistic agency and xenophobic fear that tenaciously remain' (O'Donnell 2015: 21).

For Mitchell, trauma is an aspect of human experience that spans continents and centuries, linking to the theme of predatory behaviour that marks *Cloud Atlas*'s narrative progress through time. His depictions of how trauma and traumatic memories are handed down across generations connect individual ordeals to a broader sense of both history and ethical

---

[1] Although the literal translation of the first three words of this line can be found in the secret code Hae-Joo Im teaches Sonmi~451 ('these are the tears of things'), the line as a whole seemingly has as many translations as there are editions of the *Aeneid*. For a discussion of how this quote applies to *Cloud Atlas*, see Mezey 2011, 29–30. A common translation reads as follows: 'The world is a world of tears and the burdens of mortality touch the heart' (Virgil 2006, 63).

response. *Cloud Atlas* suggests that ethical choices may arise from predatory environments and that acknowledging trauma is not only an ethical stance but also a precondition of ethical action. My analysis will focus on the two characters at the opposite ends of the novel's historical spectrum, Adam Ewing and Zachry Bailey; the former's journal opens and closes the novel and suggests a radical shift in perspective, and the latter's story marks both the furthest chronological development of the novel and in some ways the most fully realized synthesis of responses to individual and collective trauma. Viewed together, these two narratives demonstrate how *Cloud Atlas* enacts the fraught conditions under which individuals navigate the aftermath of traumatic events, prompting readers to question whether individual agency and ethical action are possible given the larger, structural inequities fuelling predation.

This chapter takes as a primary assumption that *Cloud Atlas* shares significant characteristics with postcolonial trauma novels, which

> bear witness to the suffering engendered by colonial oppression. They consider the specificity of colonial traumas and of the act of postcolonial literary trauma representation in relation to the dominant trauma discourse and attempt to arrive at alternative conceptions of trauma and of its textual inscription that might revitalize the field of trauma studies by helping it to realize its self-declared ethical potential. (Craps and Buelens 2008: 2–3)

While I would not say that Mitchell significantly revises mainstream, Westernized trauma discourse, I would argue that he deploys it in his novel in two ways to highlight how individual traumas arise from the systemic traumas brought about by colonialism, capitalism and tribal warfare.

First, the parts of Mitchell's multivocal narrative from Adam Ewing to Robert Frobisher to Luisa Rey to Timothy Cavendish to Sonmi~451 to Zachry Bailey, and back again in reverse to Adam Ewing, reside on a continuum in which the slaughter of the Moriori and the subsequent exploitation of the survivors by their Maori conquerors and Euro-American colonizers link structurally to the imperial warfare of the First World War (Frobisher), the corrupt overlap between government and corporation (Rey), the callous, shallow and dehumanizing media landscapes of twenty-first-century London (Cavendish), the perfected and even more destructive overlap between the state and the corporation in a futuristic Nea So Copros (Sonmi~451), and the murderous tribal warfare of the Kona that unlike colonialism or capitalism carries with it no pretence of human advancement (Zachry).

Second, the structure of the novel, with its reliance on interrupted narratives, mimics the processing delays and latency so frequently associated with traumatic memory. The most significant of such delays, the mid-sentence pause between the first and second halves of Ewing's journal that lasts hundreds of pages, presents alternative narratives that do not reify humankind's predatory response to traumatic events. For Mitchell, trauma is not only a matter for individual healing but also an opportunity to bear ethical witness to the predatory systems by which humans seek to establish and maintain dominance over one another.

Trauma: The wound and response

In her germinal work, Cathy Caruth focuses her analysis on a notion of trauma that 'seems to be much more than a pathology, or the simple illness of a wounded psyche: it is always the story of a wound that cries out, that addresses us in the attempt to tell us of a reality or truth that is not otherwise available' (1996: 4). For Caruth, this crying-out wound is a call to ethics, the act of heeding 'a voice that it cannot fully know but to which it nonetheless bears witness' (1996: 9), as well as a call to history: 'History, like trauma, is never simply one's own, that history is precisely the way we are implicated in each other's traumas' (1996: 24). Her advocacy for studying trauma as a means of establishing historical continuities, communications and ethical relations between those who have been traumatized and those who seek to bear witness is compelling. Likewise, her emphasis on textual gaps, which 'do not simply refer to but convey the impact of a history precisely as what cannot be grasped' (1996: 21), provides an important means of understanding the stasis in which the stories of *Cloud Atlas* remain when they are interrupted by their successors.

However, while Caruth's analysis is based on the Freudian model of trauma as a sudden shock, other theories present contrasting emphases. For example, Laura Brown borrows the term 'insidious trauma' to describe 'the traumatogenic effects of oppression that are not necessarily overtly violent or threatening to bodily well-being at the given moment but that do violence to the soul and spirit' (1995: 107); similarly, Greg Forter distinguishes sudden, 'punctual' shocks from 'mundanely catastrophic' traumas (2007: 259–60) as models of traumatic exposure. Both Brown and Forter suggest the need to embrace a broad definition of trauma that incorporates the sudden shocks of life-threatening events as well as an aggregate of microaggressions fuelled by hierarchies of somatic distinction.

Caruth has also been justly criticized for characterizing trauma as ultimately unspeakable. According to Ruth Leys, trauma in Caruth's model can only be unconsciously performed through gaps in narrative rather than consciously represented, which problematically implies that 'victims of trauma cannot witness or testify to the trauma in the sense of narrate and represent it themselves and others: all they can do is perform the experience as if it were literally happening all over again' (2000: 252). Additional points of criticism for Caruth's work include her limitation of trauma symptoms to 'amnesia, dissociation, or repression' (Balaev 2014: 6), her acceptance of trauma as linked to instinctual life rather than to more historically specific forms of social conditioning (Forter 2007: 281), and the rigid identification of her model with Western theory, culture and history, a limitation that 'risks assisting in the perpetuation of the very beliefs, practices, and structures that maintain existing injustices and inequalities' (Craps 2014: 46).

Those examining Mitchell's depiction of transgenerational trauma ought to be sensitive to the critiques offered above while still preserving Caruth's notion of trauma narrative as a call for ethical relationality. However, the narrative possibilities for representing trauma, according to Roger Luckhurst, greatly expand beyond performative gaps in the text: 'If trauma is a crisis in representation, then this generates narrative *possibility* just as much as *impossibility*, a compulsive outpouring of attempts to formulate narrative knowledge' (2008: 83). As Courtney Hopf claims, Mitchell's work 'consists of a boundless and ever-expanding world that spans across all of his novels' (2011: 106). Instead of focusing exclusively on linguistic breakdowns, Mitchell's language proliferates, demonstrating a twofold process of representing trauma: first, through the inclusion of characters to whom traumatic things happen, and second, through the confrontation between characters and the larger, long-term structures of trauma to which they bear witness. The power of *Cloud Atlas* as a trauma narrative thus lies in its depiction of events on a global scale while refusing to endorse a totalizing definition of trauma's impact on the traumatized.

Recursion and latency

Mitchell's ability to evoke the trauma of others extends in part from the narrative construction of *Cloud Atlas*, in which each narrative shell bears the traces of the previous story and is discovered by the protagonist of the following story through metalepses – 'transgressions and intrusions across narrative levels' (Hopf 2011: 116) – and recursion (Mezey 2011: 14), a process by which a set of themes reiterate through a series of stacked sub-narratives. However, most evocative for a discussion of *Cloud Atlas* as a trauma narrative is an offshoot of recursion that examines the pauses between iterations. As Ursula Heise writes:

> Recursion ... is a means of articulating a temporal interval through a narrative that is not its own, but that of another moment in time: that is, of giving it a structure of meaning while 'at the same time' leaving it semantically empty as an interval of pure chronology, since nothing can happen in the frame narrative while the framed story is being told. Recursion figures the moment as what it is not, replacing it by the story of another moment; somewhat paradoxically, it becomes narrative by not being narrated. (1997: 61)

At the halfway point of each story save Zachry's, the narrative pauses, creating an empty interval in which the next telling can begin. The pause in Ewing's narrative, occurring mid-sentence between the auxiliary verb and main verb, represents a linguistic rather than a narrative cliffhanger, an interruption in syntax akin to tmesis or infixing, in which the inserted language serves to delay the completion of the original term while simultaneously emphasizing its meaning (Adams 2004: 110). In this sense, Ewing's 'Pacific Journal' is interrupted and intensified by the chapters and passage of time that intercede between its halves. These chapters move more than a millennium into the future, spanning a continuum of privilege that extends from Ewing's established status as a white-collar, white male citizen of a rising global economic power to Sonmi's impending execution as a rebel fabricant and Zachry's constant endangerment as a future Moriori to the Kona's Maori.

While Ewing's narrative remains in stasis, the novel's readers step in to process the myriad individual and structural injustices crowding its pages. This stoppage of narrative followed by several hundred pages of processing time mimics, I would suggest, the dynamics of latency – not entirely as Caruth expresses it in terms of the 'inherent forgetting' of the traumatic event (1996: 17) but certainly as the figurative representation of the phenomena of abeyance and reactivation that characterize the delayed processing of trauma. This delay is crucial for Ewing's ethical development and the reader's broader understanding, wrought by *Cloud Atlas* as a trauma narrative, of the traumatic content of our global past and the traumatic potential of our global future.

Trauma at the end of history

To chart the novel's engagement with transhistorical trauma, I turn to the central, uninterrupted story of Zachry Bailey, who not only presents the most straightforward example of *Cloud Atlas*'s traumatic narrative but also enacts the synthesis of individual trauma with structural trauma in a way that Adam Ewing, frozen in time in his past narrative, is not yet able to understand. As Zachry narrates his childhood many years later to his own children, his account resonates with Holocaust survival testimonies, about which Lawrence Langer writes, 'Instead of integrating past and present, memory here assaults and finally divides the self' (1991: 48–9). The geographical site of Zachry's defining traumatic moment, Sloosha's Crossin', where as a nine-year-old he witnesses his father's murder and his brother's abduction, becomes a synecdoche for this divided self and the resulting weight of loss and self-recrimination he carries as a result. Zachry remains permanently riven between 'Brave' and 'Cowardy' (Mitchell 2004: 239), even as he tries to exorcise his guilt through his story: 'I'm shoutin' back more'n forty long years at myself, yay, at Zachry the Niner, *Oy, list'n! Times are you're weak 'gainst the world! Times are you can't do nothin'! That ain't your fault, it's this busted world's fault is all!* But no matter how loud I shout, Boy Zachry, he don't hear me nor never will' (Mitchell 2004: 242). However, his split self will eventually inform his choices at key moments. Deciding against attempting to rescue a group of slaves, he claims: 'This weren't Zachry the Cowardy knucklyin' Zachry the Brave, nay, it was Zachry the Soosider knucklyin' Zachry the S'viver, an' I got no shame to say which Zachry vic'tried' (Mitchell 2004: 298).

Zachry the S'viver's 'victry' over Zachry the Soosider, the more impulsive and self-destructive self who would throw away his life to expiate his helplessness at Sloosha's Crossin', demonstrates Zachry's successful processing of his past trauma even while undergoing new traumas on a much larger scale. Even before this, he takes a crucial step towards recovery, described by Judith Herman as 'reconnection' (1992: 196) – essentially, the victim must heal sufficiently to develop new relationships. Zachry does so at a moment of crisis. Seeking from the technologically advanced Prescient Meronym some 'spesh Smart' (Mitchell 2004: 266) to save his sister from the fatal sting of a scorpion fish, Zachry evokes his traumatic past: 'Sudd'nwise I finded myself tellin' her ev'ry flea o' true 'bout Sloosha's Crossin', yay, ev'rythin'. How I'd leaded the Kona to kill Pa an' slave Adam an'd never 'fessed to no un till that very beat. I din't know why I was spillin' this corked secret to my enemy' (Mitchell 2004: 267–8). By 'uncorking' his secret as leverage for Meronym to use against him in order to save his sister's life, even with the potential cost of his citizenship in the Valley, Zachry is deliberately reinserting himself as a survivor into a web of social relations that has expanded to include Meronym. Zachry's trauma does not in this case result in isolation from community, but rather a reaffirming and broadening of community, in which Valleymen can exist interdependently with Prescients. Acknowledging the trauma of his past, 'other' self allows Zachry to open new possibilities of communication and relationality.

Zachry's experiences, and the trust they enable him to build with Meronym, make him an ideal audience for her lessons about the rise and fall of human civilization (Mitchell 2004: 272–3). His response to his individual trauma becomes inflected by his understanding of a much broader communal trauma – the mass-killing and mass-enslavement of the Valley people by the Kona – and the even larger-scale, longer-term trauma of human self-destruction. By virtue of his status as a survivor, he is prepared to grasp complex webs of connection and causality that, according to Mitchell, many of us have yet to learn today, despite the fact that Zachry's story presents the novel's most primitive depiction of human existence. Mitchell's vision of the post-apocalyptic world of the year 3000 and beyond results not solely from an ingrained, human tendency towards trauma and self-destruction but also as a series of historical processes that led humanity to this pass. Such processes are not deterministic, however. It is exactly because history is always in the making that Mitchell links individual traumas to systemic and structural inequities. In addition to imposing narrative and chronological deferrals, the novel's embedded shells engender a shared sense of what might be thought of as a different order of latency: the insistent need to recognize not just one's own trauma, but also – perhaps more importantly – the traumas of others, even if they are removed demographically, socially or historically. In his long view of human experience, Mitchell locates hope in individual agency. Characters who choose connection and empathy usher in the possibility of averting the near-extinction depicted in Zachry's narrative. Zachry models how readers might step beyond their own pain to see others' suffering, thus preparing them for Adam Ewing's choice to take similar steps.

Privilege and perspective

Initially, the logic behind Adam Ewing's journey from notary to abolitionist is simple: 'Upon my return to San Francisco, I shall pledge myself to the Abolitionist cause, because I owe my life to a self-freed slave & because I must begin somewhere' (Mitchell 2004: 508). Surviving the trauma of his attempted murder by Goose crystallizes Ewing's political beliefs and motivates his pledge to activism. While this cause-and-effect chain provides a very optimistic view of an individual trauma catalysing political action, it is also somewhat one-dimensional in that Ewing's attention to the suffering of others is brought about only by his own suffering. As Knepper writes, the relationship between Ewing and Autua 'remains highly transactional – involving reciprocal self-interest rather than the kind of ethical commitments to peace intrinsic to Moriori culture' (2016: 115–16). This reading becomes more complicated by the groundwork for a less self-interested, more connected stance, laid in the first half of Ewing's narrative.

In the early pages of *Cloud Atlas*, Ewing spends most of his time off-balance, thrown into disarray by the inadequacy of his own intellectual and moral training to cope with the venality of the wider world. Frequently, Ewing attempts to right himself by resorting to racist hierarchies. After denigrating a servant for her 'tinge of black blood' (Mitchell 2004: 6), Ewing along with Goose, in an effort to track down a mysterious hum, stumble upon the spectacle of Autua being whipped. While he mildly intercedes on Autua's behalf, while he feels faint at the sight and sound of the whipping and while he is struck by Autua's uncanny look of recognition, he reserves disgust not just for the punishment but for those forced to witness it: 'The slaves, duskier and sootier than their nut-brown masters & less than half their number, squatted in the mud. Such inbred, bovine torpor! Pockmarked & pustular with *haki-haki*, these wretches watched the punishment, making no response but that bizarre, beelike "hum". Empathy or condemnation, we knew not what the noise signified' (Mitchell 2004: 6).

Failing to understand the humming noise (which he will later hear in the Conical Tor, creating a soundscape representing Ewing's imagination of the racially primitive), Ewing also fails to recognize that their comportment may have less to do with their biological make-up – their 'duskier and sootier' skin colour that puts them beneath their lighter-skinned ('nut-brown') masters; their animalistic, lethargic state ('bovine'), which is toxically innate ('inbred') – and more to do with the mental and physical abuses of slavery. Ewing relies on racist thinking even when directly confronted with its horrific extremes. Ewing's lack of follow-through in response to Autua's whipping is emblematic of his broader lack of conviction concerning racial injustice. Though his moral compass is sufficiently calibrated to reject the violently racist statements he hears from other white men (Mitchell 2004: 16), any racist sentiment that has a patina of scientific or philosophical discourse attached to it gives him pause, as seen when he reacts to Goose's suggestion to 'ameliorate the savages' sufferings by *hastening* their extinction' by quailing in the face of unethical logic confidently stated: 'Occasionally, I glimpse a truer Truth, hiding in imperfect simulacrums of itself, but as I approach, it bestirs itself & moves deeper into the thorny swamp of dissent' (Mitchell 2004: 17).

As he embarks on foot to the Conical Tor, Ewing is unwilling to challenge the racism of others and unable to reject his own. His account of his journey suggests a series of failed efforts to regain his mental balance by sorting out the world he encounters into racial taxonomies, failures that leave him distraught enough to 'come to his journal as a Catholick to a confessor' (Mitchell 2004: 18). Surprised by the inhospitable terrain forcing him to 'clamber aloft like an orang-utan', a newly simianized Ewing attempts to restore a more familiar order by describing an indolent 'Robin Black-Breast' with 'tarry as night' plumage (Mitchell 2004: 18). His racialized description of the maddeningly placid bird is typical of him, showing his reliance on his whiteness to separate himself when confronted with the unknown or undesirable. However, his sense of racial superiority leaves him vulnerable to the elements, wildlife and colonial past of the Chatham Islands. With his 'inflamed fancy' in overdrive, he imagines a mollyhawk as a wild boar and then as a Maori warrior, 'his face inscribed with the ancestral hatred of his race' (Mitchell 2004: 18–19). As a result, he finds himself identifying with the racially othered identities he rejects: first by imagining himself, shortly before his fall, as a Moriori, the original target of Maori violence on the Chatham Islands, and second by daydreaming, after he hits the crater floor, that he is speaking 'not English but the guttural barkings of an Indian race' (19). When Ewing recovers his senses, his imaginary identification turns into a more concrete one, as he finds that he has stumbled deeply into Moriori history:

> My eyes adjusted to the gloom & revealed a sight at once indelible, fearsome & sublime. First one, then ten, then hundreds of faces emerged from the perpetual dim, adzed by idolaters into bark, as if Sylvan spirits were frozen immobile by a cruel enchanter. No adjectives may properly delineate that basilisk tribe! Only the inanimate may be so alive. I traced my thumbs along their awful visages. I do not doubt, I was the first White in that mausoleum since its prehistoric inception. The youngest

dendroglyph is, I suppose, ten years old, but the elders, grown distended as the trees matured, were incised by heathens whose very ghosts are long defunct. Such antiquity surely bespoke the hand of Mr. D'Arnoq's Moriori. (Mitchell 2004: 20)

As property markers (Travers 1876: 19), representations of gods or the deceased (Dendy 1901: 129–30), or portraiture (Jefferson 1955: 409–10), the dendroglyphs have served since their discovery by Europeans as a metonymy for the Moriori themselves, demonstrated in Michael King's description: 'The eyes of the dancing Polynesian figures – many of them still vital after two hundred years – look inwards at the human observer. Of such things was the mental soil of the Moriori built up, mulched by layers of metaphorical association' (1989: 36). Ewing witnesses the same atmosphere and lifelike aspect of the tree carvings, but his initial metaphorical associations are quite different. Although he cites a lack of adjectives, he is hardly at a loss for words, summoning images of magic ('cruel enchanter'), myth ('basilisk', 'Sylvan spirits', etc.), primitivism ('idolaters', 'prehistoric', 'heathens', etc.) and death ('mausoleum'). Ewing, in short, is confronted by unknown sights in an undiscovered (by white men) location, and to react he summons whatever he can to fill in the blanks of his understanding – in this case, his violent racial fantasies. Despite his accurate identification of dendroglyphs as Moriori, and despite his knowledge that the Moriori were not cannibals, Ewing is convinced that the humming noise he hears comes from a pulsating human heart hanging from one of the trees (Mitchell 2004: 20). His exposure just two days prior to a specific counter-narrative of Moriori history is not sufficient to combat his racist preconditioning, which proffers Ewing a lurid vision of cannibalism and human sacrifice.

Upon his escape from the pit, Ewing reaches for comfort in white superiority: 'Back in the dismal cloud, I craved the presence of men of my own hue, yes, even the rude sailors in the *Musket*' (Mitchell 2004: 21). Such is the power of Ewing's reflexive turn towards white authority that he elevates Walker to the level of Consul – an honorary title not usually granted to a taverner, timber-salesman, pimp and slave-catcher (Mitchell 2004: 4, 7, 32) – to report the 'robbery of a human heart', a crime against property (Mitchell 2004: 21). Left shaken by his fantasies of race and cannibalism, Ewing's thought process illustrates, as Knepper points out, his 'ideological constraints' (2016: 116); however, I would add that, by confronting these constraints in the face of externalized artefacts of otherness in the Conical Tor, Ewing has begun an important process that he can only complete after a latency period that for him lasts several weeks, but that for readers spans hundreds of pages and a chronological journey of 1,200 years forward and an equal number back. This process will culminate in Ewing's realization in the second half of his narrative that his individual trauma, brought about by Goose's attempt on his life, is connected to and made possible by the structural inequities represented in immediate terms by Autua's whipping and in epic historical scale by the dendroglyphs Ewing encounters but at first cannot comprehend.

Buried pasts and the primal scene

At its most basic, the primal scene in Freudian thought is the sight of parental sexual intercourse by an observer too young to understand what he is seeing (LaPlanche and Pontalis 1973: 335), but more broadly it is an act of witnessing one's place in a familial and sexual economy organized around principles of male aggression, female passivity and the ever-present threat of castration (Freud 1966a: 45–6). The primal scene, in other words, confronts the viewer with his/her origins; processing this scene as a point of individual and species-wide origin, however, calls for the ability to recognize social hierarchies, the systemic/structural inequities that support them and the history of violence that maintains them. I suggest that Ewing's experiences in the Conical Tor parallel this primary act of witnessing, which later fuels his desire for social activism.

Using some of the same vocabulary he applies to trauma theory in *Moses and Monotheism*, particularly latency and phylogenetic memory (Freud 1966b: 77; 133), Freud's description of the primal scene, as a real or imagined event, shares similar dynamics of experiential overload and unwitting recall with traumatic neuroses (Freud 1966a: 44). However, Forter argues that the overload stems not from a specifically witnessed sight, but rather from a more powerful process of identity formation. He advocates 'that we view the theory of primal scenes less as a factual description of events than as an allegory for how the forces of signification and sexuality – and therefore, of history – come to inhabit the child before she has the equipment for making sense of them, and thus to dwell in her as a traumatic potentiality' (Forter 2007: 265–6). Primal fantasies do not, in this sense, derive from phylogenetic memory as Freud suggests (Freud 1966a: 97) but rather from 'the emphatically social inscription in the psyche of power relations that precede any given self' (Forter 2007: 266). Confronting the way in which one's social roles have been scripted to align with one's physical body can be traumatic; Forter identifies this process, via John Brenkman, as retrodetermination, 'an effect of the interplay between two moments, the second of which retrospectively determines the meaning of the first' (2007: 264).

Rereading the incident in the Conical Tor from this perspective, Ewing is confronted not by a glimpse of his own origins, but rather by his own place in a racist hierarchy that facilitated an act of genocide and violently exploited those who survived it. Forced to witness a vision of a primitive past that Europeans and the Maori alike have done their best to bury, Ewing registers that something profound has happened to him only initially through his defensiveness – he insists that his experiences 'were not a sickbed vision conjured up by my Ailment, but real events' (Mitchell 2004: 18) – and the dilemma he faces about reporting the theft of a human heart (Mitchell 2004: 21): 'The prospect of Walker & his ilk felling the trees & selling the dendroglyphs to collectors offends my conscience. A sentimentalist I may be, but I do not wish to be the agent of the Moriori's final violation' (Mitchell 2004: 21). At the moment, his ethical decision cannot be excused by the fact that it is right, but only by Ewing's own sentimentalism.

A future of ethical agency

After the long, latent, non-narratable phase of his development, as Ewing's narrative and the novel as a whole surge towards their conclusion, we see Ewing on the other side of his intellectual and moral shift, philosophizing during his convalescence:

> If we *believe* humanity is a ladder of tribes, a colosseum of confrontation, exploitation & bestiality, such a humanity is surely brought into being, & history's Horroxes, Boerhaaves & Gooses shall prevail. You & I, the moneyed, the privileged, the fortunate, shall not fare so badly in this world, provided our luck holds. What of it if our consciences itch? Why undermine the dominance of our race, our gunships, our heritage & our legacy? Why fight the 'natural' (oh, weaselly word!) order of things? (Mitchell 2004: 508)

Ewing acknowledges three essential points: the arbitrary, murderous hierarchies that govern human existence; the continuum of oppressors that includes mercantilist missionaries along with brutal first mates and murderous con men; and the racial, political and economic benefits he has enjoyed. Decrying the term 'natural' as a reification strategy for those who would preserve the status quo, Ewing demonstrates an impressive level of insight he did not possess at his journey's start.

While Ewing's achievement of that insight can be measured through his rising esteem for Autua, it can be tracked as a process through the extended metaphor of poisoning represented by Goose's murderous plot and made possible by Ewing's assumptions of trust and camaraderie among white men. Despite their appalling first encounter, for example, Ewing regards Goose as 'the only other gentleman on this latitude east of Sydney & west of Valparaiso' (5); their similarities of race, class and gender encourage him to gladly receive as medicines arsenic and what seems to be cocaine or heroin. Goose convinces Ewing that these drugs are necessary to combat his Ailment, which he mockingly identifies as a parasite named '*Gusano coco cervello*' (Mitchell 2004: 35). Contrasting the endemic nature of the worm in the exotic Pacific Islands with the Western sureties of science, Goose easily seduces Ewing into thinking he has a cure for the tropics. In this way, Ewing's Ailment stands in not just as a ruse for slowly administered poison, but also as a somatic register of Ewing's own racism, the bodily representation of that which keeps Ewing focused on his white loyalties at the expense of any others he might form.

As Ewing is increasingly ensnared by Goose's homicidal robbery plot, his assumptions of racial and cultural superiority begin to reach a crisis point. He starts to perceive a pattern emerging from the destructive missionary activity personified by Wagstaff, the headmaster of Nazareth Smoking School, who strives to get natives addicted to tobacco so they will wish to work and thus buy more tobacco (Mitchell 2004: 482), the flawed and self-serving ideology upheld by Preacher Horrox, who advocates a divinely ordained racial hierarchy, and the blithe and callous dismissal uttered by Goose:

> Maybe the Indians of the Societies & the Chathams would be happiest 'undiscovered,' but to say so is to cry for the moon. Should we not applaud Mr. Horrox & his brethren's efforts to assist the Indian's climb up 'Civilization's Ladder'? Is not ascent their sole salvation?
>
> I know not the answer, nor whence flew the surety of my younger years. (Mitchell 2004: 492)

Descending further into Goose's treatment, Ewing's health and surety in the laws of racial superiority crumble in equal measure. His suspicions about Goose finally crystallize, however, when the doctor repels Autua's rescue attempt by ventriloquizing Ewing as a mouthpiece of racial hatred: 'Goose then told Autua this: – that I saw in Autua a carrier of disease & a rogue planning to exploit my present infirmity to rob me even of the buttons from my waistcoat. I had begged Goose, so he claimed, to "keep that d——d nigger away from me!" adding that I regretted ever saving his worthless neck' (Mitchell 2004: 502–3). Ultimately, this string of invective tips off Ewing, leading him to realize both the extent of Goose's plot and the roots of his own gullibility.

Conclusion: 'Beyond betrayal'

The final proof of Ewing's successful retrodetermination of his primal scene in the Conical Tor arises not from his conversion to abolitionism, but from a much smaller posthumous gesture. As his account of his (mis)adventure in the Conical Tor comes to a close, a footnote appended by his son Jackson alerts readers that Ewing never laid to rest what he saw during his lifetime: 'My father never spoke to me of the dendroglyphs & I learnt of them only in the manner described in the Introduction. Now that the Moriori of Chatham Island are a race over extinction's brink, I hold them to be beyond betrayal' (Mitchell 2004: 21). Clearly, Ewing decided never to reveal what he saw in the Conical Tor, suggesting that his thoughts about the incident did not stop when his narrative did. I would argue that Jackson's footnote, which serves as the evidence for his father's continued, intentional silence about the Moriori dendroglyphs, implies that the Conical Tor took on a more significant meaning for Ewing in retrospect. His story was retrodetermined – reinvested with meaning after the fact – by his newly evolved sense of racial injustice, which also carries with it a critique of imperialism. Leaving the Conical Tor, Ewing fears not just the moral crime of dishonouring of a sacred Moriori space but also the imperial crime of materially exploiting it by felling the trees and selling dendroglyphs as exotic curiosities (Mitchell 2004: 21). Especially intriguing is the superior insight Ewing demonstrates over his son's. Jackson ultimately, and wrongly (Knepper 2016: 116), chooses to publish his father's account because 'the Moriori of Chatham Island are a race over extinction's brink' (Mitchell 2004: 21), assuming that with no people to betray, there can be no betrayal. However, Ewing understands that betrayal is still possible. The secret he keeps is thus an acceptance of transhistorical responsibility, brought about by his willingness to understand the destructive complicity of his own racism in the aftermath of the trauma suffered by the Moriori. Resisting the urge to interpret the dendroglyphs as proof of the racist hierarchies that fetishize history's march to destroy weak races, Ewing transforms the Conical Tor first through his narrative and then through his silence into a locus of respectful insight concerning the cultural remnants of a people decimated by Maori violence and European indifference.

As a self-appointed custodian of the Moriori's historical legacy, Ewing enacts Caruth's ethical imperative to acknowledge 'the story of the way in which one's own trauma is tied up with the trauma of another, the way in which trauma may lead, therefore, to the encounter with another, through the very possibility and surprise of listening to another's wound' (1996: 8). However, it is particularly noteworthy that he does not do so by anointing himself as a spokesperson for the lost Moriori or attempting to ventriloquize the gaps in Moriori history. Instead, Ewing's silence is a show of respect to the traumas of others; he bears witness not by exploiting what he has found, nor even by reporting publicly what he has seen, but by acting in the here and now through his dedication to abolitionism. Through Ewing, Mitchell presents a model for readers – who themselves have the lopsided historical and literary advantage of the intervening narratives of Cloud Atlas – to rewrite the fall of humankind as a self-inflicted, species-wide trauma. To do this, Mitchell implies, we must witness, process and undertake our own custodianship of the traumas of others.

Works cited

Adams, M. (2004), 'Meaningful Infixing: A Nonexpletive Form', *American Speech*, 79(1), 110–12.

Balaev, M. (2014), 'Literary Trauma Theory Reconsidered', in M. Balaev (ed.), *Contemporary Approaches in Literary Trauma Theory*, New York: Palgrave, 1–14.

Brown, L. S. (1995), 'Not Outside the Range: One Feminist Perspective on Psychic Trauma', in C. Caruth (ed.), *Trauma: Explorations in Memory*, Baltimore: Johns Hopkins University Press, 100–12.

Caruth, C. (1996), *Unclaimed Experience: Trauma, Narrative, and History*, Baltimore: Johns Hopkins University Press.

Craps, S. (2014), 'Beyond Eurocentrism: Trauma Theory in the Global Age', in G. Buelens, S. Durrant and R. Eaglestone (eds), *The Future of Trauma Theory: Contemporary Literary and Cultural Criticism*, New York: Routledge, 45–61.

Craps, S. and G. Buelens (2008), 'Introduction: Postcolonial Trauma Novels', *Studies in the Novel*, 40(1–2), 1–12.

Dendy, A. (1901), 'On Some Relics of the Moriori Race', *Transactions and Proceedings of the Royal Society of New Zealand 1868–1961*, 34, 123–34.

Forter, G. (2007), 'Freud, Faulkner, Caruth: Trauma and the Politics of Literary Form', *Narrative*, 15(3), 259–85.

Freud, S. (1966a), *The Standard Edition of the Complete Psychological Works of Sigmund Freud*, vol. 17, ed. and trans. J. Strachey, London: Hogarth.

Freud, S. (1966b), *The Standard Edition of the Complete Psychological Works of Sigmund Freud*, vol. 23, ed. and trans. J. Strachey, London: Hogarth.

Heise, U. K. (1997), *Chronoschisms: Time, Narrative, and Postmodernism*, Cambridge: Cambridge University Press.

Herman, J. (1992), *Trauma and Recovery*, New York: Basic.

Hopf, C. (2011), 'The Stories We Tell: Discursive Identity through Narrative Form in *Cloud Atlas*', in S. Dillon (ed.), *David Mitchell: Critical Essays*, Canterbury: Gylphi, 105–26.

Jefferson, C. (1955), 'The Dendroglyphs of the Chatham Islands', *The Journal of the Polynesian Society*, 64(4), 367–441.

King, M. (1989), *Moriori: A People Rediscovered*, Auckland: Viking.

Knepper, W. (2016), 'Toward a Theory of Experimental World Epic: David Mitchell's *Cloud Atlas*', *Ariel: A Review of International English Literature*, 47(1–2), 93–126.

Langer, L. (1991), *Holocaust Testimonies: The Ruins of Memory*, New Haven: Yale University Press.

LaPlanche, J. and J.-B. Pontalis (1973), *The Language of Psycho-Analysis*, trans. D. Nicholson-Smith, New York: Norton.

Leys, R. (2000), *Trauma: A Geneaology*, Chicago: University of Chicago Press.

Luckhurst, R. (2008), *The Trauma Question*, London and New York: Routledge.

Mezey, J. H. (2011), '"A Multitude of Drops": Recursion and Globalization in David Mitchell's *Cloud Atlas*', *Modern Language Studies*, 40(2), 11–37.

Mitchell, D. (2004), *Cloud Atlas*, New York: Random House.

O'Donnell, P. (2015), *A Temporary Future: The Fiction of David Mitchell*, New York and London: Bloomsbury.

Travers, W. L. T. (1876), 'Notes on the Traditions and Manners and Customs of the Morioris', *Transactions and Proceedings of the Royal Society of New Zealand 1868–1961*, 9, 15–27.

Virgil (2006), *The Aeneid*, trans. R. Fagles, New York: Penguin.

5

Raids on the inarticulate: The stammering narrative of *Black Swan Green*

Courtney Hopf

Chapter summary

This chapter situates *Black Swan Green* within Mitchell's oeuvre by highlighting the structural and formal elements that align it with his other work, while also striking out into new territory by examining that oeuvre through the lens of disability studies. After outlining the various appearances of disability narratives in Mitchell's work, this chapter turns to *Black Swan Green* (2006a), which, as a semi-autobiographical novel about a protagonist with a stammer, is uniquely placed to highlight Mitchell's humanist focus on the intersections of power, language and identity. Unlike most representations of speech disfluency in literature, which use stammers and stutters as quick metaphorical 'cheats', *Black Swan Green* incorporates Jason Taylor's stammer as a fundamental formal aspect of the novel's construction, eliding it in text but using such elisions as one of many forms of silence that appear throughout the narrative. Ultimately, the formal and narratological silences that permeate the text are overcome as Jason learns to articulate his own fears and hesitancies, thus successfully elevating the representation of disability beyond the level of the cursory symbol to become an essential component of narratological meaning making.

Introduction

When *Black Swan Green* was first published, it became standard practice among reviewers to open with a commentary about how the novel sits apart from David Mitchell's other works. In opposition to the rest of his oeuvre, regularly labelled with grand descriptors like 'dizzying' (Bissell 2004) and 'a firework display' (Lively 1999), reviewers have called *Black Swan Green* everything from 'startlingly unmannered' (Zalewski 2006) and 'uneventful' ('Wonder Year' 2006) to 'traditional as could be' (Shriver 2006). The *Independent* went so far as to say that 'those already familiar with Mitchell's work, especially the brilliantly metafictional *number9dream* and the exhilarating structural adventure that is *Cloud Atlas*, may be forgiven for wondering what exactly is going on here' (Thomas 2006). Indeed, the novel's apparently complete departure from the tropes and styles that so mark Mitchell's previous and subsequent works – multiple narrators spanning time and space, shifting narrative frames and genres, technology giving way to futuristic apocalypse – these driving forms and themes are, at least at first glance, wholly missing from the story of the thirteenth year in the life of Jason Taylor.

Nevertheless, the novel does bear some of Mitchell's recurrent structural hallmarks. The author has noted that 'the book wanted to be a sequence of miniatures' (Birnbaum 2006), and like *Ghostwritten* (1999), it is written in discrete chapters that could each stand alone as short stories, but which ultimately come together in a coherent whole. The thirteen episodes each chronicle a month in the year 1982, ending with a final chapter set in January 1983. Over the course of this year, Jason experiences many of the awakenings and epiphanies typical of the *Bildungsroman*, from battles with self-esteem and omnipresent bullying to a first kiss and the dawning realization that his parents' lives are just as complicated as his own. This very ease of categorizing the novel among coming-of-age narratives is perhaps what has stymied reviewers as they attempt to classify it in the context of Mitchell's canon.

Literary critics, too, seem to struggle with where to place *Black Swan Green*, if the relative lack of literature published on the novel is anything to go by. Most commonly, they will address how it places individual experience alongside national and global events (see Olson 2012; O'Donnell 2015), thus aligning Mitchell's broader interest in globalization with this much more localized text. The chapter titled 'Rocks' is most often invoked here, as it takes place during May 1982 and juxtaposes the rising Falklands conflict with the growing animosity between Jason's parents. Patrick O'Donnell draws a variety of wider links 'between village culture and a globalized "Cold War"' (2015: 106), citing scenes of adolescent hierarchy writ large, as when the neighbourhood boys play a vicious game of 'British bulldogs'. However, it is worth noting that the novel's emphasis on social hierarchy is as much a critique of the entrenchment of class division within British society as it is a commentary on global assertions of power.

As much as it appears to be the outlier on the scatterplot of his novels, *Black Swan Green* is also an opportunity to examine a prominent theme in Mitchell's work that has been thus far largely ignored: narratives of and about disability. Mitchell has stated specifically that one of his reasons for writing the novel was that he wanted to address speech disfluency, in part because 'people who have the affliction or impediment sometimes literally can't talk about it' (Birnbaum 2006). But *Black Swan Green* is far from the only example of such an impetus in Mitchell's oeuvre. If we tug at the thread of disability themes in his work, what unravels is a persistent focus, a feature that helps to expose his emphasis on the intersections of power, language, inequality and predacity. The adjectives most commonly applied to Mitchell and his body of work – 'global', 'maxmimalist', 'cosmopolitan' – might seem fundamentally at odds with the necessarily individual and personal nature of disability, yet in this chapter I will demonstrate how Mitchell's concerns with disability can be incorporated into an understanding of his wider aesthetic and thus argue that it is a fundamental and critical element of his canon. Further, through *Black Swan Green* particularly, I will show that the lens of disability studies can provide a valuable critical framework for reading narrative, identity and structure in Mitchell's work.

Most recently, discourses of disability became linked to Mitchell through his translation, with his wife Keiko Yoshida, of *The Reason I Jump* (2013), a memoir/fiction hybrid by a thirteen-year-old Japanese boy named Naoki Higashida, and its follow-up, *Fall down Seven Times, Get up Eight* (2017). In these books, Higashida expresses with poetry and clarity what it is like to be a person with autism. Mitchell's son is autistic, and in an article for the *Guardian* he wrote a moving account of his family's experience as it strove to adapt to the challenge now faced by so many. After years of difficulty, Mitchell describes his experience of reading Higashida's book as transformative: 'I felt as if my own son was responding to my own queries about what it's like to live inside an autistic mind. Why do you have meltdowns? How do you view memory, time and beauty?' (Mitchell 2013). The translations of Higashida's books are evidence for the ways in which Mitchell's craft naturally intersects with his lived experience. *Black Swan Green*, too, is widely acknowledged as his most autobiographical work, boasting a narrator growing up in a fictional Worcestershire village much like Mitchell's early 1980s home of Hanley Swan. Most importantly, Jason Taylor's main struggle in life is that he has a stammer, a challenge also dealt with by Mitchell himself.

Beyond these two prominent examples, disability narratives crop up more obliquely throughout Mitchell's oeuvre. In his most recent novel, *Slade House* (2015), Mitchell has crafted a narrator in chapter one who clearly has a behavioural disorder of some kind, though an exact diagnosis is never given.

However, it is notable that this chapter is a revision of the short story 'The Right Sort' (2014), which Mitchell initially published on Twitter and which sparked the ideas for the expanded novel. In 'The Right Sort', the narrator, Nathan, comes off as a generically bratty teenage boy, but in chapter one of *Slade House*, which covers the same events, the character has clearly evolved. Through hints of synaesthesia – 'I don't know any Jonahs. It's a maroon-coloured name' (12) – and difficulty with social interaction – 'Jonah's face may mean he's puzzled. Mrs Marconi and me have been working on "puzzled"' (16) – we can presume that while Nathan may not be diagnosed autistic, he is likely on the spectrum. It is clear that over the course of translating the narrative from short story to novel, Mitchell's investment in understanding autism found its way into the work.

Similarly, across his short fiction Mitchell has employed disability and social care as both minor tropes and central themes. 'Lots of Bits of Star', a very short story released as part of a boxed set of work by the artists Kai & Sunny, has a clearly autistic narrator (Harris-Birtill 2016). 'The Massive Rat' (2009) features a narrator called Nick Briar (also a minor character in *Black Swan Green*) who suffers from what he calls a 'not real Tourette's Syndrome' that causes vocal ejaculations and physical tics like hitting his head with his knuckles. In 'Muggins Here' (2010), about a woman who has worked many years in a supermarket checkout, the narrator discovers by chance that she has a gift for caring for others and is offered a more life-affirming job in a care home. On their own, these small gestures may not speak as loudly as the more bombastic themes we have come to associate with Mitchell's oeuvre, but together they point towards a humanist emphasis that is driven by personal experience and curiosity – a desire to understand and empathize with those who see the world in a different way. As Mitchell notes in the interview at the end of this volume, 'the more different the skin is to yours, the more interesting it is to be in it' (Hopf 2019: 192).

Silence as structuring ethos

It would seem a fairly clear-cut observation to state that novels are generally built around narration. Utterance, the act of telling – this is fundamental to the complex, debated notion of what we mean by 'narrative'. However, I will argue here that *Black Swan Green* is constructed largely through its absences, around the not-said. This ethos is signalled to the reader in the very opening scene, when, from the moment we begin reading, the telephone in Jason Taylor's father's office has been ringing for several minutes ('*Fifty* rings'. Jason tells us. 'That's just not normal' (1)). Despite his father's absolute injunction about the kids entering his office, Jason finally relents and goes in to answer the phone. He is greeted only with silence: 'They breathed in like they'd cut themselves on paper. ... When people listen they make a listening noise' (2). We can't know it at the time, but both reader and Jason will come to understand by the end of the novel that it is his father's mistress on the other end of the line.

Black Swan Green is populated with such silences, most notably through the representation of Jason's stammer. It is worth clarifying that the term 'stutter' is more commonly used in North America, while 'stammer' is more standard in the UK, and there is disagreement even among specialists over whether the two terms should be used interchangeably. For Jason's part, he sees them as two very different conditions:

> Most people think stammering and stuttering are the same but they're as different as diarrhoea and constipation. Stuttering's where you say the first bit of the word but can't stop saying it over and over. *St-st-st-st*utter. Like that. Stammering's where you get stuck straight after the first bit of the word. Like this. *St … A*Mmer! (30)

When we consider how Jason's stammer is narratively represented, this distinction is in fact quite apt. Most examples of characters with speech disfluency in narrative follow Jason's definition of stutterers – the text overflows with the utterances, usually creating a simultaneously comic and tragic effect. Consider, for example, the character of S. S. Sisodia in Salman Rushdie's *The Satanic Verses*:

> Sisodia, seeing the legendary features of the vanished demigod squashed up against the limousine's windshield, was tempted to answer: *Baback where you bibi belong: on the iska iska iscreen.* – 'No bobobones broken,' Sisodia told Allie. 'A mimi miracle. He ista ista istepped right in fafa front of the weewee wehicle.' (337)

Sisodia's speech is played for laughs as disfluency so often and unfortunately is, but it also sustains the musicality and rhythm that is emblematic of Rushdie's style. Alternatively, the representation of Wilfred Owen in Pat Barker's First World War novel *Regeneration* invokes the common trope of the stammer as a signifier for anxiety and trauma:

> 'I've b-brought these.'
> A stammer. Not as bad as some, but bad enough. Sassoon exerted himself to be polite. 'What is it? I can't see.'
> Books. *His* book. Five copies, no less. 'My God, a reader.'
> 'I wondered if you'd b-be k-kind enough to s-sign them?' (80)

Daniel Martin has noted that this very metaphorical-ness of the stammer 'all too often seduces theorists from awareness of the actual disability of developmental disfluency in preference for seductive descriptions of the "stuttering" rhythms of modern life, literature, art, and aesthetics' (2015). Given these examples, along with representations of characters in major works by Ken Kesey, Kurt Vonnegut, Herman Melville and Philip Roth,[1] to name a few, it is unsurprising that theorists latch on to the figurative power of the stammer. Literary discourse almost universally represents speech disfluency mimetically, the way it might present an accent or dialect, as an effusion of sounds that must be textually evoked for the reader to comprehend them. In short, the stutter is a spectacle, inherently symbolic.

Black Swan Green, however, offers up an alternative. Instead of the common stream of sounds and hyphens, Jason's stammer is represented only by its absence and thus more directly mimics his definition of stammering as a widening, traumatizing silence. Jason signals when it has happened, but only through parenthetical narration: '"Why d'you" (Hangman blocked "nick" *then* "steal" so I had to use the naff "pinch") "pinch the fags?"' (78). The only time the reader sees the stammer literally represented is when others are mocking him, or through Jason's internal monologue as he imagines such moments: 'Stammerers can't win arguments 'cause once you stammer, H-h-hey p-p-presto, you've l-l-lost, S-s-st-st-utterboy!' (40). Notably, both the real and imagined attacks always follow his definition of *stuttering*, not stammering, thus further emphasizing his tormenters' lack of understanding and Jason's own isolation. Mitchell himself has noted having experiences like this as a teenager: 'During a dispute any antagonist could, and happily did, mimic a stutter, bystanders would laugh and, of course, win the day' (2006b). With Jason's stammer being the central obstacle of the novel, and his desire to overcome it his fundamental desire, it is fitting that silences, gaps and absences are the organizing principles of the narrative.

In his evocative essay for the British Stammering Association, 'Let Me Speak' (2006b), Mitchell has written in detail about his experiences growing up with a stammer. We learn that he views the stammer/stutter distinction in the same way as Jason, but he also argues further that the silence produced by a stammer, 'an ever-widening hole in the sentence', might also be viewed as a kind of opportunity: 'I believe that in this hole, this gap, you can find the silence, the calmness, you need to get the next word out' (2006b). Much writing about speech disfluency, whether clinical or literary, has focused on the imperative to *overcome* such silences, yet as Mitchell indicates, he has never quite conquered his stammer or utterly eradicated the silences it can produce, but merely found to a way to, like a 'teetotaller alcoholic ... exist in a state of peaceful coexistence with it' (Begley 2010). As such, 'writing, in effect, is the means for filling in the blanks that speech cannot' (O'Donnell 2015: 117). It would thus seem that both Mitchell and the novel posit that

---

[1]Kesey's Billy Bibbit in *One Flew Over the Cuckoo's Nest*, Vonnegut's Alexander Hamilton McCone in *Jailbird* and Melville's Billy Budd all exhibit disfluency that functions as a query of the characters' masculinity. Roth's Merry Levov in *American Pastoral* is a rare example of a female stuttering character.

such silences, holes and voids are in fact necessary formal elements in both the creation of fiction and the formation of identity.

In addition to a speech disfluency that is not textually reproduced, though, I suggest that through its construction around absences and hesitation, the novel as a whole 'stammers' its way through the plot. This is partially accomplished because it is structured as thirteen discrete chapters, and there are thus inherent narrative gaps between each one. However, the chapters also consistently end without resolution – they are hesitations, sharp intakes of breath like the woman on the other end of the phone in the first scene. Sometimes these arrested moments reflect the minor dramas of adolescence, as in the chapter titled 'Souvenirs', when Jason is waiting in a long queue outside the cinema to see *Chariots of Fire* with his mother, a film he has been trying to see throughout the chapter. A cinema employee is walking down the line, counting to see how many more people can fit inside. Jason's internal monologue conveys his desperation for just this one thing to go right, but the chapter ends on these lines, leaving us uncertain about whether it does: '*Please*, let your feet come just a *few* extra paces along the pavement, just a few more, come *on*, just a few more … *Please*' (248). At other times the irresolution hinges on a moment of horror or fear, as at the end of 'Spooks', which sees Jason standing on the doorstep of the house of a man the local kids have tormented, trying to force himself to knock because his friend Moran has just fallen through the man's greenhouse roof during a club initiation gone wrong (178).

If, as in the *Bildungsroman* form that this novel so clearly invokes, each chapter contains a 'lesson' that helps Jason on his road to adulthood, these endings are fulcrums on which those lessons hang, the moments when Jason will choose whether to evolve or regress as a result of his growing experience. The actual moments of decision-making – the moment when that sharp intake of breath is let out – however, are elided. We never learn explicitly whether Jason and his mum got to see *Chariots of Fire*, and while we find out much later that he must have owned up to the greenhouse incident as he references a punishment in the following chapter, we never see the actual confrontation. Instead, the accumulation of Jason's experiences become visible as his self-awareness and self-sufficiency increase, so that by the end of the novel he is finally able to stand up to his bullies. It is only then that Jason is able, on his own terms, to push through the silences in his narrative, by laying claim to the gaps in his identity.

Is it fair for the literary critic to invoke the stammer as a narratological metaphor in this way? A central debate of literary disability studies has been the idea that disability is too often used as a 'metaphorical shortcut' (Hall 2015: 4), a shallow, character-making trope quickly serving to signal personal or societal anxieties. In their seminal text, *Narrative Prosthesis* (2000), David T. Mitchell (not to be confused with our eponymous novelist) and Sharon Snyder argue that disability in narrative is rarely invoked with a view towards interrogating social identity or communicating the disabled experience. Instead, it is what they call a 'prosthesis', a discursive tool that drives a narrative or quickly signals characterization but rarely challenges stereotypes or public perceptions. Rosemary Garland Thomson has argued similarly, and has highlighted how representation of the feminine in narrative is often similar to representation of the disabled, showing that both are objectified: 'The more the literary portrayal conforms to the social stereotype, the more economical and intense is the effect; representation thus exaggerates an already highlighted physical difference' (1997: 11). Snyder and Mitchell as well as Garland Thomson were the loudest voices to hone in on the problem of metaphor in disability representation, and many since have argued for a disability studies that calls out metaphorical shortcutting and seeks to eliminate them from narrative literature. As such, applying a metaphorical 'stammer' to literary discourse itself could be deemed problematic.

Yet, while most novelistic representations of stammerers and stutterers are guilty of the above simplifications, it is also interesting to note that there is a relative lack of literary disability scholarship that looks specifically at speech disfluency. This absence may seem ironic, for what is more implicated in literary discourse than the one disability that has solely to do with impeded linguistic expression? However, it is not surprising once the difficulty of classifying speech fluency disorders is addressed. From a medical standpoint, it is generally agreed that speech impediments are the result of some combination of neurological, psychological and hereditary causes, but how we might address their effects in literature is still highly up for grabs. Disability studies theorists often make a distinction between cognitive and physical disability and will focus on one or the other. This leaves speech disfluency with nowhere to go – it is neither a solely cognitive nor a solely physical disability, but there is no doubt it can be a source of trauma, social exclusion and isolation in the same way as any other disability.

Jason himself grapples with this problem, with being able to 'pass' for 'normal' until he needs to speak, and he marvels at the ill luck of having a disability that opens him up to ridicule instead of one, like the local boy nicknamed 'Squelch', that excuses him from the hierarchy: 'Who decides which defects are funny and which ones are tragic? Nobody laughs at blind people or makes iron lung jokes' (45). While waiting at a medical centre to see his speech therapist, he notices 'a freckly girl … in a wheelchair. One of her legs wasn't there' (34). He ponders their fates and acknowledges that she would probably swap him and have her leg back if it meant taking his stammer. 'That cuts both ways, mind. People'll look at me … and think, *Well, my life may be a swamp of shit but at least I'm not in Jason Taylor's shoes. At least I can talk*' (34, italics in original). The liminal nature of speech disfluency has left it outside of established theoretical categories, and Jason personifies that conflicted identity: because they *seem* 'normal', 'unlike the experience of being blind or deaf, stutterers are clearly expected to perform on the same terms as the able-bodied' (St. Pierre 2013: 18).

Disability studies theory is generally underwritten by the social model of disability, which asserts that 'the "physically disabled" are produced by way of legal, medical, political, cultural and literary narratives that comprise an exclusionary discourse" (Garland Thomson 1997: 6). In other words, it is societal structures that fail to accommodate difference which actually 'disable' people, not physical or cognitive characteristics in and of themselves. Thus, theorists have been unsurprisingly reluctant to tackle linguistic disability, as it is difficult to articulate how the social world (other than simple human impatience) figuratively 'disables' a person with a stammer. Bringing speech disfluency into literary theory has also been a slow process and had not been attempted until very recently, with books like *Talking Normal: Literature, Speech Disorders and Disability* (2013, ed. Christopher Eagle), *Dysfluencies: On Speech Disorders in Modern Literature* (Eagle 2014) and James Berger's *The Disarticulate: Language, Disability and the Narratives of Modernity* (2014). The *Did I Stutter Project*, launched in 2014 by three disability studies scholars, has taken a particularly bold stance in relation to the social model, arguing first and foremost that speech disfluency is not a medical or psychological disorder, but a form of social discrimination. They state that 'stuttering is only a problem – in fact is only abnormal – because our culture places so much value on efficiency and self-mastery' (didistutter.org). Such debates will inevitably continue, but in this chapter I will argue that speech disfluency's very unquantifiability can be its strength. In the next section, I show how this categorical liminality makes Jason's stammer integral to the meaning making of *Black Swan Green* and its representations of identity formation and social exclusion.

Stuck in the middle

As I have established, speech disfluency occupies an uncertain middle ground between definitions of cognitive and physical disability and, thus, 'as a liminal form of oppression ... dwells in the periphery of the cultural imaginary and is the result of ambiguous social anxieties, not well-defined taxonomies' (St. Pierre 2013: 18). While Jason's stammer positions him in this ontological no man's land, he also feels, like most thirteen-year-olds, trapped between the signifying categories of boyhood and adulthood. Jason thus manoeuvres through the pressures of family, school and social hierarchy via adept management of both his stammer and his social persona:

> The only way to outfox Hangman is to think one sentence ahead, and if you see a stammer-word coming up, alter your sentence so you won't need to use it ... but you have to remember who you're talking to. (If I was speaking to another thirteen-year-old and said the word 'melancholy' to avoid stammering on 'sad', for example, I'd be a laughing stock, 'cause kids aren't s'posed to use adult words like 'melancholy'.) (31–2)

There are numerous other ways in which Jason and *Black Swan Green* occupy liminal spaces, particularly when we consider the semi-autobiographical nature of the novel. In 'Body Solitaire: The Singular Subject of Disability Autobiography', David T. Mitchell makes the usual assertion that in literature disability is most often deployed as a metaphor for character weakness or 'social collapse', but notes that 'in autobiography disability represents the coordinates of a singular subjectivity' (2000: 311). Rosemary Garland Thomson, too, has argued that autobiography 'eliminates the dynamics of sympathy and the potential for objectification that often emerge when a narrator mediates between the reader and a marginalized character' (1997: 126). Through its less mediated form and perceived closeness to lived personal experience, autobiography is thus deemed less problematic than fictional representations of disability. *Black Swan Green*, though, is not entirely autobiographical and thus once again easy categorizations are scuppered. Mitchell was Jason's age in the 1980s and lived in a small village in Worcestershire; he does have a stammer and both author and character are fans of similar popular media, but at that point the similarities fade. Mitchell makes the distinction between 'autobiographical' and 'personal' to define his relationship to the novel, which he considers the latter: 'Autobiographical is when you and everybody around you is represented in the book. Personal is when you are represented in the book, but the rest of the book is peopled by relatively fictional creations' (Mudge 2006). If *Black Swan Green* is 'personal' but not 'autobiographical', where does that leave it with regard to its representation of disability?

At the heart of this distinction is an important question about representation and identity in narrative, especially considering that one of literary disability studies' major projects has been the act of reframing disabled characters in literature. This task has been, as Michael Bérubé notes, to critique the novels in which such characters appear 'for their failure to do justice to the actual lived experiences of people with disabilities' (2005: 570). And yet, Bérubé argues, while that project was and is still necessary, such an approach 'sometimes proceeds as if characters in literary texts could be read simply as representations of real people' (570). In other words, *all* characters in a literary text *signify*, whether they bear a clichéd characterological trope or not. Further, as James Berger asserts, metaphor is not a simple one-to-one exchange of signification (2014: 149) – to argue that a character can 'stand for' one specific metaphorical concept is to misunderstand the complexity of literary discourse. Though we can acknowledge the conditions from which the sometimes hyperbolic critiques of disability-as-metaphor arise, Berger and Bérubé contest arguments that insist disabled characters are *only* portrayed as spectacles serving, in their otherness, to uphold notions of what it means to be 'normal'.

Neither Bérubé nor Berger are actively arguing in favour of disability-as-metaphor, but they do challenge the notion that figurative representation is inherently problematic, and thus usefully provide two poles that illustrate the stakes in this area of research. To what extent should literary disability studies remain focused on the embodied, lived experience of real people, and to what extent can the disabled body appear as figural? As described above, there is already a difficulty in placing stammering within disability studies' established conceptual boundaries, so examinations of speech disfluency are ideally placed to shake up the dominant binaries. *Black Swan Green* here provides us with a unique narrative through which to test these ideas. As a novel narrated by a young man with a stammer, Jason is the classic example of a character who is at least partially defined by his disability. At the same time, he is a talented budding writer who himself *characterizes* his stutter, evolving a personification of it that he calls 'Hangman': 'Pike lips, broken nose, rhino cheeks, red eyes 'cause he never sleeps. ... But it's his hands, not his face, that I really feel him by. His snaky fingers that sink inside my tongue and squeeze my windpipe so nothing'll work' (31). Thus, in Jason we have a character who *literalizes the process of narrative prosthesis* – he conceptualizes a prosthetic, discursive persona for a disability that is otherwise invisible. As a result, Jason is not easily reduced to a character who is defined solely by his disability, because through his disability he discovers a way to define himself; he becomes a storyteller.

It is clear here that the liminalities are legion – Jason is neither disabled nor abled, neither boy nor man, both fictional and autobiographical, both a well-rounded character and inherently symbolic. He is also trapped by class distinction, not working class enough to be respected by the other kids, but not middle class enough to be respected by his aspirational aunt and uncle's family. He lives in Black Swan Green but his family hasn't been there for generations, so he will never truly belong. Even the landscape through which he moves, the rural Worcestershire of the 1980s, is in transition, and through this landscape Mitchell plots, in his own words, 'the long, slow death of agrarian England' (Birnbaum 2006). Given the sheer number of middle grounds and neither-nors, it would seem that the equally difficult-to-categorize stammer is, in fact, the ideal figuration for representing Jason's journey into selfhood. The novel as a whole is thus evidence for how a disability can narratively transcend the charge of 'metaphorical shortcut' – the stammer is indeed a metaphor, but rather than acting as a shortcut to elucidate Jason's character, it is a metaphor for its own liminality and the many gaps that Jason inhabits.

Conclusion: Raiding the inarticulate

There is one more persistent textual absence in *Black Swan Green* and that is Jason's own writing. We know he submits poems to the parish newsletter under the name of 'Eliot Bolivar', but we are never privy to the poetry itself. Rebecca L. Walkowitz has argued that Mitchell's parenthetical technique, 'introducing the stammer word as well as the replacement ... creates subjunctive editions: glimpses of sentences that might have been, or might be' (2015: 145), and indeed the text as a whole is one of narratological potentialities. The closest we get to a literal representation of what Jason writes is when Madame Crommelynck reads a line aloud: 'Venus swung bright from the ear of the moon' (185). In this moment, we realize we have been reading the poems all along, because 'Venus swung bright from the ear of the moon' (166) is a line of narration in the previous chapter. As we process this revelation, Madame Crommelynck attempts to educate Jason about beauty and poetry and at the same time explains to us how we should be reading the novel: '*The poem exists before it is written*', she tells both Jason and reader. 'T. S. Eliot expresses it *so* – the poem is a raid on the inarticulate' (186, italics in original). And so it is with *Black Swan Green*, as the reader discovers that *all* its utterances can be viewed as the inarticulate thoughts and perceptions from which Jason will draw his art, and hidden among them are the lines that will make up each poem. In the penultimate chapter, this inarticulation becomes the articulated, as Jason sits down to write a poem and what emerges is a 'confession' (331). The lines he writes, in fact, are the opening lines of the previous chapter, 'Goose Fair': 'That song Olive's Salami[2] by Elvis Costello and the Attractions drowned out whatever Dean yelled at me' (331). As Lisa McNally has noted, this narrative move casts the possibility of isolating the moment of composition into a space of limitless deferral:

> If we want to read its entirety, we should reread the earlier chapter. But when does Jason's writing stop? Nothing marks its end. If we continue to read we return once again to the point at which Jason begins his 'confession'. We are caught in a loop; Jason writes his confession and, as he writes, he recalls the moment at which he began to write and thus begins once again to write his confession. And so on, *ad infinitum*. (2011)

The story we have been reading, then, is the raw material of Jason Taylor's inner life, and therefore it is the beginning of the self-narrativization through which Jason will attempt to understand his experience and thus shape his identity. Yet this process is never complete, but merely an act of drafting and re-drafting, something Jason alludes to in the final chapter: 'The world won't leave things be. It's always injecting endings into beginnings' (360).

Ultimately, Jason stands up to his bullies not by conquering his stammer but by arresting this eternal deferral, overcoming the hesitations that have so narratively marked him and finally taking action. This shift occurs in the penultimate chapter, 'Disco', which has a markedly different structure from

---

[2] Jason's mishearing of 'Oliver's Army' as 'Olive's Salami' is of significance if we consider it as a signal that the text we are reading consists of these unformed and unmediated thoughts before the process of writing and revision.

the others. Where the preceding chapters are arranged, as I have established, around hesitations that elide moments of choice, 'Disco' opens *in media res*, as Jason tells us, 'Rule one is *Blank out the consequences*' (327, italics in original), and then proceeds to destroy his classmate Neal Brose's expensive calculator. Throughout the novel, consequences have plagued Jason, as time and again he has hesitated to act for fear of what might happen. This chapter is different – we see the action and the consequences before we even learn the cause. Within a few pages, Jason is in the headmaster's office and through their conversation we find out what prompted his rash act: Neal Brose, a boy popular with both students and adults, has been extorting money out of the unpopular kids, and the only way to end it without 'grassing' is for Jason to get into trouble himself, so that he can then explain why he did it. So much of *Black Swan Green* consists of the reader encountering the influences that will shape Jason, but not the *result* of that shaping. This, suddenly, is the reverse, and it signals Jason's climactic coming-of-age moment.

Early in the novel, Jason laments that popular narratives have convinced the public that all a stammerer needs to conquer their disability is a 'baptism of fire' (49), after which they are magically cured. 'Just go back and check up on that "cured" stammerer one week later.' He tells us. 'You'll see' (49). And indeed, rather than a baptism of fire, Jason's journey to achievement is a slow burn, and his success arises from his willingness to step out of the realm of the inarticulate and into the realm of self-expression. His ultimate moment of victory occurs later in the day after the calculator incident, during a class discussion in which, Jason notes, 'Hangman'd handed me a free pass for the afternoon' (332). Basking in the freedom he has won for himself to stop caring what others think, Jason shocks the other students with his newfound nerve when he candidly speaks to his teacher in front of the whole class about how Neal Brose's behaviour and has 'buggered' (339) his 'golden boy' (338) reputation. Ultimately, through his acts of literal and figurative speaking up, Jason confronts both the structures of the novel and the strictures of the world in which he lives and defies the absences that organize both. The satisfaction he expresses is both that of the victim who has triumphed over his enemies and the stammerer who has, for once, at just the right moment, found his voice and left *others* dumbstruck: 'That appalled silence was *my* handiwork. Words made it. Just words' (339).

Works cited

Begley, A. (2010), 'David Mitchell, The Art of Fiction No. 204', *The Paris Review*, 193. Available online: http://www.theparisreview.org/back-issues/193 (accessed 21 July 2016).

Berger, J. (2014), *The Disarticulate: Language, Disability and the Narratives of Modernity*, New York: New York University Press.

Bérubé, M. (2005), 'Disability and Narrative', *PMLA*, 120, 568–76.

Birnbaum, R. (2006), 'David Mitchell', *The Morning News*, 11 May. Available online: http://www.themorningnews.org/article/david-mitchell (accessed 8 March 2016).

Bissell, T. (2004), 'History Is a Nightmare', *New York Times*, 29 August. Available online: http://www.nytimes.com/2004/08/29/books/history-is-a-nightmare.html (accessed 22 January 2016).

Eagle, C. (ed.) (2013), *Talking Normal: Literature, Speech Disorders and Disability*, London: Taylor and Francis.

Eagle, C. (2014), *Dysfluencies: On Speech Disorders in Modern Literature*, London: Bloomsbury.

Freudenberger, N. (2006), 'Wonder Year', *The New York Times*, 16 April. Available online: http://www.nytimes.com/2006/04/16/books/review/16freudenberger.html?pagewanted=all (accessed 22 January 2016).

Garland Thomson, R. (1997), *Extraordinary Bodies: Figuring Physical Disability in American Culture and Literature*, New York: Columbia University Press.

Hall, A. (2015), *Literature and Disability*, Abingdon: Routledge.

Harris-Birtill, R. (2016), 'Reading the Collections, Week 48: David Mitchell / Kai & Sunny Collaboration', *Echoes from the Vault*, 11 February. Available online: https://standrewsrarebooks.wordpress.com/2016/02/11/reading-the-collections-week-48-david-mitchell-kai-sunny-collaboration/

Higashida, N. (2013), *The Reason I Jump: One Boy's Voice from the Silence of Autism*, trans. David Mitchell and K. A. Yoshida, London: Sceptre.

Higashida, N. (2017), *Fall down Seven Times, Get up Eight: A Young Man's Voice from the Silence of Autism*, trans. David Mitchell and K. A. Yoshida, London: Sceptre.

Hopf, C. (2019), 'Building a Fictional Universe: An Interview with David Mitchell', in *Contemporary Critical Perspectives: David Mitchell*, London: Bloomsbury, 183–94.

Lively, A. (1999), 'Inside Every Psychopath Is a Jazz Buff Trying to Get Out', *The Observer*, 8 August. Available online: http://www.theguardian.com/books/1999/aug/08/guardianfirstbookaward1999.guardianfirstbookaward (accessed 22 January 2016).

Martin, D. (2015), 'Floating Academy: Stuttering in Victorian Studies', *Victorian Review*, 8 May. Available online: http://web.uvic.ca/victorianreview/?p=1303 (accessed 29 March 2016).

McNally, L. (2011), 'Fictions of Composition in the Novels of David Mitchell', *Dandelion*, 2(1). Available online: https://dandelionjournal.org/article/doi/10.16995/ddl.240/ (accessed 28 June 2017).

Mitchell, D. (1999), *Ghostwritten*, London: Sceptre.

Mitchell, D. (2006a), *Black Swan Green*, London: Sceptre.

Mitchell, D. (2006b), 'Let Me Speak', *The British Stammering Association*, 1 June. Available online: http://www.stammering.org/speaking-out/article/let-me-speak (accessed 2 February 2016).

Mitchell, D. (2009), 'The Massive Rat', *The Guardian*, 1 August. Available online: http://www.theguardian.com/books/2009/aug/01/david-mitchell-short-story-rat (accessed 29 March 2016).

Mitchell, D. (2010), 'Muggins Here', *The Guardian*, 14 August. Available online: http://www.theguardian.com/books/2010/aug/14/david-mitchell-summer-short-story (accessed 29 March 2016).

Mitchell, D. (2013), 'Learning to Live with My Son's Autism', *The Guardian*, 29 June. Available online: http://www.theguardian.com/society/2013/jun/29/david-mitchell-my-sons-autism (accessed 22 January 2016).

Mitchell, D. (2014), 'The Right Sort: David Mitchell's Twitter Short Story', *The Guardian*, 14 July. Available online: http://www.theguardian.com/books/2014/jul/14/the-right-sort-david-mitchells-twitter-short-story (accessed 22 January 2016).

Mitchell, D. (2015), *Slade House*, London: Sceptre.

Mitchell, D. T. (2000), 'Body Solitaire: The Singular Subject of Disability Autobiography', *American Quarterly*, 52(2), 311–15.

Mitchell, D. T. and S. Snyder (2000), *Narrative Prosthesis: Disability and the Dependence of Discourse*, Ann Arbor: University of Michigan Press.

Mudge, A. (2006), 'David Mitchell: Second Childhood', *Bookpage*, April. Available online: https://bookpage.com/interviews/8342-david-mitchell (accessed 10 March 2016).

O'Donnell, P. (2015), *A Temporary Future: The Fiction of David Mitchell*, London: Bloomsbury.

Olson, C. (2012), 'The Nightmare of History: A Look at Time in the Novels of Eliade, DeLillo and Mitchell', *Theory in Action*, 5(1), 81–102.

Shriver, L. (2006), 'Down to Earth', *Financial Times*, 5 May. Available online: http://www.ft.com/cms/s/0/3c2cd322-db3f-11da-98a8-0000779e2340.html (accessed 22 January 2016).

St. Pierre, J. (2013), 'The Construction of the Disabled Speaker: Locating Stuttering in Disability Studies', in Christopher Eagle (ed.), *Talking Normal: Literature, Speech Disorders and Disability*, London: Taylor and Francis, 9–23.

Thomas, S. (2006), '*Black Swan Green* by David Mitchell', *The Independent*, 6 May. Available online: http://www.independent.co.uk/arts-entertainment/books/reviews/black-swan-green-by-david-mitchell-362616.html (accessed 22 January 2016).

Walkowitz, R. L. (2015), *Born Translated: The Contemporary Novel in an Age of World Literatures*, New York: Columbia University Press.

Zalewski, D. (2006), 'Thirteen Ways: A Portrait of Adolescence from the Puzzle Master of British Fiction', *The New Yorker*, 17 April. Available online: http://www.newyorker.com/magazine/2006/04/17/thirteen-ways (accessed 22 January 2016).

6

History, globalization and the human subject in *The Thousand Autumns of Jacob de Zoet*

William Stephenson

Chapter summary

Jacob de Zoet and Aibagawa Orito, the protagonists of *The Thousand Autumns of Jacob de Zoet* (2010a), think and act like people of their time and place. As such, Mitchell's novel falls into step with Georg Lukács's classic Marxist account of historical fiction as a genre that represents the struggles of history through the horizons and perspectives of characters. The gestures, hints and fantasies that characterize Jacob and Orito's unconsummated affair suggest in microcosm the state of world-historical relationships in the novel, where the expansionist West and isolationist Japan imagine one another, creating spectres of race and nation. *The Thousand Autumns of Jacob de Zoet* alludes to its own time by advancing Mitchell's project, begun in *Ghostwritten*, of engagement with the contemporary globalized world where civilizations clash in a state of mutual ignorance. Even as *Thousand Autumns* confronts the realities of the past, it alludes to contemporary cultural conflicts via the historical setting of Mitchell's Japan. As such, the novel's articulation of a disjointed present/past works to defamiliarize and shed light critically on the historical (dis)continuities of a global capitalist world.

Introduction

The Thousand Autumns of Jacob de Zoet,[1] David Mitchell's fifth novel, is his first to be set entirely in the historical past.[2] This chapter considers Mitchell's novel as a historical fiction, considering the ways *Thousand Autumns* addresses history as well as negotiates relations between the past and present of globalization. As a fictionalized chronicle of history, the novel follows the career of Jacob, a Dutch bookkeeper and colonial official, from July 1799 when he arrives on Dejima, a tiny artificial island just off Nagasaki. For over two hundred years, Dejima was the sole foreign trading post permitted by the Shogunate, whose isolationist policy severely limited the Japanese people's contact with other cultures. Despite the barriers of law and custom separating him from the Japanese, Jacob falls in love with Aibagawa Orito, a midwife with ambitions to learn from Western science, who is studying medicine on Dejima. Jacob and Orito's relationship is never consummated but exists at the level of symbols, hints and dreams. The protagonists imagine each other far more than they have actual contact; they exist more as traces or spectres in each other's lives than as physical presences.

Thousand Autumns resembles Mitchell's first novel *Ghostwritten* (1999), in which linear chronology is 'replaced by the presence of a potentially endless procession of "Nows", the present of one narrator's narrative also containing the present of the novel's other narrations as traces' (Griffiths 2004: 84). *Ghostwritten*'s overlapping narrative traces prevent the emergence of a dominant storyteller with a reliable point of view; the novel advocates 'a turning-away from linear chronology and the truth-value of historical representation ... [in order to replace] absolutism with the pluralism of focalization' (Griffiths 2004: 80). *Thousand Autumns* develops this technique by adding the complicating factor of historical context. Though written almost entirely in the third person, the novel is focalized through a succession of characters of different race, ideology, gender and social status. The first section narrates Jacob's experience on Dejima in detail. The second section follows the journey of Ogawa Uzaemon into the interior of Japan

---

[1] The novel's title is abbreviated hereafter to *Thousand Autumns* in the main text.
[2] To date, *Thousand Autumns* is Mitchell's only historical novel, but his other fictions all engage with history to a greater or lesser extent. *Ghostwritten* (1999) has one section, 'Holy Mountain', set around and after the Communist Revolution in China. *Number9dream* (2001), although set in modern Japan, quotes extensively from the journal of its narrator's great-uncle, a kamikaze submarine pilot during the Second World War. *Cloud Atlas* (2004) begins in the nineteenth century and ends there, with its opening and closing sections, the two halves of 'The Pacific Journal of Adam Ewing'. The same novel incorporates the interwar period in 'Letters from Zedelghem'. In *Black Swan Green* (2006), set in 1982, the narrator is upset when an admired older boy dies in the Falklands War. Mitchell's sixth novel, *The Bone Clocks* (2014), ranges from the 1980s to a global environmental collapse in the 2040s, following the same protagonist through past, present and the contemporary reader's future.

to rescue Orito, whose viewpoint is also given. The third section introduces several new focal characters: the slave Weh; Penhaligon, the captain of a British frigate approaching Nagasaki; and Magistrate Shiroyama. This decentres the narrative by preventing any single unifying viewpoint from imposing closure on the subject matter.

In this respect, the novel echoes the globalized conditions of the world in which it was written. Globalization represents a decentred form of the imperialism of previous centuries; under globalization, the formerly all-powerful nation-state now takes a peripheral role, and the sovereignty of capital extends everywhere, without limits (Hardt and Negri 2001: xii). As Jan Nederveen Pieterse observes, 'Globalization is being shaped by technological changes, involves the reconfiguration of states, goes together with regionalization, and is uneven ... globalization involves more intensive interaction across wider space and in shorter time than before, in other words the experience of a shrinking world' (2004: 8). Although the decentred character of globalization is new, the figurative shrinking of the world through the global expansion of capital has taken place in successive phases throughout history. The imperialism of the eighteenth and nineteenth centuries, the time of *Thousand Autumns*, was one of these.

Thousand Autumns investigates the globalized economy of the contemporary world by foregrounding the imperialist economics of the past. Before he meets Orito, Jacob's main focus on Dejima is his work, and he is fully aware of the commercial underpinnings of his role. Much of the novel's first section consists of conversations about trade. One valuable commodity, copper, is 'the bride for whom we Dutch have danced in Nagasaki' (40–1) which gives the first section of *Thousand Autumns* its title (1). At the start of the novel, the eager, career-minded Jacob strongly resembles one of *Ghostwritten*'s avatars of globalization, the corrupt late-twentieth-century banker Neal Brose of the 'Hong Kong' section, 'a synecdochic figure of imperial complicity, representing one branch of the ideological state apparatus that operates to maintain and replicate the ideological structures of late capitalism and its neo-colonial aspects' (Dunlop 2011: 210). Unlike Neal, Jacob comes to realize the immorality of the corruption in which he is complicit and chooses to reject 'the hypocrisy, ideological myopia, and ongoing enactment of economic and social relations of dependency implicated in this "reinterpretation" (or renegotiation)' of the rules of manipulating capital (Dunlop 2011: 211).

Although both Neal and Jacob are immersed in the grubby mundanity of finance, neither is immune to fantasy. At the ends of their respective stories, each man dies in the company of a spectral oriental female. Jacob sees 'amber shadows in the far corner coagulate' into the form of an imaginary Orito, who leans over and kisses his forehead (546). Neal's ghostly Chinese girl walks with him 'hand in hand ... up the steps of the Big Bright Buddha, brighter and brighter, into a snowstorm of silent light' (Mitchell 1999: 109). There is a shared awkwardness here, as each female ghost could be a figure of redemption or a patriarchal orientalist fantasy, or both. Jacob's final vision of Orito situates his dying mind as an uncanny space, poised on the verge of otherness, in a way that accords with the Enlightenment positioning of the ghost as a hallucination: 'With the new habituation of ghosts, spectres and spirits in the mind of the percipient (during the Enlightenment), the realm of psychological space itself becomes a deeply haunted and uncanny site' (McCorristine 2010: 33). Yet, this haunted space is also a contemporary one, characteristic of a world in which subjectivity is disturbed by feeling itself permanently connected. In Mitchell's fiction, 'haunting indicates that one is not fully present to oneself. If, as with Mitchell's characters, the world that enframes and discloses a self is shot through with other beings, places and times, then a lone self cannot be fully grasped, for it always depends on a chain of relations' (Trimm 2018: 24).

This uncanny mental space on the edge of otherness reappears several times in *Thousand Autumns* as different characters enter it, usually at moments of intense emotion. 'A Mountain Fastness', the second section, ends when Ogawa is betrayed and handed over to the ruthless Abbot Enomoto, Jacob and Ogawa's antagonist and Orito's captor. Ogawa's death at Enomoto's hands gives 'A Mountain Fastness' a powerful yet unstable moment of closure:

The pistol rests on Ogawa Uzaemon's forehead ...
He expends his last moment on a prayer. *Avenge me.*
A click, a spring, a strangled whimper nothing now but
Now Now Now Now now now now now nownownow—
Thunder splits the rift where the sun floods in. (363, italics in original)

Menaced by Enomoto's gun, Ogawa knows he is a split second from oblivion. His final utterance is not his prayer for vengeance but a mentally stuttered 'now'. The word repeats itself and changes case and spacing. This undermines the usual function of 'now', which is to delimit a distinct instant. Instead, time is broken. Ogawa's inner voice is trapped in a loop, frantically copying itself, as his subjective space cracks apart. His terminal thoughts vividly demonstrate how presence, meaning the lived experience of a human subject at a given moment, is ephemeral and vulnerable to forces the subject cannot control.

As this scene demonstrates, presence is problematic as well as fragile. Jacques Derrida has addressed this problem in *Specters of Marx* (1994), a text which differs from Derrida's earlier deconstructionist writing in that it engages strongly with the need for social justice. His later work, with its 'call for an economically aware human rights vision' (Spivak 1999: 431) has strongly influenced feminist, ecocritical and postcolonial voices in the contemporary globalization debate.[3] Derrida characterizes subjectivity as

---

[3]Gayatri Chakravorty Spivak acknowledges Derrida's emphasis on the value of subjectivity, or its 'unconditional dignity' (Derrida 1994: xx) that lies above mere economics: 'In order to

riven with internal differences rather than unified by structure. He describes the present as disjointed, because at any given moment, consciousness is also located elsewhere. The moment is lived partly in memory, partly in anticipation. Within this paradox lies the basis of historical consciousness and responsibility to the future:

> Without this *non-contemporaneity with itself of the living present*, without that which secretly unhinges it, without this responsibility and respect for justice concerning those who *are not there*, of those who are no longer or who are not yet *present and living*, what sense would there be to ask the question, 'where?' 'where tomorrow?' 'whither?' ... It must therefore exceed any presence as presence to itself. At least it has to make this presence possible only on the basis of the movement of some disjointing, disjunction, or disproportion: in the inadequation to self. (Derrida 1994: xix, italics in original)

This point is demonstrated in *Thousand Autumns* when characters find themselves living intensely in the moment, yet their consciousness is disrupted by memory and anticipation, and especially by visions of significant others who are absent. Agency is undermined, as the novel's characters find themselves 'moving targets in a rapidly passing present that is reliant on equally indeterminate senses of anteriority and posteriority' (O'Donnell 2015: 142). Mitchell's novels construct subjectivity as fundamentally disrupted, hence his work's many references to uncanny doubling, ghosts or spirits: '[Mitchell's] ghost stories do not build toward suspense but haunt from the start, a possession originating from not being fully oneself, a founding dispossession. The experience is of being inside oneself but feeling the frames of one's world changing' (Trimm 2018: 23).

Caroline Edwards has shown how *Ghostwritten* and *Cloud Atlas* offer 'a non-contemporaneous narrative present' of the sort described by Derrida (Edwards 2011: 192). Taking a cue from Edwards's point that this disjointed present exists in Mitchell's fiction to defamiliarize and critically examine

---

mobilize for non-violence ... one relies, however remotely, on incanting the sacredness of human life' (Spivak 1995: 115). She goes on to advocate a setting-to-work of Derrida's deconstructive philosophy that 'breaks hesitantly into an active resistance to the inexorable calculus of globalization' (Spivak 1999: 430). Michael Hardt and Antonio Negri cite approvingly Derrida's point that compassion for the victims of terrorist atrocities must be applied to *all* victims of the war on terror, regardless of nation or background, taking to its logical conclusion the White House's term 'infinite justice', the early name for Operation Enduring Freedom, the US invasion of Afghanistan (Hardt and Negri 2004: 361). Derrida's emphasis on the value of *every* human subject, especially absent others, is shared by Mariano Siskind, who situates it in its wider philosophical context: 'In the tradition formalized by Kant in his moral and political philosophy, cosmopolitanism is most often thought of as an ethical mandate to concern oneself with the good of others ... , as an obligation to those who are beyond the people who are close to us like our kin or our compatriots' (Siskind 2004: 8).

'the globalized capitalist world of his readership' (Edwards 2011: 192), my analysis now turns to the cultural conflicts played out in the historical setting of *Thousand Autumns*. I will explore how subjective experience is shaped and constrained by history, offering an analysis of what happens when individuals and cultures do not understand each other but resort to fantasy. At the same time, through indirect allusions to the twenty-first century, *Thousand Autumns* becomes 'markedly contemporary as a fiction of the global present' (O'Donnell 2015: 150), especially through its account of the structural and economic inequalities of its historical setting. As will be shown, the novel's focus on injustice stems from its 'cosmopolitan mandate to map the asymmetric interaction of hegemonic and subaltern cultural and economic forces that account for the historical formation of the unevenness of the globe' (Siskind 2004: 58).

'There are spies everywhere': Dejima and the prison of history

'The (historical) novel's ace of spades is subjective experience, which is a merit or demerit depending on how the card is played and who you are' (Mitchell 2010b: 558). Mitchell's way of playing this card is to remain faithful to history by ensuring that Jacob and Orito never become modern lovers in disguise. The oriental historical setting does not degenerate into a mere backdrop for the protagonists' romance, as in the exotica of *Madame Butterfly* or of 'yet another book where there's a beautiful, rather dim geisha who swoons at the feet of someone who's tall and blond and foreign' (Mitchell 2010c). Instead, Mitchell sets his novel in a historically accurate and therefore isolated and xenophobic Japan, stratified by rigidly enforced caste distinctions. Orito's membership of a samurai family is enough to prevent her from ever becoming Jacob's mistress: 'Women of her class do not become Dejima wives … what hopes of a decent marriage after being pawed by a red-haired devil?' (135). Sex between them is unattainable, let alone a relationship. Japan is policed by omnipresent surveillance, where a consummated affair between a foreign man and any Japanese woman other than a prostitute is all but impossible, not least on Dejima, 'a place where there are spies everywhere' (Wood 2010: 29).

Jacob and Orito's relationship must take place largely in the imagination because the lovers think and act like people of their period and culture. *Thousand Autumns* thus falls into step with Georg Lukács's classic Marxist account of the historical novel as a genre that 'endeavours to portray the struggles and antagonisms of history by means of characters who, in their psychology and destiny, always represent social trends and historical forces' (1989: 34). Mitchell allows such forces to determine identity and shape presence. Every character is trapped by circumstances. The Japanese in their isolated empire are permitted almost no contact with foreigners; the British sailors are confined to their ship and by naval discipline; the slaves are punished by their masters. In the second section, 'A Mountain Fastness', the Sisters are subjected to rape and forced to bear the children of the evil Enomoto and his monks. Enomoto's shrine at Mount Shiranui creates an oriental parallel to those castles and labyrinths that have haunted Western Gothic literature as spaces 'for the sovereign exercise of selfish, vicious and illegitimate desires: remote, inaccessible and gloomy, their malevolence impersonates that of the villain' (Botting 1999: 29). Indeed, the entire world of *Thousand Autumns* is 'colonized by different levels of imprisonment' (Dillon 2011: 12). The tiny artificial island of Dejima, with all the constraints it imposes on Jacob and the other traders, is the most obvious image of historically generated incarceration in the novel, and yet at the same time, it is the image that most subverts colonial stereotypes. In Mitchell's words, 'Dejima inverts the common Orientalist terms – on this tiny man-made island, it was the whites who were corralled, fleeced, and exoticized' (Begley 2010).

Jacob's entrapment in this offshore prison proves an insurmountable obstacle to his love for Orito and to her desire to connect with him. Pursued by Enomoto's men, and hoping Jacob will rescue her, she calls at Dejima's Land-Gate, its one point of contact with the mainland. As a subject of the Shogun, and especially as an unaccompanied woman, Orito cannot simply visit the foreigners on Dejima but must present her pass to the guard, who must believe her explanation. Observing that she is pursued by the hirelings of a powerful man, he does not let her through. Moreover, Jacob hesitates fatally before rushing to try to rescue her: '*It's not you she wants*, whispers Pride. *It's incarceration* [at the shrine with Enomoto] *she wants to avoid*' (198, italics in original). He believes it is Dejima's status as a sanctuary that attracts Orito, not his own qualities as a man; therefore, he dithers and all is lost. Thus, the protagonists' failure to reconnect is caused by their respective historical backgrounds. Jacob feels 'everything is happening too slow and too fast and all at once' (198). This sentence encapsulates his subjective situation. From the perspective of the present moment as lived by the subject in history, progress in some respects is too quick, in others not quick enough, and yet these contradictory flows of time seem simultaneous. This temporal paradox points to the way Mitchell's historical novel manipulates the disjointed, self-contradictory basis of presence outlined by Derrida.

This does not mean that the individual is simply at the mercy of events in *Thousand Autumns*. Historical forces shape the subject, but the subject is permitted, in its own small way, to shape history. Orito founds a progressive school of midwifery based on her learning from Western texts. Jacob composes a Dutch-Japanese dictionary known to Orito's students under the Japonified form of its author's name as the 'Dazûto' (536). Ogawa is translating Adam Smith (31–2). Enomoto has translated Antoine Lavoisier (84). These examples all give the subject an active role in social change through his or her dissemination of discourse.

Thousand Autumns also gives room to those who have no chance to articulate their aspirations except in internal monologue: 'Turning the colonial tables, seeing the encounter through the eyes of the other, is one of Mitchell's recurring obsessions and one that imparts greater depth to his novels' (Larsonneur 2015: 142). At the start of the third section, the narrative briefly shifts to the first person as it enters the mind of Weh, a slave on Dejima (367–73). Weh speaks of an uncanny sense of spectrality. He feels excluded from his own flesh, because he does not own his body. Even his name has been imposed on him and is a mistake; on account of an error in translation, he has been named Weh after his place of origin. He owns his true name but keeps this to himself and from the reader. Denied the agency permitted to the whites and Japanese, Weh becomes a form of organic machine without full rights, paralleling Sonmi~451 in *Cloud Atlas* as a 'marginalized and enslaved technical object of colonialism' (Dunlop 2011: 217).

Weh's first-person narrative contributes to the novel's 'prevailing theme [of] ... incarceration and, in opposition to the cannibalism of predacity, the sustenance of stories that make imprisonment tolerable' (Dillon 2011: 12). To compensate for his alienation, Weh retreats to what he calls his 'mind-island', where 'I am as free as any Dutchman. There, I lie with Master van Cleef's wife in the warm sand. There, I build boats and weave sails with my brother and my people. If I forget their names, they remind me' (369). He cuts himself off from his surroundings by withdrawing into a utopia based on memory and fantasy, which is repeatedly shattered when history, hierarchy and slavery intrude: 'Then, I hear, "Are you *listening* to me, idle dog?"' (369, italics in original). His Dutch masters see themselves as trapped on Dejima, which to them feels like 'a prison' (370), but they will eventually leave, whereas Weh's slavery is permanent. *Thousand Autumns* here advances Mitchell's project, begun in *Ghostwritten*, of engagement with the contemporary globalized world that juxtaposes mobile international independence for the rich with static wage slavery for the poor, in which 'an elevated sphere travelled by the privileged is upheld by innumerable lower levels whose apparent solidity depends on their inhabitants' social immobility and hopeless economic entrapment' (Schoene 2010: 44). *Thousand Autumns* also extends the carceral project of *Cloud Atlas*, which offers its own 'history of imprisonments', from the nineteenth-century conquest of the Moriori by the Maori through to the enslavement of the Valleysmen by the Kona in the far future (Jameson 2013: 311).

As this shows, nations can be enslaved as well as individuals. Just as Weh can be imprisoned, humiliated and marginalized, so too can the isolationist, backward-looking Japan in the increasingly imperialistic world of late-eighteenth-century international trade and European colonization. During a debate about overseas threats to Japan, the scholar Yoshida constructs the present as a field of military and ideological conflict, where 'new machines of power are shaping the world. ... The present is a battleground ... where rival what-ifs compete to become the future "what is"' (231–2). This can be connected to the novel's key moments where the protagonists make important decisions or experience intense emotion; all of these moments are themselves battlegrounds in the sense that they demonstrate the struggles of the subject to realize its envisioned future, and the entrapment of the subject by historical forces. Ogawa's silently stuttered syllable ('now'), Weh's creation of his mind-island and Jacob's sense of time flowing at several rates at once all suggest in different ways how, for the individual caught up in the present, identity is disrupted and far from self-contained. Both for the nation and for the subject, the future struggles into being out of the unstable matrix of the moment.

'Justice is served': The moral order of *Thousand Autumns*

'Historical authenticity means [faithfulness towards] ... *the quality of the inner life*, the morality, heroism, capacity for sacrifice, steadfastness, etc. peculiar to a given age' (Lukács 1989: 50, italics added). At first sight, *Thousand Autumns* seems to abandon this authenticity in one key area: its depiction of fantastical and supernatural inner lives, even among those characters who advocate the linear march of progress or the civilizing replacement of superstition by science. Doctor Marinus is the resident physician on Dejima and is Orito's teacher. Although the wisest man in the novel, Marinus is not a didactic personification of all-conquering Reason. Instead, as Mitchell has revealed in an interview, he is a *noncorpum* or immortal transmigrating spirit: 'Readers of this book don't know it, but in *Thousand Autumns* he's on his twenty-eighth lifetime' (Begley 2010). Weh senses this intuitively: 'His skin is a White man's, but through his eyes you can see his soul is not a White man's soul. His soul is much older ... an ancestor who does not stay on the island of ancestors' (370).[4] Marinus is not the only fantastical character in *Thousand Autumns*. Abbot Enomoto appears to be able to wake a sleeping boy and kill a butterfly simply by passing his hands over them in the air (84, 511) as well as to have attained a six-hundred-year lifespan by ingesting Oil of Souls, the elixir he derives from murdered babies (361). Mitchell has pointed out that Enomoto is a fundamentally different kind of immortal from the body-shifting Marinus: 'By cannibalizing souls, he [Enomoto] ensures that his soul can never be severed from his body' (Begley 2010).[5]

---

[4]Marinus's life as a character extends beyond *Thousand Autumns*. He has reappeared in female form as Dr Iris Marinus in Mitchell's libretto to Michel van der Aa's opera *The Sunken Garden* (2013). Marinus returns in various incarnations in *The Bone Clocks* (2014).
[5]The conflict between the two types of immortal is played out at greater length in *The Bone Clocks* (2014) in the war between the Horologists like Marinus, who are reborn in a new body each time they die, and the Anchorites like Enomoto, who depend on killing others in order to remain immortal in the same body.

It seems difficult to reconcile such supernatural, time-defying characters with the Enlightenment setting of the novel and the historically accurate surface detail of its locations. However, the paradox can be resolved by considering the social and historical impact of Enomoto's actions. The wicked schemes of the Abbot have an ambiguous role in that they preserve the feudal, superstitious status quo, with all its irrational fears and beliefs, and yet they advance science. Dying from the poison secretly administered by Magistrate Shiroyama near the end of the novel, the indignant Enomoto insists his mysterious powers are genuine and have impressed some very important people: 'How could an abbot earn the favour of the Empire's most cunning men with quackery?' (526). His monastic Order has helped uphold the reactionary feudal Shogunate that is denying Japan access to the outside world except through the tiny portal of Dejima. Despite this, the Abbot is far from a slavish upholder of tradition. He is the translator of Lavoisier and advocate of mercury as a cure for syphilis. Moreover, Enomoto is well versed in Western economics: 'A fifty-strong Order needs a constant supply [of Oil of Souls] for its own use, and to purchase the favours of an elite few. Your Adam Smith would understand' (361). Mitchell here fuses vampirism with classical political economy. He defamiliarizes the theories of Smith by placing them in the mouth of a deranged Buddhist cleric who is also a serial killer. The fantastical is employed as part of the novel's interrogation of its historical context, through which it 'invites us to think and feel about a clash, or convergence, of civilisations in a fierce new light' (Tonkin 2010).

Thousand Autumns further defamiliarizes clashes within and between cultures through the game of *Go*, played towards the end of the novel by Shiroyama and Enomoto. The game is a constant and ever-shifting struggle for territory between opposed forces. This *mise en abime* encapsulates wider class struggles and international conflicts in miniature, forming a 'microcosm of the novel' (O'Donnell 2015: 152). Several juxtapositions help suggest this. The players place fresh stones on the board. Meanwhile, on the previous page, a new stone in the game of world affairs, Captain Penhaligon's HMS *Phoebus*, disguised under a Dutch flag, has just entered Nagasaki Bay. With one of his pet moneylenders at his side, Enomoto advocates to the impoverished Shiroyama the benefits of credit and his cherished political economy (402–3). However, once news of the *Phoebus* arrives, Shiroyama refuses the offer of a loan, believing he is relieved of the need for debt by the arrival of the supposed Dutch ship, which will bring him a fortune in trade (409). The players' struggle on the board also represents the transient efforts of the individual to make his or her mark on the world: '*One is here and one is gone*, thinks Shiroyama. ... The game of *Go* reasserts itself' (405, italics in original). Shiroyama tricks the Abbot into taking poison with him and, in their final throes, the game pieces scatter around them: 'Shiroyama's heart stops beating. ... An inch away is a *Go* clam-shell stone, perfect and smoothed. ... a black butterfly lands on the

White stone, and unfolds its wings' (527, italics in original). The opening of the butterfly's wings suggests not only the reincarnation of the soul, in accordance with Buddhist doctrine, but also the temporary triumph of the subject over history.

Even in death, Shiroyama has fulfilled his plan and Ogawa's dying wish, by avenging the Abbot's victims: 'Those souls may rest now. Justice is served' (526). Shiroyama has acted in the service of an urgent sense of moral responsibility that defies the heartless economic logic of the Abbot and his Order: 'To be just: beyond the living present in general – and beyond its simple negative reversal ... [in the name of] that unconditional dignity (*Würdigkeit*) that Kant placed higher, precisely (*justement*), than the economy, any compared or comparable value, any market price (*Marktpreis*)' (Derrida 1994: xx). In its own indirect way, *Thousand Autumns* seeks to impose a moral order on the societal conflicts to which its protagonists' dilemmas allude. This moral order is most apparent to the individual closest to death, such as Ogawa praying for vengeance or Shiroyama collapsing among the scattered *Go* stones. The subject perceives its own value and its own presence most acutely when it is about to become absent or a spectre: 'The sameness of the self, what remains irreplaceable in dying, only becomes what it is, in the sense of an identity as a relation of the self to itself, by means of the idea of mortality as irreplaceability' (Derrida 1995: 45). It is precisely when presence is perceived as ephemeral, vulnerable and affected by outside forces that the subject becomes most aware of itself and its agency, however limited that may be.

Thousand Autumns deals with not only presence and absence but also the ambiguous liminal state between them: spectrality. Although Jacob and Orito's relationship is one of love, at least on Jacob's side, the two protagonists meet alone only four times: in 1799 at the warehouse, at Marinus's seminary and in the garden, then finally in 1811, twelve years after the main action of the novel, at Marinus's funeral. They connect more frequently in the imagination: in Jacob's erotic dreams of her, Orito's ambiguous thoughts about him and lastly when he sees her ghost on his deathbed. The central relationship of the novel is thus based on memory and desire, on presence disjointed by imaginary pasts and futures. Jacob's love object becomes a spectre. Mitchell believes this improves the novel by allowing fresh possibilities: 'The price I have to pay [for a historically accurate depiction of Japanese isolationism] is a lack of consummation ... but then, that opens the way to a relationship that's based on haunting' (Wood 2010: 29). The impossibility of frequent meetings between the lovers means that the focus of the novel can shift to the imaginative construction of the other and all the failings and errors this involves.

The sexuality in Jacob and Orito's relationship is never physical but is instead mental and psychological, acted out on a symbolic plane. The closest they come to sex is the exchange of objects. Jacob sends Orito a fan on which he has drawn her likeness. She gives him a persimmon. The exchange stems from Mitchell's deep interest in Japanese culture; it alludes to how Japanese artists use 'details from the scenery such as insects, flowers or stones, as frameworks for the plot and as objective correlates for the protagonists' state of mind. Cherry blossoms, moss, moonlight or autumn leaves tend to be used and valued for their symbolism rather than as depictions of reality' (Larsonneur 2016: 30). Orito keeps Jacob's fan for years (535) whereas Jacob eats her persimmon within hours of their meeting, relishing its flesh in a manner pregnant with suggestiveness: 'He takes a nip of waxy skin between his incisors, and tears; juice oozes from the gash; he licks the sweet smears. ... Jacob's stomach ingests Orito's slithery gift' (146).

Having figuratively consummated their affair in this way, Jacob reflects on the disjointed relationship of identity and time: '*Creation never ceased on the sixth evening. ... Creation unfolds around us, despite us and through us, at the speed of days and nights, and we like to call it "Love"*' (146, italics in original). Jacob sees love as a process of non-linear, decentred creativity in which the godlike subject moulds not only the love object but also the world in the image of the emotion. Jacob holds the fruit up to the light and 'eclipses the sun with her persimmon; the planet glows orange like a Jack O'Lantern' (146). The noun 'persimmon' here carries echoes of 'permission', suggesting Orito's consent. However, Jacob's rapturous rhetoric is uttered entirely without her knowledge. With a hyperbole that becomes unwittingly comic, Jacob is improvising a love of biblical proportions based on the flimsy evidence of a piece of fruit.

This incident gives dramatic form to the situation of the West and Japan, when at this point in history contact was severely limited by Japan's strictly isolationist foreign policy. In Jacob's besotted mind, even the seeds of the persimmon embody a facet of the oriental other: 'in its heart he finds ten or fifteen flat stones, brown as Asian eyes and the same shape' (146). Jacob thinks of his fiancée at home in the Netherlands and denies her claim on him: '*But Anna*, he thinks uneasily, *is so far away in miles and in years; and she gave her consent, she as good as gave her consent, and she'd never know*' (146, italics in original). Jacob embodies the cliché of the Westerner tempted by Eastern beauty here, except that the exotic woman to whom he is attracted is as absent as the betrothed he has left behind. Both are generated by Jacob's imagination, which works instead on the persimmon as a symbol of Orito. The description is deliberately purplish, suggesting Jacob's overactive imagination: 'the pulp disintegrates into fermented jasmine, oily cinnamon, perfumed melon, melted damson' (146). Orientalism, sexuality and consumption are neatly combined, implying Jacob's infatuation but also suggesting metonymically the sexual and consumerist predations at the heart of Western fantasies of the Orient.

Hauntology: The spectres of clashing civilizations

The imprecision and ignorance that characterizes Jacob and Orito's never-consummated affair operates on a world-historical level, as each culture haunts the other, creating spectres of race and nation. Alluding ironically to Francis Fukuyama's prematurely optimistic theory of the global victory of Western democracy in *The End of History and the Last Man* (1992), Derrida coins a neologism, *hauntology*, to describe the return of the unwanted spectre. He has in mind the spectre of Marxism that will reappear despite the triumphalism of pro-capitalist intellectuals like Fukuyama: 'Each time (it returns) is the event itself, a first time is a last time. Altogether other. Staging for the end of history. Let us call it a *hauntology*' (Derrida 1994: 10, italics in original). By following the hauntological returns of Orito to Jacob, *Thousand Autumns* dramatizes not only a love affair but also an awkward clash of civilizations. This is part of the complex patterning of overlapping cultures in Mitchell's work that positions him 'as a global writer, a writer who fully addresses what globalization entails: the coexistence of a variety of distinct societies, irreducible one to another yet overlapping' (Larsonneur 2015: 146).

Thousand Autumns is far from a simplistic allegory of contemporary politics. But Mitchell has acknowledged that his novel's focus on encounters between widely different cultures, shot through with mutual misunderstandings, means that it echoes modern problems. He observes, 'I didn't set out to write a novel that alludes to Afghanistan or Iraq ... [but] collisions between East and West and their consequences and their fallout and the large doses of mutual ignorance on both sides ... these are themes that haunt the past as well as the present' (Mitchell 2011). The novel deals with the collapse of the Dutch East India Company and the loss of imperial status that this involved. By exploring the consequent damaged careers and lost chances among both the colonists *and* the natives, and the greedy opportunism of the invading British, *Thousand Autumns* refuses to embrace 'the politically unengaged nostalgia for a national or imperial past' that has characterized much British historical fiction since the 1960s (Boccardi 2009: 133). Instead, Afghanistan and Iraq remain the novel's recurring spectres.

The clearest appearance of these spectres is in the third section, where the appearance of HMS *Phoebus* signifies the arrival of an alien intruder, the defamiliarized and aggressive British, intent on imposing upon Japan 'anarchy, rapine, slaughter and John Bull' (40); or in Captain Penhaligon's more optimistic formulation, the rule of 'a market, sirs, for the fruits of *your* mills, mines, plantations and manufactories' (376, italics in original). This rule will be imposed through offshore bombardment, an early form of shock and awe. Penhaligon, the instigator of the raid, is motivated by the egocentric desire to make his mark on history. With unintended comedy, he is fantasizing about a future maiden speech to the House of Lords at this point. This is part of the novel's metafictional commentary on the process of the construction of history: 'This scene points to the ambivalence of contemporary testimonies, part true, part mock-heroic, part fabrication' (Larsonneur 2015: 140). The second person *your* in Penhaligon's fantasized speech also points to the reader, implicating him or her in the British imperial adventures of the present. At the critical moment, however, the adventure stops. Penhaligon sees Jacob remove his hat. Jacob's red hair triggers a ghostly vision: 'Penhaligon sees Tristram, his beautiful, one-and-only red-haired son, waiting for death' (499). The spectre of Penhaligon's son, killed in 1797 at the naval battle of Cape St Vincent (380), cuts across the trajectory of the narrative of imposed bombardment, and the shaken captain withdraws.

In the final analysis, *Thousand Autumns* is subjective in focus. Without offering clumsy allusions to the present, it reclaims history for the human subject by allowing the grand narrative of historical change to be interrupted by moments of presence that are infused with uncanny feelings and ghostly apparitions, when non-linear forms of subjective temporality disrupt the historical chronicle. The novel concentrates on key moments in the lives of individuals, on the spectres that haunt these moments and on the resulting dialectic of presence and absence. The dying Jacob imagines Orito emerging from the shadows to stand over him:

> She places her cool palms on Jacob's fever-glazed face.
> Jacob sees himself, when he was young, in her narrow eyes.
> Her lips touch the place between his eyebrows.
> A well-waxed paper door slides open. (546)

This is a symbolic inversion of Ogawa's death. Instead of a pistol held to the viewpoint character's forehead, there are lips. The dying man's skin is graced with a kiss. Instead of thunder ripping open a rift through which pours light, a door opens. The door is paper, therefore Japanese, suggesting a trace of oriental otherness remains in Jacob's mind, despite his return to the Netherlands. The door is well waxed, implying an often-repeated transition, from life to death, through the unknowable yet uncannily familiar terminal moment that initiates the subject's passage out of presence and into spectrality and history.

Works cited

Begley, A. (2010), 'David Mitchell, The Art of Fiction No. 24', *The Paris Review*. Available online: http://www.theparisreview.org/interviews/6034/the-art-of-fiction-no-204-david-mitchell (accessed 25 June 2014).

Boccardi M. (2009), *The Contemporary British Historical Novel: Representation, Nation, Empire*, Basingstoke: Palgrave Macmillan.

Botting, F. (1999), 'The Gothic Production of the Unconscious', in G. Byron and D. Punter (eds), *Spectral Readings: Towards a Gothic Geography*, Basingstoke: Palgrave Macmillan, 11–36.
Derrida, J. (1994), *Specters of Marx: The State of the Debt, the Work of Mourning, and the New International*, trans. P. Kamuf, New York: Routledge.
Derrida, J. (1995), *The Gift of Death*, trans. D. Wills, Chicago: University of Chicago Press.
Dillon, S. (2011), 'Introducing David Mitchell's Universe: A Twenty-First Century House of Fiction', in S. Dillon (ed.), *David Mitchell: Critical Essays*, Canterbury: Gylphi, 3–23.
Dunlop, N. (2011), 'Speculative Fiction as Postcolonial Critique in *Ghostwritten* and *Cloud Atlas*', in S. Dillon (ed.), *David Mitchell: Critical Essays*, Canterbury: Gylphi, 201–23.
Edwards, C. (2011), '"Strange Transactions": Utopia, Transmigration and Time in *Ghostwritten* and *Cloud Atlas*', in S. Dillon (ed.), *David Mitchell: Critical Essays*, Canterbury: Gylphi, 177–200.
Fukuyama, F. (1992), *The End of History and the Last Man*, New York: Free Press.
Griffiths, P. (2004), '"On the Fringe of Becoming" – David Mitchell's *Ghostwritten*', in S. Glomb and S. Horlarcher (eds), *Beyond Extremes: Repräsentation und Reflexion von Moderniesierungsprozessen im Zeitgenossichen Britischen Roman*, Tübingen: Gunter Narr Verlag, 79–99.
Hardt, M. and A. Negri (2001), *Empire*, Cambridge: Harvard University Press.
Hardt, M. and A. Negri (2004), *Multitude: War and Democracy in the Age of Empire*, New York: Penguin.
Jameson, F. (2013), *The Antinomies of Realism*, London: Verso.
Larsonneur, C. (2015), 'Revisiting Dejima (Japan): From Recollections to Fiction in David Mitchell's *The Thousand Autumns of Jacob de Zoet*', *SubStance*, 44(1), 136–47.
Larsonneur, C. (2016), 'Weaving Myth and History Together: Illustration as Fabrication in David Mitchell's *Black Swan Green* and *The Thousand Autumns of Jacob de Zoet*', *Image (&) Narrative*, 17(2), 24–33.
Lukács, G. (1989), *The Historical Novel*, trans. H. Mitchell and S. Mitchell, London: Merlin Press.
McCorristine, S. (2010), *Spectres of the Self: Thinking About Ghosts and Ghost-Seeing in England, 1750–1920*, Cambridge: Cambridge University Press.
Mitchell, D. (1999), *Ghostwritten: A Novel in Nine Parts*, London: Sceptre.
Mitchell, D. (2001), *number9dream*, London: Sceptre.
Mitchell, D. (2004), *Cloud Atlas*, London: Sceptre.
Mitchell, D. (2006), *Black Swan Green*, London: Sceptre.
Mitchell, D. (2010a), *The Thousand Autumns of Jacob de Zoet*, London: Sceptre.
Mitchell, D. (2010b), 'On Historical Fiction', in *The Thousand Autumns of Jacob de Zoet*, London: Sceptre, 555–60.
Mitchell, D. (2010c), 'David Mitchell on *The Thousand Autumns of Jacob de Zoet*'. Available online: http://www.youtube.com/watch?v=S5kEtjTdvMo (accessed 26 March 2014).
Mitchell, D. (2011), 'Author Video: David Mitchell Talks about *The Thousand Autumns of Jacob de Zoet*'. Available online: https://www.youtube.com/watch?v=vNpwR7ByeoU (accessed 30 June 2014).
Mitchell D. (2014), *The Bone Clocks*, London: Sceptre.

Mitchell D. and M. van der Aa (2013), *The Sunken Garden* (opera), London: English National Opera.
O'Donnell, P. (2015), *A Temporary Future: The Fiction of David Mitchell*, London: Bloomsbury.
Pieterse, J. N. (2004), *Globalization and Culture: Global Mélange*, Lanham: Rowman.
Schoene, B. (2010), '*Tour du Monde*: David Mitchell's *Ghostwritten* and the Cosmopolitan Imagination', *College Literature*, 37(4), Fall, 42–60.
Siskind, M. (2004), *Cosmopolitan Desire: Global Modernity and World Literature in Latin America*, Evanston: Northwestern University Press.
Spivak, G. (1995), 'Supplementing Marxism', in B. Magnus and S. Cullenberg (eds), *Whither Marxism? Global Crises on International Perspective*, London: Routledge, 109–20.
Spivak, G. (1999), *A Critique of Postcolonial Reason: Toward a History of the Vanishing Present*, Cambridge: Harvard University Press.
Tonkin, B. (2010), 'Review of *The Thousand Autumns of Jacob de Zoet*', *The Independent*, 7 May 2010. Available online: http://www.independent.co.uk/arts-entertainment/books/reviews/the-thousand-autumns-of-jacob-de-zoet-by-david-mitchell-1965088.html (accessed 25 June 2014).
Trimm, R. (2018), 'Spirits in the Material World: Spectral Worlding in David Mitchell's *Ghostwritten* and *Cloud Atlas*', *C21 Literature: Journal of 21st-Century Writings*, 6(3), 1–28. Available online: https://doi.org/10.16995/c21.63 (accessed 5 October 2018).
Wood, E. (2010), 'The Magical Worlds of David Mitchell', *Books Quarterly*, 36, 26–32.

7

Voicing tragedy in David Mitchell's libretti: *Wake* and *Sunken Garden*

Rose Harris-Birtill

Chapter summary

This chapter discusses David Mitchell's libretti for the operas *Wake* (2010), composed by Klaas de Vries and with an electronic score by René Uijlenhoet, and *Sunken Garden* (2013), composed by Michel van der Aa. Drawing on interviews with *Sunken Garden*'s original cast and *Wake*'s composer, this chapter investigates how Mitchell's texts contribute to each opera as a *Gesamtkunstwerk*, or total work of art, analysing each opera's secular reworking of Buddhist approaches to mortality as a response to personal and collective tragedy, and identifying key traits that situate these works as integral facets of Mitchell's wider textual universe.

Introduction

Any critical study that seeks to understand the entirety of David Mitchell's textual universe cannot afford to ignore his writing for the stage. His libretti for the operas *Wake* (2010), composed by Klaas de Vries and with an electronic score by René Uijlenhoet, and *Sunken Garden* (2013), composed by Michel van der Aa, remain almost entirely overlooked as part of his oeuvre, with few mentions in Mitchellian literary criticism. Yet, while each libretto requires no previous knowledge of the author's works, they feature several interconnections with his wider fiction, offering visualizations of the reincarnated character of Marinus and the blurring of realism and fantasy explored in several of Mitchell's novels. The author notes in his 2013 interview with Jasper Rees that all his works are 'chapters in one bigger über-novel', and that 'the libretti are also chapters in the über-novel'; as such, to ignore Mitchell's libretti is to leave part of this continuous 'über-novel' unread (Rees 2013).

At the heart of each opera lies a shared focus on mortality and grieving; *Sunken Garden* explores the theme of suicide, while *Wake* was commissioned to commemorate the Enschede fireworks disaster in the Netherlands, which occurred on 13 May 2000, killing 23 people and injuring nearly 1,000. Both operas have Dutch composers and English-language libretti – *Wake* also has an opening Latin requiem – and each includes both sung text and spoken dialogue.[1] Using interview material from *Wake*'s composer and the original cast members of *Sunken Garden*, this chapter investigates how Mitchell's texts contribute to each opera as a form of *Gesamtkunstwerk*, or total work of art. Identifying the shared traits that make these works integral facets of Mitchell's larger fictional world, this chapter also analyses each opera's secular reworking of Buddhist approaches to mortality as part of a wider response to personal and collective tragedy.[2]

Mitchell's libretti in performance

Wake was first performed at the Nationale Reisopera in Enschede in May 2010, opening on the tenth anniversary of the fireworks disaster. The opera begins with a requiem sung by a chorus on stage, with the opera's main characters in tableau in the foreground. The second act then depicts a cross-sectional view of the lives of nine characters and their dramatic counterparts in a single apartment building, using a grid of nine video screens to show the action within the individual apartments unfolding simultaneously on screen and stage (see Figure 7.1). The building's occupants include the apartment's owner and her housekeeper; Vita, a biology student; Otto, a guilt-ridden accidental hit-and-run driver; and Marinus, his mysterious friend who is 'cursed and blessed' with premonitions. *Wake*'s composer Klaas de Vries emphasizes how Act Two presents this 'very condensed information'

---

[1] *Wake*'s libretto and score are available from Donemus, while *Sunken Garden* is published by Boosey & Hawkes. A documentary on *Sunken Garden* and excerpts from the opera can be found at https://vimeo.com/vanderaa/videos; see http://www.paulkeogan.com/wake-nationale-reisopera.html for photographs of *Wake* by Marco Borggreve (accessed 21 June 2016).
[2] Tragedy is defined here as 'an event, series of events, or situation causing great suffering, destruction, or distress, and typically involving death (esp. on a large scale or when premature)'. See 'tragedy, n'. *OED Online*. Oxford University Press, June 2016. Web (accessed 15 June 2016).

FIGURE 7.1 *Photograph of Act 2 of* Wake. *Reproduced courtesy of Marco Borggreve.*

through the characters' apartment rooms, shown on nine screens behind the live actors, depicting their everyday lived experiences with this 'small drama background' (Harris-Birtill 2014).

Shared domesticity gives way to collective tragedy in Act Three, an electronic soundscape interwoven with the characters' spoken experiences as they describe the night of an unnamed disaster. No single narrative is allowed to dominate, the cacophony of overlaid voices suggesting the many victims and individual stories competing for recognition. The final act is a requiem with spoken interludes, bringing a collective chorus to the stage as the voices of a shared memory, the living and the dead take part in what de Vries imagines as an 'impossible conversation' on the disaster's aftermath, ending the performance with a choral rendition of William Wordsworth's poem 'A Slumber Did My Spirit Seal'.

Sunken Garden was first performed by the English National Opera at London's Barbican theatre in April 2013, with sold-out runs at the Holland Festival in Amsterdam in June 2013, Lyon's Théâtre National Populaire in March 2015, and further performances at the Dallas Opera, Texas, in March 2018.[3] The opera begins as documentary-maker Toby secures funding from wealthy patroness Zenna Briggs to investigate the disappearance of Simon Vines. Filming interviews with Simon's landlady, Rita, and friend, Sadaqat, Toby tracks down another missing person, Amber Jacquemain, whose disappearance seems mysteriously connected. As Courtney Hopf highlights

---

[3]See 'Sunken Garden' on the Dallas Opera website (n.d). Available online: https://dallasopera.org/performance/sunken-garden/ (accessed 4 October 2018).

in 'The Stories We Tell: Discursive Identity through Narrative Form in *Cloud Atlas*' (2011), 'nearly all of Mitchell's characters are storytellers of some kind', and *Sunken Garden* is no exception (133). Toby is another Mitchellian storyteller, an 'artist' constructing a fragile identity through visual narrative, becoming lost in the video footage that he encounters and creates (Scene 1); his film project soon becomes his obsession. He finally finds the missing people – and himself – lured into the magical sunken garden of the supernatural soul-stealer Zenna, who extends her lifespan by feeding off grief-stricken victims inside her lair, its colourful setting depicted using 3D film. Helped by Dr Iris Marinus, a psychiatrist from Sadaqat's mental hospital, Toby escapes by jumping into Zenna's body in the real world, while Simon and Amber must decide whether to leave and find ways of living with their personal tragedies or remain in the garden forever. While *Wake* depicts an unspecified disaster in order to create a more universal approach to tragedy and regeneration, *Sunken Garden* explores a specific facet of human tragedy: why an individual becomes 'disengaged from life' – as Toby puts it in the opera's first scene – to the point of deciding to end it and where alternative solutions may lie.

Speaking in a 2014 Goodreads interview, David Mitchell notes that in writing these libretti he 'wanted to learn about the opera world' and was fascinated by the freedom of combining so many art forms. He notes, 'It's a peculiar form – a total art form. You have narrative, visual arts, costume, choreography, orchestral, and vocal music. All glued together with the logic of dreams. It's a strange, beautiful art form, and I am intrigued by it' (Goodreads 2014). While Mitchell's libretti provide the words and storyline for each opera, these form the basis for vivid collaborative performances which use music, orchestral scores, film and live actors to bring his text to life. Each opera uses the genre-crossing hybridity of Mitchell's narratives to create performances whose multimedia approaches reflect the author's fascination with the intersection between music and text, and the narrative possibilities of sound. Mitchell's libretti in performance reflect an author intrigued by boundary crossings, both within narrative and between art forms, exploring the ability of language and music to augment each other to create a 'total art form'.

As such, in performance each libretto effectively becomes part of a *Gesamtkunstwerk*, a term coined by German composer and writer Richard Wagner in *Das Kunstwerk der Zukunft* or *The Artwork of the Future* (1849), signifying a total work of art in which many art forms – for example, music, dance and poetry – work together to express a continuous world view. Although the *Gesamtkunstwerk* has a complex sociopolitical history – Matthew Wilson Smith notes the form's multiplicitous legacy in *The Total Work of Art* (2007), citing its visibility in artworks of the Third Reich, Disney, Warhol and *World of Warcraft* alike – the term is used here in its 'most widely understood' definition as a form which synthesizes mixed media to create an immersive world (Smith 9). Approaching *Wake* and *Sunken Garden* as contemporary *Gesamtkunstwerks* emphasizes the importance of the contrasting elements that create each of these shifting forms, each depicting a Mitchellian 'world-machine' built on juxtapositions, simultaneously 'massive, unjust, beautiful, cruel, miraculous', as Simon puts it in *Sunken Garden*. Interpreting these operas as *Gesamtkunstwerks* draws attention to their revaluing of artistic diversity by which heterogeneous elements become integral units of difference, forming a mosaic of interconnected approaches. This typically Mitchellian perspective surfaces throughout David Mitchell's works – for example, in the complex web of narrative interconnections in *Ghostwritten* (1999) and the simultaneous narrative perspectives in the short story 'Variations on a Theme by Mister Donut' (2014b).

The mixed media used to stage Mitchell's libretti integrate diverse components to form an artistic whole, each creating its own expansive fictional world. As Klaas de Vries notes of *Wake*'s combined 'electronics, and film, and stage': 'It's a question if it's a real opera … it has aspects of opera, but it also has a requiem, it has poetry, it has all these aspects' (Harris-Birtill 2014). Mitchell's libretto provides just one part of the opera's compositional ingenuity as a collaborative synthesis of film, electronic soundscape, orchestral score, choral and solo operatic voices; its ambitious narratorial approach combines Latin requiem with sung libretto and spoken dialogue, newly commissioned operatic lyrics with romantic poetry. *Sunken Garden* takes this ambitious use of mixed media even further, integrating electronic music into operatic score and augmenting live action with 3D film. This stylistic breadth creates an immersive, dreamlike world of contrasting forms, its bold juxtapositions an embodiment of Mitchell's wider artistic hybridity in his genre-crossing novels. The opera combines the realism of Toby's film documentary with abstract representation; the set's darkly lit minimalism contrasts with the 3D visuals of the ultra-colourful garden, the fusion creating an opera which challenges the boundaries and expectations of its genre. The use of 3D film begins midway through the opera as Toby enters the sunken garden, creating a visual hyperreality in which it becomes difficult to differentiate between live and filmed action, blurring the boundaries between the real and the fantastic – a narrative technique which is also visible in *The Bone Clocks* (2014a) and *Slade House* (2015).

While the combination of film and live action contributes to the creation of an immersive world whose many elements work together as a continuous whole, the juxtaposition of stage and screen also emphasizes each opera's portrayal of the self as fragmented, reflecting the conflicted lives and fractured identities that each opera explores. For example, in *Sunken Garden*, a moving virtual duet takes place between Toby and Amber, Amber's image multiplied across five screens in a visual fragmentation that emphasizes her vulnerability (Scene 2). The repeated lyric 'backstreets of waking and sleeping', at first sung tenderly between the live actor and the filmed actress, moves from a harmonious duet to a swarming crescendo of looping image glitches and vocal repetition, the fragmented images and overlayered sounds emphasizing their deepening instability, using the abstract to confront the real.

Operatic baritone Roderick Williams, who played Toby in all four of *Sunken Garden*'s productions to date, emphasizes Michel van der Aa's 'investigation of the blurred lines between live and filmed action', observing that the juxtapositions 're-orientate (rather than disorientate!) his audience into believing the screen and live performance are one', using film and live action to blur reality and fantasy (Harris-Birtill 2015b). Toby's connection with Amber may be purely virtual, but her filmed narrative becomes part of his lived reality, his fascination with her story leading him to the sunken garden. In *Wake*, the abstract and the real intermingle in the orchestral score as a clamour of background voices resurfaces intermittently throughout the second act's domestic scenes, a metatheatrical counterpoint that prevents the audience from forgetting the tragic shared victimhood behind its commonplace events. Similar to *Sunken Garden*'s use of overlayered sounds, although these are musical rather than textual expressions, they become inseparable facets of Mitchell's libretti in performance; as Nina Penner states in 'Opera Singing and Fictional Truth' (2013), within opera 'the orchestra music is also part of the ontology of the fictional world', an inextricable feature of each narrative realm (84).

'I'd make more sense in Sanskrit; or better yet, Tibetan'

Mitchell's libretti contain an ecosystem of shared tropes and characters that situate his writing for opera within his Über-novel. However, as this section will demonstrate, the shared Mitchellian tropes that resurface in the libretti cumulatively evoke Buddhist philosophies of reincarnation within a secular framework, building on each opera's approach as a total work of art with the inclusion of Eastern philosophical influences alongside Western perspectives. Significantly, the libretti provide early clues to the reincarnated character of Marinus from *The Thousand Autumns of Jacob de Zoet* (2010), *The Bone Clocks* and *Slade House*. Marinus is consistently depicted as a compassionate figure across Mitchell's Über-novel, a role also explored in each of his libretti. In *Wake*, Marinus befriends the elderly Otto who lives alone, tortured by guilt; realizing that Otto 'punishes himself more than any judge could', Marinus continues to visit Otto as a non-judgemental source of support (Act 3). When Marinus experiences a premonition of imminent disaster, he tries to 'persuade Otto to come night-fishing' three times in an effort to save his life, concerned that alerting the police risks adding to the 'carnage'. Dr Iris Marinus's compassionate role is also visible in *Sunken Garden*, as she helps Toby to come to terms with his grief over helping his terminally ill mother to die and finally risks her own life to save those trapped in Zenna's supernatural garden.

This reincarnated character also hints that an understanding of Tibetan Buddhist mythologies is relevant to her past. In *Sunken Garden*, Dr Iris Marinus – who reappears in *The Bone Clocks* and *Slade House* – describes its garden setting as a metaphysical space connecting life, death and rebirth. She explains, 'If Life be Day and Death be Night, then … the Soul must cross the Dusk that lies between. Where we stand was built inside the Dusk' (5). However, she immediately clarifies her cryptic description with 'I'd make more sense in Sanskrit; or better yet, Tibetan', the languages of Tibetan Buddhism – an important assertion that will be explored later in this chapter.[4] Marinus's references to the twilight realm of the 'Dusk' as a space between life and death, combined with her own status as a reincarnated character, evoke samsara, or the cycle of life, death and rebirth.

This twilight space between life and death is explored further through the trope of the otherworldly underpass which features in both *Sunken Garden* and *Wake*, signifying a shift between real and imagined worlds. In *Sunken Garden*, a journey through an underpass leads to Zenna's fantastical sunken garden – itself an imagined place of escape for the depressed and suicidal. Similarly, in *Wake*, 'grief' becomes a three-dimensional space, a 'hole that keeps the shape of what is lost', described as an 'underpass' into another realm (Act 2). In *The Bone Clocks*, Holly's journey 'down into the underpass' also marks the tale's descent into a realm between fantasy and realism (43). In each of these works, both the underpass and dusk explore a passage between two states of being: the moment of transition between life and death.

Each libretto's acceptance of death underpins a wider humanistic belief system, offering an ethically driven response to human tragedy. Dealing with the inseparability of life and death and the passage through the 'Dusk' between them, the 'underpass' as a journey between the known and unknown, and Marinus's reincarnations as a healing force in each opera, the resurfacing of these tropes in the libretti cumulatively evoke a specific Buddhist philosophy: that of samsara, a concept that refers to the cycle of life, death and rebirth. Mitchell refers to his wider interest in Buddhist philosophies in several interviews; in an interview with Christopher Wallace, Mitchell reveals that while living in Japan he briefly stayed at a Buddhist temple and notes, 'The belief system which is most helpful to me is Buddhism' (Wallace 2014). In a 2012 Shanghai TV interview, he notes, 'Of the great world religions, Buddhism … strikes the strongest chord inside me, seems to

---

[4]In a 2015 interview, Claron McFadden, who played Dr Iris Marinus in *Sunken Garden*'s first three performance runs, explains that she interprets this remark as symptomatic of Marinus's past as a 'reincarnated healer' (Harris-Birtill 2015a). She notes, 'The references to Sanskrit, the Buddhistic references … the way I've interpreted it is that Sanskrit was in one of her lives, that's what she actually spoke, so she's quite an old soul … it's not so much that she's studied these things, but that she's actually been them.'

suit me best' (Shanghai TV 2012), while he reveals in a 2013 interview with Andrei Muchnik, 'I am a kind of secular Buddhist' (Muchnik 2013).

Wake's composer Klaas de Vries similarly remarks on the influence of Eastern spiritualities on his works, revealing a shared interest visible in the opera's approach to its difficult subject matter in a 2014 interview. He explains, 'I regard myself as an atheist – but if I had to choose a religion, it would be Taoism,' noting he is drawn to its cyclicality and lack of a 'redeemer': 'The wheel finally returns around, and nothingness. There are of course resemblances with Buddhism, but I think that appeals' (Harris-Birtill 2014). While Taoism is a distinct set of philosophical principles, the importance it places on harmony, balance and compassion is shared with Tibetan Buddhist approaches. Klaas de Vries emphasizes that this overall 'harmony' and 'balance' in *Wake* was widely noted in its critical reception: 'The word "harmony" was used a lot. And not only regarding my music, which is also very much about harmony ... but also harmony between all these elements. The balance was there' (Harris-Birtill 2014).

It is significant that both Mitchell and de Vries express the importance of Eastern religious philosophies within secular world views. De Vries notes his atheism in tandem with his interest in Taoism, while Mitchell mentions to Christopher Wallace that while he isn't part of a group of Western Buddhists, 'the books and conversations, these are very important to me' (Wallace 2014), its philosophies a notable interest to the author even from outside a formal religious practice. For each of these artists, there is a sense that their Taoist and Buddhist interests and their non-religious beliefs are not mutually exclusive but create a secular hybridity of approach which infuses their works, each world view enriching the other to build a total art form whose influences move beyond traditional Western Judeo-Christian approaches to tragedy.

Reflecting this approach, each libretto's samsaric resonances are firmly rooted in the ethical dimensions of Mitchell's writing. As Rosita Dellios notes in 'Mandala: From Sacred Origins to Sovereign Affairs in Traditional Southeast Asia' (2003), samsara is a 'lesson' to be learnt within Buddhist teachings (3). Once realized, as Dellios argues, 'such a state, in Buddhist thought, permits a greater openness to life' and a Marinus-like 'compassionate disposition to others'; an acceptance of the cycle of death and rebirth helps the individual abandon 'the delusion of a self' and develop 'a life-affirming practice of helping others to avoid suffering and to fulfil their potential' (3). Samsaric acceptance aims to transform perception of the self as a fixed, central and independent entity into a realization of the self as a transitory part of a collective identity in constant flux, viewing mortality as a single facet of a larger system – just as each opera creates a world view which extends beyond individual tragedy to envisage collective strategies to adapt, recover and keep on living.

In drawing together this particular group of recurring samsaric motifs, *Wake* and *Sunken Garden* extend their approaches to human tragedy through a shared exploration of life and death as cyclical processes, evoking Buddhist philosophies of reincarnation within a secular format to offer humanistic approaches to healing after inexplicable tragedy. This depiction of life and death as part of an interlinked cycle – 'a theme both ancient and modern' (Scene 1), as Toby puts it in *Sunken Garden* – becomes a dramatic vehicle that allows each libretto to move towards acceptance, evoking samsaric resonances within a secular format to present a humanistic rather than overtly religious approach to tragedy. *Sunken Garden* also begins and ends cyclically; Toby's journey ends when, having shed his 'old life' and been reincarnated into Zenna's body, he accepts the inevitability of his own death, realizing '*It Must End and Shall*'; his samsaric journey comes full circle by the opera's end (Scene 9). Similar reminders of life and death as inseparably and cyclically bonded also feature in *Wake*. For example, Ursula, the midwife, for whom birth and death are a daily reality, realizes that her existence, both experientially and bodily – 'life' and 'organs' – is a mere 'loan' and 'what is loaned is repossessed' in a samsaric return (Act 2). This concept resurfaces throughout the opera. Tom, playing a video game, sings, 'The dead don't want to stay that way,' death's finality undermined by the possibility of reincarnation, while McCroom remarks that 'a nebula is both the blasted open urn of a dead star' and 'the womb and the seeds of new stars', part of a larger system of beginning, ending and rebirth. In interview, Klaas de Vries emphasizes that beginning and ending the opera with a general commemorative chorus, rather than individual characterization, 'brought everything to kind of a reconciliation, as far as that is possible with such serious loss'.[5] As in *Sunken Garden*, *Wake*'s sense of reconciliation is imagined through the opera's secular suggestion of death as part of a universal, cyclical return to the pantheistic Wordsworthian 'slumber' evoked in its final chorus, rather than a single incomprehensible tragedy; as Vita and McCroom note in *Wake*'s final act, 'The universe uncrumples, indifferent and unfussed' (Act 4).

Elements of Buddhist narratives are particularly evident within each libretto's approach to death. Discussing human mortality, Mitchell notes in interview with Wallace: 'You need to find some kind of acceptance. Buddhist monks spend all of their lives preparing for death, accepting it, and seeing it as a facet of life. And this yearning, this longing for immortality is pernicious and dangerous ... it's a kind of disease of your soul, and you have to cure yourself of it' (Wallace 2014). *Sunken Garden* and *Wake* both show an

---

[5] *Wake*'s basis in real-life events meant its Dutch audiences came to each performance already aware of its traumatic subject; at its Enschede performance, many audience members would have been personally affected by the disaster it represented. In interview, Klaas de Vries highlights the importance of taking a 'general' and 'universal' approach to a 'politically very tricky' and '*omstreden* [controversial]' commission, ending not with a specific depiction of events in Enschede, but an unspecified disaster (Harris-Birtill 2014).

ontological search for and a finding of 'some kind of acceptance' of human impermanence, embedding a Buddhist-influenced contemplation of death within each opera's secular framework.

'Right yourself as best you may'

A further recurring trope in Mitchell's libretti and his wider oeuvre is that of life and death as contractual bond. In *Sunken Garden*, Marinus sings, 'We are born already bound by a contract with life,' its terms 'non-negotiable' (Scene 7). This metaphor is extended throughout the libretto; the contract's first clause is described as '*You Will Suffer*' and its second as '*You May Hope*', while Toby explains 'Life's Third Clause: *It Must End and Shall*', the final term of the contract envisaged as death itself (Scene 7 and Scene 9). This contractual motif also surfaces in *Wake*, in a conversation between the living, dead and memory, who remind the audience of life's 'small print': 'All that is here shall cease to be' (Act 4). This trope of life and death as contractually inseparable also resonates with Mitchell's wider writing, imagined extensively in *The Bone Clocks* as even immortality comes with its own 'terms and conditions' (407).

As this extended contractual metaphor illustrates, Mitchell's libretti draw from Buddhist ethical philosophies to offer their own form of secular guidance within each work's contemplation of mortality. This can be seen in the three clauses of life's contract in *Sunken Garden*: '*You Will Suffer*', '*You May Hope*' and '*It Must End and Shall*' (Scene 7 and Scene 9) can be read as a secular reworking of the Four Noble Truths, or foundational principles, within Buddhist teachings. To briefly summarize these, the first clause in *Sunken Garden*'s contract corresponds with Buddhism's first Noble Truth, which refers to the universality of suffering; the second can be read against the second Noble Truth, which states that suffering stems from desire. Although the idea of an end to existence, as in the third clause ('*It Must End and Shall*'), at first appears incongruous with reincarnation's cyclicality, the third Noble Truth suggests a productive alternative reading. This states that removing desire will end suffering, reworked in *Sunken Garden* as '*It Must End and Shall*' and echoed in *Wake* as the dead sing '"All that is here shall cease to be" the not-so-very-small print reads' (Act 4). Buddhist philosophies interpret death as a facet of change within a vast system of impermanence, a single end in a *Cloud Atlas*-like (2004) multiplicity of endings; '*It Must End and Shall*' evokes the Buddhist striving for acceptance of life's impermanence, but also the third Noble Truth's reference to the end of suffering itself. At the end of the opera, Toby, now in Zenna's body, is struggling to accept the change. He mournfully notes, 'Youth is gone; my gender's switched; My old life's obsolete' (Scene 9). Yet this desire for his past life is followed with his invocation of 'Life's Third Clause: *It Must End and Shall*. Let these words prise open every January dawn, usher in my finite

Springs,' the promise of an end to his suffering becoming a mantra of sorts that allows him to accept the change and keep on living.

Sunken Garden only identifies three clauses of life's contract – yet there remains a fourth Noble Truth. This directs Buddhist practitioners towards further guidance, recommending the everyday, practical steps of the Noble Eightfold Path as core actions to help alleviate suffering, including understanding how actions affect others, the practice of compassion, and aspiring not to harm others or oneself.[6] While *Sunken Garden*'s 'contract' stops at the first three steps, both *Wake* and *Sunken Garden* can be seen as a form of secular embodiment of the fourth Noble Truth's principle of lived action, each offering practical guidance to the living to help them find their own way out of private suffering. In *Wake*, the narrative shifts from the mimesis of the central acts, which enact the characters' daily lives, to the diegesis of the final act, in which the situations of the living, dead and memory become stylized, the action narrated to allow each group to comment on their situation to the audience. The dead impart practical steps to the living, telling them to abandon suffering and embrace life: 'Your prize must not be pain, but duty. Honour us, by living fully' (Act 4).

This dramatic movement from naturalistic action to direct commentary blurs the division between actors and audience, evoking German playwright Bertolt Brecht's alienation effect, or *Verfremdungseffekt*. Brecht first refers to this concept in '*Verfremdungseffekte in der chinesischen Schauspielkunst*' (1936), or 'Alienation effects in Chinese Acting', describing a theatrical technique that undermines the dramatic illusion of a 'fourth wall' between actors and audience. By directly addressing the disaster's survivors, *Wake*'s chorus of the dead also metatheatrically addresses the opera's original Enschede audience as survivors of an all-too-real tragedy. The final role of the dead in the opera is therefore not to leave grief, but to offer guidance to the living, imagined as navigating a perilous journey: 'So navigate by maps or stars; Meet trouble and capsize, And right yourself as best you may; And improvise; and improvise' (Act 4).

Wake's depiction of human existence as a journey to be actively navigated forms a secular echo of the Eightfold Path. This nautical metaphor conceals a humanist imperative, to 'right yourself as best you may' and take self-directed practical steps to continue 'living fully' after tragedy, a conclusion that lies at the heart of each libretto's reconciliation. The repetition of 'and improvise' emphasizes the human condition's theatricality, the living cast as unscripted actors and directed to find solace in personal resourcefulness. In *Sunken Garden*, a similar message is given to those contemplating

---

[6]As described in *The Buddhist Religion* (1996) by Richard Robinson and Willard Johnson, the Noble Eightfold Path is a series of practical actions that lead to greater insight in the practitioner, including '(1) right view, (2) right resolve, (3) right speech, (4) right action, (5) right livelihood, (6) right effort, (7) right mindfulness and (8) right concentration' (32).

suicide, envisaged as a premature terminus along life's journey: 'Why soldier on, then ... ? Because Clause Two reads, *You May Hope*' (Scene 7). The knowledge that death is the unavoidable destination is presented as solace to those seeking it: 'The most painless way to die is to live.'

In this scene, the word 'hope' is repeated five times in as many lines, deployed each time as a verb to be actively pursued rather than an abstract noun. This sense of hope as an imperative, a positive action to be chosen, also underpins Tibetan Buddhist approaches to life and death as part of a larger cycle. As Robert Goss notes in 'Tibetan Buddhism and the Resolution of Grief' (1997), 'Tibetans recognize death all around them: The deaths of those they know and love cause them to search for the meaning of life with a sense of hope' (388). While it is important to acknowledge this statement's cultural generalization, it usefully recognizes the coexistence of hope within a narratological acceptance of death. Acknowledging that 'rebirth does not remove the pain of loss', as Goss explains, the Tibetan Buddhist framework of samsara provides a non-Judeo-Christian source of secular inspiration for a constructive approach to tragedy that can still find the 'sense of hope' and reconciliation that remains a hallmark of each libretto and also of Mitchell's wider writing. As Diana sings in *Wake*, 'hope may be displaced, disappointed, but hope cannot be wrong' (2). A reading of the Buddhist influences within Mitchell's libretti therefore prompts a broadening of the *Gesamtkunstwerk*'s form to include non-Western influences, offering an ethical approach whose secular content is enriched by echoes of Buddhist philosophies, its combination of Eastern and Western influences suggesting the value of cross-cultural approaches to tragedy and healing.

Mitchell's libretti in the Über-novel

Spanning libretti, novels and short stories, Mitchell's Über-novel shares similarities with the *Gesamtkunstwerk*'s form as a total work of art, a continuous fictional world which spans many genres. While several characters from the libretti resurface in his other works (Iris Marinus, Sadaqat and Prudence Hanson), their thematic resonances also merit far greater discussion than space permits here. *The Bone Clocks*, as an extended exploration of mortality, perhaps shares the strongest thematic ties with Mitchell's libretti, reflecting a confrontation of the Western cultural reluctance to discuss death's inevitability and drawing on Tibetan Buddhist mythologies to do so.[7]

---

[7]*The Bone Clocks* is also perhaps Mitchell's most musically-influenced work to date, from its references to American rock group Talking Heads, to the eerily foreseen breaking of the bust of composer Jean Sibelius (392). In its superimposition of contrasting musical genres to create an immersive world, *The Bone Clocks* offers a blueprint of the *Gesamtkunstwerk*, the polyphony of musical references using one art form to inform another in a form of compact figurative evocation.

Mitchell remarks in a 2014 interview with James Kidd that he read *The Tibetan Book of the Dead* (2006) while writing *The Bone Clocks* and that when it comes to a cultural contemplation of death, 'it's right that we think about it and do what we can to prepare for it. I don't like this aspect of our culture that sees death as the taboo' (Kidd 2014). Popularly known in English as *The Tibetan Book of the Dead*, the *Bar-do Thos-grol Chen-mo* – 'Great Liberation by Hearing in the Intermediate States' – provides guidance through the processes of death and rebirth. Its transmigration mythology is embedded in *The Bone Clocks* as Marinus explains that after death, her kind 'wake up as children forty-nine days later', the period between death and rebirth spent in 'the Dusk' – illuminating Marinus's reference to 'the Dusk' in *Sunken Garden* (413, 461). The influence of *The Tibetan Book of the Dead* is clearly visible; in this text, the state between life and death is a dusk-like 'greyness, like autumn twilight, with neither day nor night', which lasts for 'up to forty-nine days' before rebirth (277). By re-incarnating Marinus across *The Bone Clocks*, *Sunken Garden* and *Slade House* (as Iris Marinus); *The Thousand Autumns* (as Lucas Marinus); and *Wake* (as a male character known simply as 'Marinus'), this background retrospectively infuses each work with Tibetan Buddhist mythologies, reinforcing her suggestion in *Sunken Garden* that her world would 'make more sense' when approached through its philosophies, an important facet of Mitchell's wider confrontation of the Western 'taboo' surrounding mortality.

Samsara is also discussed in *The Bone Clocks*; the venal 'sociopath' Hugo Lamb dismisses it as 'self-deception', remarking, 'Our culture's coping strategy towards death is to bury it under consumerism and samsara' (149, 116). Hugo's cynicism reflects his heightened sense of self-preservation, displaying the antisocial attitudes which spur him to join the soul-stealing Anchorites. Yet, his care for Holly finally makes him save her life instead of his own, choosing death in order to let her survive (518–20). Hugo's life may be finally saved by Marinus, but it is his concern for another's wellbeing that makes him voluntarily give up immortality; read within a Buddhist framework, the realization of his own compassionate capabilities allows him to accept his own death (518–20).

However, Hugo's remark also evokes the opposing perspective, that samsara – like any redemptive philosophy of death as part of life – can be seen as a 'coping strategy' to avoid death's finality. In typical Mitchellian fashion, both sides of the argument are presented, displaying what Timotheus Vermeulen and Robin van den Akker's 'Notes on Metamodernism' (2010) describes as the oscillatory metamodern 'double-bind' of encountering conflicting perspectives simultaneously (5). With Hugo's wry remark, the topic of reincarnation becomes caught in what Vermeulen and van den Akker recognize as a pendulous contemporary movement between 'modern enthusiasm and a postmodern irony, between hope and melancholy, between naïveté and knowingness'(5–6), evoking samsaric sacrality alongside ontological secularity in order to create a text in which the real must be inescapably read within a framework of the mythological, and vice versa.

Conclusion: 'When remembered, we exist'

As the chorus sing in *Wake*'s final act, 'when remembered, we exist' (Act 4). It is as an act of remembrance that the world views offered by each of these fleeting performances survives, finding a voice for the silenced victims that they represent – whether the thousands of suicides registered in the UK and Netherlands every year, or the 947 people injured and 23 killed in the Enschede disaster. Each opera portrays this act of remembering as multifaceted; at the heart of each opera lies the recognition that 'each grain of memory is – look close – of smaller grains composed' (Act 4), the pain of remembered grief inseparable from the sustaining shared memories that it contains. Both *Sunken Garden* and *Wake* present communities threatened by internal and external destruction, encouraging their audiences to re-evaluate their own responses to demonstrate the importance of shared approaches to collective tragedy. This engagement with real-world social issues is a powerful presence in each libretto's finding of hope after tragedy, each offering its own form of guidance to 'right yourself as best you may' (*Wake* Act 4) and again dare to hope for renewal: 'Hope the hydras run out of heads; hope endurance triumphs; hope for friendlier cards; hope that suffering is fractured by change' (*Sunken Garden* Scene 7). Each opera's constructive approach evokes a metamodern revaluing of hope, noted by Vermeulen and van den Akker as an '(often guarded) hopefulness and … sincerity that hint at another structure of feeling' (2). *Sunken Garden* ends not with Amber's suicide but with Simon's choice to live, while *Wake*'s reminder that 'to re-remember, recreates' presents memory as transformative, a force able to make something from nothing: 'when remembered, we exist' (Act 4). In each libretto, it is this act of evoking shared memories that gives voice to the voiceless, collectively bearing witness to human tragedy in order to find acceptance.

Acknowledgements

This chapter is a reworked version of part of Chapter 2 of *David Mitchell's Post-Secular World: Buddhism, Belief and the Urgency of Compassion* (London: Bloomsbury Academic, 2019) and is reprinted courtesy of Bloomsbury. My heartfelt thanks to David Mitchell, Klaas de Vries, Claron McFadden, Roderick Williams and Katherine Manley for their time in interview, the English National Opera and Silbersalz for access to *Sunken Garden* and *Wake*'s video footage, Michel van der Aa and Intermusica for providing access to *Sunken Garden*'s libretto, the University of Amsterdam and Donemus for providing access to *Wake*'s recording and score, and Marco Borggreve for permission to reproduce the photograph of *Wake*.

Works cited

Brecht, B. (2014), '*Verfremdung* Effects in Chinese Acting', 1936, trans. Jack Davis et al., in Marc Silberman, Steve Giles and Tom Kuhn (eds), *Brecht On Theatre*, London: Bloomsbury, 151–9.
Dellios, R. (2003), 'Mandala: From Sacred Origins to Sovereign Affairs in Traditional Southeast Asia', *CEWCES Research Papers*, 8, 1–15.
Goodreads (2014), 'Interview with David Mitchell', *Goodreads.com*, September. Available online: https://www.goodreads.com/interviews/show/975.David_Mitchell (accessed 12 June 2015).
Goss, R. (1997), 'Tibetan Buddhism and the Resolution of Grief', *Death Studies*, 21(4), 377–95.
Harris-Birtill, R. (2014), Interview with Klaas de Vries, Personal Interview, 15 December.
Harris-Birtill, R. (2015a), Interview with Claron McFadden, Personal Interview, 22 February.
Harris-Birtill, R. (2015b), Interview with Roderick Williams, Personal interview, 13 January.
Hopf, C. (2011), 'The Stories We Tell: Discursive Identity through Narrative Form in *Cloud Atlas*', in Sarah Dillon (ed.), *David Mitchell: Critical Essays*, Canterbury: Gylphi, 105–26.
Kidd, J. (2014), 'Time and Again', *The National*, 9 October. Available online: http://www.thenational.ae/arts-lifestyle/the-review/time-and-again-the-critically-acclaimed-novelist-david-mitchell-on-life-death-and-everything-in-between (accessed 12 March 2015).
Mitchell, D. (1999), *Ghostwritten*, London: Sceptre.
Mitchell, D. (2004), *Cloud Atlas*, London: Sceptre.
Mitchell, D. (2010), *The Thousand Autumns of Jacob De Zoet*, London: Sceptre.
Mitchell, D. (2014a), *The Bone Clocks*, London: Sceptre.
Mitchell, D. (2014b), 'Variations on a Theme by Mister Donut', *Granta: Japan*, 127, 39–61.
Mitchell, D. (2015), *Slade House*, London: Sceptre.
Muchnik, A. (2013), 'David Mitchell Talks about Moscow, Literature and the Future', *Moscow Times*, 13 September. Available online: http://www.themoscowtimes.com/arts_n_ideas/article/david-mitchell-talks-about-moscow-literature-and-the-future/485995.html (accessed 2 October 2014).
Penner, N. (2013), 'Opera Singing and Fictional Truth', *Journal of Aesthetics and Art Criticism*, 71(1), 81–90.
Rees, J. (2013), '10 Questions for Writer David Mitchell', *Theartsdesk.com*, 10 April. Available online: http://www.theartsdesk.com/film/10-questions-writer-david-mitchell (accessed 23 September 2014).
Robinson, R. and W. Johnson (1996), *The Buddhist Religion*, 4th edn, Belmont: Wadsworth Publishing Company.

Shanghai TV (2012), Interview by Shanghai TV, '2012 Shanghai Book Fair', *Reading Tonight*, 21 August. Available online: https://www.youtube.com/watch?v=8Y1zPJ9xpFo&list=PLsMDs0SXlAFWQOlLiNdnDdbntJkMkyeRA&index=57 (accessed 2 October 2014).

Smith, M. W. (2007), *The Total Work of Art: From Bayreuth to Cyberspace*, New York: Routledge.

Sunken Garden (2013), Comp. Michel van Der Aa, Lib. David Mitchell, English National Opera, London, 12 April. Performance.

The Tibetan Book of the Dead (2006), trans. Dorje, Gyurme. ed. Graham Coleman and Thupten Jinpa, London: Penguin.

Vermeulen, T. and R. van den Akker (2010), 'Notes on Metamodernism', *Journal of Aesthetics and Culture*, 2. Available online: https://doi.org/10.3402/jac.v2i0.5677 (accessed 17 April 2015).

Wake (2010), Comp. Klaas de Vries and René Uijlenhoet, Lib. David Mitchell, *Nationale Reisopera*, Enschede, 13 May. Performance.

Wallace, C. (2014), 'The Expansive David Mitchell', *Interview Magazine*, 1 October. Available online: http://www.interviewmagazine.com/culture/david-mitchell-the-bone-clocks (accessed 12 March 2015).

8

David Mitchell's representations of environmental crisis and ecological apocalypse

Treasa De Loughry

Chapter summary

This chapter examines David Mitchell's concern with eco-crisis and civilizational collapse across several works from his oeuvre, paying close attention to his speculative and global treatment of contemporary narratives of scarcity. This includes *Ghostwritten*'s (1999) depiction of simultaneous planetary crises and the wave of infestations and infections that brings about *Cloud Atlas*'s (2004) future dystopian narrative. This chapter also examines Mitchell's short story 'The Siphoners' (2011) and its account of a roving band of paraffin stealers in the post-energy dystopia of 2033, and Mitchell's novel, *The Bone Clocks* (2014), which portrays the brutal aftermath of global civilizational collapse in 2043 due to overconsumption. Yet, thinking 'ecologically' means imagining progressive change beyond eco-apocalypse. I conclude by examining how storytelling is the essential kindling for post-apocalyptic civilizations and how depictions of other social groups gesture towards sustainable social and ecological relations.

Introduction

David Mitchell has long been preoccupied with the prospect of ecological apocalypse, and this chapter will map Mitchell's concern with eco-crisis and civilizational collapse across several works from his oeuvre, paying close attention to his speculative and global treatment of contemporary narratives of scarcity and crisis. As ecocritic Greg Garrard observes, apocalyptic environmental imaginaries are always 'proleptic' (2004: 85) – they are a narrative and imaginative response to the future yet to come, and the global scope of an emergent eco-catastrophe registers urgently in Mitchell's works. This includes *Ghostwritten*'s (1999) depiction of the strange weather of simultaneous planetary crises, and the disorderly tidal wave of infestations and infections which brings about *Cloud Atlas*'s (2004) future dystopian narrative, where a malachite statue of eighteenth-century overpopulation catastrophist Thomas Malthus surveys an arid plain and a consumerist dystopia commodifies nature, from rural hinterlands to fabricant bodies.

More specifically, this chapter will examine the intersection of scarcity and eco-crisis in Mitchell's oeuvre through, firstly, an analysis of power as a brutally competitive law of survival based on competitive individualism that, secondly, manifests as an ecological relation which leads to narratives of overpopulation and resource scarcity. For example, in *Cloud Atlas* the journalist Luisa Rey uncovers a plot by oil corporations to sabotage the safety of nuclear reactors, and in the futuremost tale, the narrator, Zachry, ekes out a subsistence existence in a post-Fall, post-oil world. Put simply, ecological degradation from overpopulation and overconsumption are linked in these works to configurations of power and social values. This chapter also examines Mitchell's short story 'The Siphoners' (2011), which depicts a roving band of paraffin siphoners amid the establishment of geronticide as a desperate population-control measure in a 2033 post-energy dystopia. Finally, Mitchell's novel, *The Bone Clocks* (2014), is well placed to expand on *Cloud Atlas*'s world-mapping and concern with ecological crisis by portraying the immediate and brutal aftermath of a 2043 global petro-collapse brought on by overconsumptive behaviours.

The environmental historian Jason W. Moore states that scarcity is socially produced and operates as a means of opening up new commodity and energy frontiers by exploiting the supposedly limitless 'wealths' of nature. Although the world has witnessed several economic crises in the past several years, Moore argues that all of these events are rooted in complex causes or a 'world-ecology' in which hegemony, the production of nature and capital accumulation are interlinked processes (Moore and Keefer 2011: 42). The hyphenation of the term 'world-systems' refers to the argument that capitalism is a 'system *that is a* world' (Wallerstein 2004: 98), without referring to *all* the world's economic systems. A world-ecology thus refers to the ecology of the capitalist world-system, rather than the ecology of the entire world (Moore 2003: 447).

Moore defines capitalism as a 'gravitational field' through which human and extra-human natures have been integrated, surveyed and commodified on a global scale for over five hundred years. However, the current moment of neo-liberal capitalism differs from previous eras in that it relies solely on speculative financial capital and drives down the price of food, labour and resources without a concurrent 'revolution in labour productivity' (2011: 48). Neil Smith likewise describes how a 'crisis in the regime of intensive accumulation' (Aglietta qtd in Smith 2007: 18) in the 1970s brought about a 'new phase of accumulation and a restructured capitalism dominated by neoliberalism and so-called globalization' in which nature was constitutive of capitalism's reconfigured 'accumulation strategy' and search for surplus value. The result was the 'extensive production of nature' (Smith 2007: 16) through its transformation into another market frontier, with the financialization of nature leading to the emergence of new ecological commodities, among them gene therapies, genomed flora and fauna, and seed patents (6). However, in recent times the impact of climate change, the suppression of crop yields and the lack of new frontiers of investment or cheap natures to exploit, have generated a crisis of cheap nature (Moore 2010: 229–30) specific to the contemporary juncture.

This chapter examines how Mitchell's works, with their speculative account of future environmental crisis and world-mapping trajectories, are a means of coming to terms with the contemporary intensified degradation of the world-ecology. The dual meaning of power in Mitchell's works, as both predacious human behaviour and scarce energy resource, suggests an assemblage of social values and ecological affects that coproduce eco-crisis, or what theorist Timothy Morton describes as an emergent global environmental culture that intimates the networked 'mesh' or cognitive map of interlinked economic, ecological and political phenomena (2010: 102). Additionally, Morton claims that 'ecological thought' necessarily imagines progressive change beyond eco-apocalypse, and this chapter will conclude by examining, first, how storytelling is the essential kindling for post-apocalyptic civilizations in *Ghostwritten*, *Cloud Atlas* and *The Bone Clocks* and, second, how the depiction of other social groups like the 'Prescients' in *Cloud Atlas* and *Bone Clocks* gestures towards the possibility of sustainable social and ecological relations after the 'Fall'.

Ghostwritten's eco-global imaginary and 'strange weather'

Ghostwritten (1999) is David Mitchell's first novel. With its narrative echoes and expansive geographic horizons – nine stories are set in different locations including Tokyo, Okinawa, Mongolia, St Petersburg and London – it has been described as a 'novel of globalization' (Vermeulen

2012: 381) and a prescient twenty-first-century 'global novel', in line with contemporary composite films like *Babel* (Barnard 2009) or Kieslowski's interconnected *Three Colours* films (Lively 1999). However, the text's globality is constructed not just by its scope of reference but also by eco-global tropes that interknit diverse narratives, like the reappearance of a comet in each tale, the strange weather efflorescence of social and ecological disruption or the implication that 'ghostwritten' forces structure its account of chance and fate, which Mitchell in interview describes as the novel's main thematic (Begley 2010). The text's epigraph is, fittingly, a quote from Thornton Wilder's *The Bridge of San Luis Rey* (1963), a novel about a priest's search for the divine cause of a bridge's collapse. In Mitchell's final story, an artificial intelligence inhabiting a satellite acts out Wilder's premise by discarding its rule 'to preserve visitors' lives' (427) and impairs a strut on a bridge, which stops an Eritrean militia from attacking a village (428).

Ghostwritten's search for 'meaning in randomness' (Begley 2010) is carefully plotted throughout the text, with each story concerned with causality and connected through chance encounters. In the seventh chapter, Marco the ghostwriter is told by his publisher Timothy Cavendish, 'We're all ghostwriters, my boy. And it's not just our memories. Our actions, too. We all think we're in control of our own lives, but really they're pre-ghostwritten by forces around us' (295–6). Cavendish's cryptic remark suggests that the author is the 'ghostwriter' of the text's fictional universe, but also that other unexplainable forces structure fate, from strange weather to opportune artificial intelligences. Timothy Cavendish is also a central narrator in *Cloud Atlas*, meaning that both novels inhabit the same literary universe. This speaks to Mitchell's admission in interview that his books constitute a vast 'Über-book' (Schulz 2014): an element that necessitates this chapter's ecological critique across Mitchell's oeuvre.

The final and ninth chapter about a bodiless artificial intelligence called the Zookeeper or 'Zooey', who flits between satellites and tries to stabilize global stock markets and halt nuclear war, is an exemplary story from which to examine *Ghostwritten*'s account of an alternate 'force' intervening in and narrating global ecological crisis. Zooey is charged by its maker, physicist Mo Muntervary, with safeguarding the earth's citizens and with being 'accountable'. In the pursuit of the latter, Zooey rings Bat Segundo's New York 'Night Train' radio show annually to confess to its actions, which includes halting a nuclear strike and destabilizing a bridge to stop an African militia from committing further atrocities. However, the Zookeeper's virtuous attempts to offer humanity a way out of its reliance on fossil fuels, weapons and war is thwarted by human ingenuity, and by the time of its final and fourth phone-in, instead of producing order its repeated interventions have sowed the seeds of new crises. In a lengthy passage from a 'MedSat' over the Central African Republic, Zooey extraordinarily mentions all the classic causes of civilizational breakdown in dystopian fiction including plague, viral mutations, war, rising sea levels, refugee crises, nuclear meltdowns, famine and out of control GM crops (425). Zooey's recitation of these eco-statistics is shocking because their simultaneity, as extra-human natures, from infections to infestations, erupt in an impenetrable planetary wave of ecological and social disruption. Zooey's inability to parse this complex 'strange weather' of interrelated events leads it to conclude that it will discharge itself of its duties by locking out the visitors to its earthly zoo in a fortnight's time when a comet is due to fly past. Rather than directly hurting its earthly charges, Zooey fails to interrupt the comet's path. Despite the frustrating inconsistencies between Mitchell's novels (for instance, that Mo Muntervary dies in *Ghostwritten* but reappears in *Bone Clocks*), the dreadful ecological conditions of Sonmi~451's world in *Cloud Atlas*, of a far-future Korean peninsula affected by rising sea levels, toxicity and nuclear fallout, appears to be the result of Zooey's disastrous rejection of its role as the policer of the 'earthly' zoo.

Ghostwritten's depiction of epidemics, economic fluctuations and political change as a tsunami of eco-global 'strange weathers' has a recent genealogy in weather reports as a means of naturalizing such unusual and simultaneous events. For example, Andrew Ross describes how 1987 North American weather reports linked the falling prices of the Wall Street stock market with the freezing temperatures of America's Eastern seaboard (1991: 238). Bat Segundo's radio show in *Ghostwritten* follows the same format described by Ross, and immediately after the Zookeeper's attack on a US military facility, the radio presenter announces his next segment of music 'Bob Dylan's "World Gone Wrong"' (392), followed by wartime news reports and the weather. McKenzie Wark similarly notes that the political turmoil of 1989 to 1991, which included the Wall Street stock crash, the Tiananmen Square protests, the fall of the Berlin Wall and the Gulf War, were interrelated by a series of 'media vectors' or 'vectors of communication' (1994: x, 5) which drew seemingly unrelated occurrences into a comprehensible narrative. This turbulent period in world politics forms an important backdrop to *Ghostwritten*, with multiple references made throughout the text to the Gulf War: Mo Muntervary's 'quantum cognition' technology is used against her will by the US military for surgically precise cruise missiles, and the language of the 'New World', 'New Earth' and nuclear 'White Nights', which recalls the 'New World Order', a catchphrase of US foreign policy during the Gulf War, appears nearly twenty times throughout the novel (examples include 5, 25, 28, 31, 127, 130, 293, 331, 372 and 436). The analogically similar treatment of economic and political turmoil in *Ghostwritten* is a means of simplifying the ungraspable correspondences between such events, with 'strange weather' a symptom of the structural processes that produce unrepresentable but existing links between diverse processes, ecologic and economic. This emergent global environmental imaginary is what Timothy Morton describes as the 'stunningly vast and disturbingly decentered' (2010: 102) ecological mesh now brought to visibility by capitalism's intense transformations of the environment. However, Zooey's aerial mapping of the compound irruption of civil wars and rising sea levels, viruses and famines, and inability to stop fossil fuel consumption or arms dealing despite its frequent interventions, more accurately literalizes Jameson's pithy statement that it is easier to imagine the continued degradation of the earth than the end of late capitalism (1998: 50).

In another 'strange weather' correspondence the entire text is dogged by the reappearance in every story of 'Comet Aloysius'. The comet reappears nineteen times in total throughout *Ghostwritten* and loosely connects disparate events, from Quasar's millenarian beliefs that the comet will usher in the 'New Earth' (28) to Zooey's last phone-in to Segundo's show on 'Aloysius Night, Brink Night, and Zookeeper Night' (425) and the prophetic Chinese peasant in the fourth story who senses that the comet is not a shooting star but a 'man's eye' (141) that bathes the world in evil even before the space race begins. Despite *Ghostwritten* lacking the strong thematic structure and consistency of *Cloud Atlas*, its most powerful global trope is a 'butterfly effect'-like paranoia, of which 'strange weather' is an important trope through which events are networked with other stories and amplified in their consequences. For instance, the collapse of Denholme Cavendish's bank in Hong Kong precipitates the betrayals and murders at the centre of the art heists in the St Petersburg story, enables the prosperity of the great-granddaughter of an elderly woman in the Chinese 'Holy Mountain' chapter and leads to Marco being thrown out of his lover's house and therefore saving Mo Muntervary from an oncoming taxi. Similarly, *Ghostwritten*'s account of Neal Brose's actions is a fictionalized version of Nick Leeson's disastrous futures trading at Barings Bank, which was laid bare by the 'strange weather' occurrence of an earthquake in Kobe in 1995, and in turn drove down the price of Leeson's predictions and caused irreparable losses for the bank. The character of Neal Brose is brought low by an auditing check rather than an earthquake, but the text's butterfly effect serves to create new patterns that are beyond the scope of either artificial intelligences or 'ghostwriters' to map in their totality.

Predacity and ecological crisis in David Mitchell's *Cloud Atlas*

Cloud Atlas's global environmental imaginary also maps unusual correspondences, not just between characters but through historical timeframes, with a comet-shaped birthmark reappearing on each of the text's main figures. Unlike *Ghostwritten*, *Cloud Atlas*'s six story narrative form has an innovative matryoshka doll format, meaning that each narrative, bar the futuremost one, is broken in half, midway through scenes and sometimes sentences, and then returned to in reverse order. Connecting the text's diverse array of narratives is the novel's eponym which refers to the immutability of human nature (Naughtie 2007), which Mitchell defines in interview as 'predacity' (Martin 2010). Predacity is informed throughout the text by frequent references to Nietzschean 'will-to-power' struggles. In the second chapter, composer Vyvyan Ayrs, a self-professed fan of Nietzsche, names his newest composition *Eternal Recurrence* (2004: 84), and in Luisa Rey's story, energy executive Alberto Grimaldi asks himself how some men achieve positions of Übermensch-like dominance while others die as subordinates, concluding that the answer is the 'will *to power*' (131, italics in original) and human nature (132). Predacity scales from the individual to the nation-state in what minor character Morty Dhondt also describes as the 'will to power', which is observable in 'bedrooms, kitchens, factories, unions and the borders of states' (462). It also operates as a metonym for the text's historical recurrence with each main figure a reincarnated or recannibalized soul of previous characters, and each plot a reiteration of characters trying to escape compromising positions of predacious exploitation.

The text's account of Nietzschean will-to-power struggles is informed by nineteenth-century social Darwinism, which anthropomorphized Darwin's account of natural selection by interpreting society as the 'survival of the fittest' of competitive individuals (Clayton 2013: 57–8). Such sociobiological rhetoric, inasmuch as it treats human and animal natures as analogically similar, provides ecological reasonings for unequal social structures and destructive behaviours (Ross 1993: 101). Examining *Cloud Atlas*'s account of predacious human natures and the immutability of the will to power therefore provides a crucial insight into the text's environmental imaginary. In the penultimate story, 'An Orison of Sonmi~451', about a revolutionary clone fomenting agitation in a hyper-consumerist Korean dystopia, predacity becomes a means of exacting control over the regime's consumers by advancing anti-hoarding consumption laws and monetizing nature. On a visit to an exiled mountain community, the leader explains to Sonmi that the ruling *juche* (a term for the corporacy's ruling junta, originating from North Korea), 'castigates' the 'colonists' for stealing natural resources from corporations including 'rain from WaterCorp; royalties from VegCorp patent holders; oxygen from AirCorp' (349). Neil Smith describes how capitalism's treatment of nature as an accumulation strategy has changed not only the production but also the consumption of nature (2007: 17), and likewise Sonmi's narrative is a nightmare of perfectly commodified nature. The production of clones for every imaginable landscape from 'disastermen' for 'deadlands' (215) to fabricants for uranium mines (340) and the advertisements beamed onto the moon by a 'lunar projector on far-off Fuji' (236) owned by 'SeedCorp' are examples of the treatment of nature, from genomes to lunar landscapes, as sites of potential wealth.

In Sonmi's flight from the regime, her account of the landscape surrounding Neo-Seoul marries predacity as a principle of overconsumption with environmental degradation. She describes how monocrop 'hybrid' plants replace indigenous fauna as a 'sterile wind' swishes 'blunted needles'

(344), and on a hill overlooking lakes filled with fish effluence stands 'mighty corp logos' alongside which 'a malachite statue of Prophet Malthus surveyed a dust bowl' (344). The lesson is clear: the regime's pursuit of consumption at any cost has exhausted the region's bioenvironmental conditions. This loss of ecological diversity is a general principle in its own right and corresponds with the peninsula's cultural and political banality – fittingly, the corpocratic regime is named 'Unanimity'. *Cloud Atlas*'s account of environmental collapse is therefore defined by the overproductive and overconsumptive tendencies of a consumerist *juche* which leads directly to the dreadful plagues, '*crazed atoms*' (286, italics in original), and violent tribalism of Zachry's tale. As Morty Dhondt warns, the will to power and human civilization are 'the same faculties that'll snuff out *Homo sapiens* before this century is out!' (462), and the competitive advantages gained within each narrative by Pacific-based colonialists, America's Cold War energy complexes and Korean corporations are eventually undercut by a disastrous future of wars and civilizational collapse.

The narrative's account of environmental catastrophe is couched in terms that suggest a sociobiological and deterministic account of human behaviour. But it also foregrounds Thomas Malthus's 'discovery' of what Marx ironically described as 'the beautiful trinity of capitalist production: over-production, over-population and over-consumption' (Marx 1978: 787, fn 15; Medovoi 2010: 126–7). Ecocritic Greg Garrard states that Malthus's 'An Essay on the Principle of Population' (1798) represents the 'most influential forerunner to the modern environmental apocalypse' (2004: 93). Malthus argues that nature has a 'limit' that when exceeded by overpopulation leads to nightmarish boom and bust population cycles that alternately exhaust and replenish earth's 'natural' resources through scarcity and epidemics ((1798) 2009: 55). Contemporary variants of Malthusianism manifest in anxieties surrounding the depletion of fossil fuels, and *Cloud Atlas*'s narrative of ecological crisis is likewise conditioned by the exhaustion of nature in terms that recall the 'limits to growth' and 'peak oil' anxieties of 1970s oil shock discourses. 'Oil shock' discourses include prose pieces, films and novels that imagine the effects of future energy scarcity against a backdrop of anticipated problems like overpopulation, such as Paul Ehrlich's *The Population Bomb* (1968) and the Club of Rome's report *The Limits to Growth* (1972) (cited in Heise 2008: 71). These works peaked after the 1973 oil shock crisis, caused when OPEC, a Middle Eastern oil conglomerate, decided to enact an oil embargo in response to the Yom Kippur War, driving up global oil prices and fears of fossil fuel shortages (Harvey 2005: 12, 27).

In *Cloud Atlas*, such 'resource angst' is coproduced by predacity, with will-to-power struggles to control decreasing resources inciting rapacious behaviours in terms that scale the metaphors of nature and society through sociobiological language. Predacious nature turns into predacious *human* nature, and power as a verb, supplying force, energy and surging kinetic action becomes power as a noun or the exertion of authority. The exemplary link between 'will-to-power' and resources occurs in Luisa Rey's story, a potboiler detective thriller following the journalist as she uncovers a plot to bury a safety report about Seaboard Corporation's dangerous nuclear reactor. Written in the form of an airport thriller in short 'chapteroids' (164), the story is a breathless account of corrupt nuclear executives in the pay of oil companies, double-crossing environmental activists and unscrupulous politicians. Significantly, Luisa Rey's story is titled 'Half-Lives: The First Luisa Rey Mystery': the 'Half-Lives' of the title refers to the recursive format of the novel with stories split into 'half-lives', and also to the shortened temporalities of characters like Timothy Cavendish who is 'retired' into a nursing home, and the clone Sonmi who can only live for twelve years. 'Half-lives' is also of course a reference to the measurement of time, the 'half-life' it takes for nuclear isotopes to decay, conjoining the 'half-lives' of nuclear isotopes to the text's structure and its short-lived characters.

Graeme Macdonald states that a 'resource-angst' (2013: 19) has permeated most discourses about starvation, extinction, and 'bioenvironmental degradation' since the oil shock era of the 1970s, and similarly *Cloud*'s Malthusian account of ecological crisis is defined by repeated references to a 'resource-angst' of convergent biophysical exhaustion which manifests in shortened lifespans – most noticeably in the continuities between Timothy Cavendish's narrative, a tragic-comic tale about his entrapment in a nursing home, and Sonmi's story. When Timothy Cavendish tries to escape nursing home Aurora House, he roars, 'Soylent Green is made of people!' (179), in a reference to the 1973 film about the recycling of human body matter into a protein food substance called 'soap'. By Sonmi's story Cavendish's enforced obsolescence is taken to extreme principles with speed and efficiency realized in grotesque biopolitical measures: fabricants are euthanized at twelve years of age and dismembered into a *Soylent Green* 'soap' foodstuff, in a speeded-up growth regime that supplies the *juche* with vigorous and obedient workers.

Predacity is thus linked in *Cloud Atlas* to cannibalism in what Wendy Knepper describes as a 'sustained allegory' (2016: 106), for 'the endemic predations of capitalist accumulation'. Cannibalism as allegory operates literally, with clones being recycled into 'soap', and figuratively, referring to the social cannibalism of class hierarchies and inequality (Knepper 2016: 110). This gruesome doubling of cannibalism as the predacious feeding on bodies and labour exposes what Knepper calls the 'necropolitical and necro-economic tendencies of the one and unequal world-system' (111), in an allegory that forcefully rejects a progressive outlook on history (Ng 2015: 112, 118). The novel's recursive structure, together with its cannibalist tropes, critiques the capitalist processes that damage social relations and implies, as Jason Mezey notes, that the 'cannibalistic behavior of the past' extends to the 'systemic cannibalism of the future' (2011: 26).

Cloud Atlas's critique of capitalist accumulation extends to environmental degradation or the systemic and recurring capitalist forces that exhaust not just the world-system but also the world-ecology. In Sonmi's tale, the *juche*'s turn to consumerism and state-sanctioned cannibalism implies a backdrop of extreme biophysical exhaustion. Sonmi notes that a key difference between her era and Cavendish's is that in his time people 'uglified as they aged' (244), without access to the 'fixed-term lifespans' and 'euthanasium' provided by the *juche*'s maximization of humans as another source of calorific energy to buttress its failing sources of food. Cavendish is initially tricked into entering 'Aurora House' after he approaches his brother Denholme for a loan to stave off thuggish clients, with Denholme telling Timothy that the only assistance he can offer is a place to 'lie low for a while' (160), without confiding that this place is Aurora House. Cavendish's forcible imprisonment and Sonmi's account of cannibalistic behaviour in a future corporate dystopia neatly conjoins present and future financial crises with the rationalization and eradication of 'surplus' humans, literalizing what Moore describes as the messy bundle of interpenetrating 'human and extra-human natures' (2015: 42), or the interrelation of socio-ecological transformations and economic crises.

While Cavendish's and Sonmi's narratives are linked by fears of senescence and emerging biophysical exhaustion, David Mitchell's 2011 short story 'The Siphoners', with its gruesome account of geronticide as a population-control measure, is an important bridging narrative between both chapters. 'The Siphoners' is set in 2033 in an unspecified location of a new Russian-Chinese empire called Jìndàn-TransUral. The narrator, anthropologist Avril Bredon, ekes out an existence in a remote cabin with her husband Bruno who suffers from Alzheimer's disease, with Avril battling the compound pressures of socio-ecological and pathological degeneration: '*Economics has eaten itself; dementia is eating you; climate change has crippled global agriculture; our government only has the means to hold the Cordon because Jìndàn-TransUral needs order on their farm*' (132, italics in original). Ironically, Avril's former profession as an 'anthropologist' is rendered obsolete by the post-anthropos threat of human extinction in the transition to a post-oil world, with paraffin now a valuable commodity for the government, and Avril's use of 'old' fuels like firewood and peat signals her return to the 'Middle Ages, step by step' (137).

Energy scarcity also intimates wider social transformations. A roving band of teenage militia who siphon Avril's remaining paraffin supply her with suicide 'mercy pills' to hasten the liquidation of the regime's newly surplus population with immigration bars of 'Thirty-five years old for men, … and thirty for women' (138), echoing the 1976 movie *Logan's Run* about the enforced euthanasia of anyone over thirty amid a similarly depleted post-collapse landscape. Likewise, in 'The Siphoners' geronticide as a form of targeted eugenicism coincides neatly with the peninsula's energy crisis and turn to a neo-Malthusian vision of tribalistic warfare, just as clone recycling in Sonmi's tale and Cavendish's forced retirement telescopes the shortened timeframes of human lives by wider networks of biophysical scarcity. 'The

Siphoners' and *Cloud Atlas*'s account of ecological crisis therefore owes much to 1970s discourses foretelling imminent disaster due to fossil fuel depletion but reconfigured for present-day crises.

Although *Cloud Atlas*'s recursive structure foregrounds the inescapability of cycles of history that wax and wane, from progressive social movements to regressive tribalism, occasionally characters embark on radical utopian journeys that emphasize the necessity of battling the forces of greed. Sonmi and Adam Ewing both join Abolition movements that are over three hundred years apart, with Sonmi advocating revolution at the 'molecular level' (342) by slipping an ascendancy catalyst into fabricant soap. At the close of his narrative, Adam Ewing similarly promises to pledge himself to abolitionism, 'because I owe my life to a self-freed slave & because I must begin somewhere' (528). Additionally, that the latter half of *Cloud Atlas* is a composition of endings which unravels from the future to the past suggests that the recirculation and transmission of previous narratives and characters in the shape of holograms, clones and video recordings can change the course of the future.

Mezey notes that *Cloud Atlas*'s play on the fictionality of its characters, a trope established earlier in *Ghostwritten*, produces a text which is 'still in the process of its fictionalizing' (2011: 27). This emphasis on fictionality offers a means for positively reconsidering both fictions, as characters build narratives which seek alternate futures and paths beyond the exploitative actions of corporations and greedy individuals. For instance, despite the potentially crushing conclusion of *Ghostwritten* – that the Zookeeper abstains from saving the earth – a final stream-of-consciousness coda by the narrator Quasar links all the previous stories through fleeting impressions. This leaves open the possibility that it is a narrative within a narrative and that world-preserving actions may yet be imagined. The environmental consciousness of both works is thus rooted in a speculative praxis of embedded storytelling or the political possibilities engendered by imagining alternate ecological futures.

The Bone Clocks and near-future disaster

Mitchell's *The Bone Clocks* (2014) continues *Ghostwritten*'s and *Cloud Atlas*'s experimentation with form by using Mitchell's now signature structure of the composite novel form and retaining a concern with predacity and future socio-ecological collapse, and should rightly be read as a 'novel of the Anthropocene' (Parker 2018: 3), given its account of anthropogenic climate change. The novel is composed of six consecutive chapters from 1984 to 2043 that track Holly Sykes and her involvement in the battle between immortal 'atemporals' or 'Horologists' and evil soul-stealing 'psychodecanters' or 'Anchorites'. As in *Cloud Atlas*, in which predacity unifies the text's different historical periods, spaces and characters, predacity also forms a core element of *Bone Clocks*'s narration, with the psychodecanters literalizing the cannibalistic qualities of predacity by 'decanting' the souls of the young to ensure their own mortality. In the second story Hugo Lamb, a young Cambridge graduate, is a paradigmatically rapacious and amoral figure. He steals the valuable stamps of an elderly stroke victim, causes the suicide of an indebted friend and defines humans deterministically as 'walking bundles of cravings' (144). Hugo is soon recruited by Anchorite Immaculée Constantin, who tells him that 'psycho-decanting' offers a means to refuse the decrepitude and vulnerability of old age, instead defining power as an amoral and indifferent force that moves 'from host to host' (96) and structures the 'plot of history' (96).

While multiple similarities conjoin *Bone Clocks* and *Cloud Atlas*, chief among them is their treatment of predacity as a principle that structures both texts' account of coercive social forms and ecological disaster. In Sonmi's narrative in *Cloud Atlas*, the overconsumptive behaviour of the Korean *juche* is the final warning bell of coming civilizational collapse, and *Bone Clocks*'s final story, set in the west of Ireland, mines a similar thematic in portraying the dreadful consequences of oil-based consumerism. By the sixth narrative, set in 2043, Holly Sykes is largely cut off from the rest of the world after a series of 'NetCrashes' and depends on the largesse of a Chinese consortium to supply fuel and ration boxes. After the consortium withdraws from West Cork, Holly is nearly stripped of her solar panels by roving thieves who excuse their behaviour by appealing to the carelessness of their parent's generation who continued burning oil during a time of 'creature comforts' (571). Reproducing the enforced immigration quotas and geronticide of Mitchell's short story 'The Siphoners', Holly is given anti-emetic 'huckleberries' (572) by the group as potential insurance from the horrors of post-endarkenment pillaging (572).

Reflecting on the prior conditions that led to this civilizational collapse, Holly describes the combined effect of catastrophic rising sea levels, dreadful 'gigastorms', 'deadlanded' regions, mass extinction, and epidemics of Ebola and 'Ratflu' as a 'plotless never-ending disaster movie I could hardly bring myself to watch' (525). Her account of the sudden onset of ecological disaster resonates with recent 'climate change' or 'cli-fi' fiction by imagining the sudden transition from a world of air travel, relative comfort and constant energy, to one ravaged by the compound irruption of extreme weather conditions and oil depletion – Holly's adopted son Rafiq is incredulous of the abundant electricity and technological marvels of her era (524). The atemporal Marinus states, 'Some magic is normality you're not yet used to"' (492), and the ending of *Bone Clocks*'s is grimmer than either *Ghostwritten* or *Cloud Atlas* in imagining a generational shift towards an unrecognizable tribal future as a compound efflorescence of events speeds up the Mitchellian trope of historical regression. *Bone Clocks*'s crucial difference to *Cloud Atlas* is that the former imagines the *near*-future collapse of society due to climate change and fuel shortages, or the Anthropocene, in contrast to the latter's displacement of environmental catastrophe into the distant future, no doubt due to the financial crash of 2008 and the now daily evidence of man-made climate change which demands cognisance of the earth's worsening climatic conditions (see also Shaw 2018: 12).

That actual historical-social conditions structure *Bone Clocks*'s future imaginary is further evinced in the text's frequent lapses into a journalistic register. Holly's husband, war correspondent Ed Brubeck, narrates the third story and recounts his final expedition in Iraq prior to returning to a wedding in Brighton in 2004. Diagnosing Iraq's present difficulties, Brubeck segues into a pithy condemnation of Paul Bremer's military rule, in which tens of thousands of civil servants, members of the Ba'ath Party and Iraqi Army members lost their jobs and the security of their incomes, thus creating '375,000 potential insurgents' (241). Brubeck's largely accurate report of Iraq's regional instability is one instance among many in *Bone Clocks* in which historical veracity and political condemnation crucially define the text's account of imminent ecological disaster. Similarly, Marinus's indictment of the pharaonic inequality of 2025 has shades of the Occupy movement, and his dreadful report card to the recently awoken Horologist Esther Little combines the worst eco-apocalyptic tropes with a pithy summary of the grisly excesses of recent governments:

> 'Oil's running out,' I say, checking Holly's pulse and the second hand of the clock. 'Earth's population is eight billion, mass extinctions of flora and fauna are commonplace, climate change is foreclosing the Holocene Era. Apartheid's dead, as are the Castros in Cuba, as is privacy. The USSR went bankrupt; the Eastern Bloc collapsed; Germany reunified; the EU has gone federal; China's a powerhouse – though their air is industrial effluence in a gaseous state – and North Korea is still a gulag run by a coiffured cannibal. The Kurds have a *de facto* state; it's Sunni versus Shi'a throughout the Middle East; the Sri Lankan Tamils got butchered; the Palestinians still have to eke out a living off Israel's garbage dumps. People outsourced their memories to data centres and basic skills to tabs.' (476–7)

The verisimilitude of *Bone Clocks*'s diagnoses of contemporaneous ills conditions the imperative register of its near-future environmental imaginary, and, as eco-Marxist Leerom Medovoi notes, the 'trope of eco-catastrophe' (2010: 136) is frequently a means of exerting 'biopolitical reform' and changes to the environment 'before it is too late'. Although the supernatural war between Anchorites and Horologists jars somewhat with the text's condemnatory political critique of various governments and supra-national actors, the novel's oscillation between journalism and preternaturalism foregrounds the impossibility of narrating a near-future text without recourse to the political and social failings of the present. Despite the text's dominant strand of speculative realism, it remains, like the immortal souls themselves, shackled to earthly concerns, especially the 'slow violence' of 'attritional' damage caused by anthropogenic environmental destruction (Nixon 2011; Parker 2018: 17). In the final narrative, the Horologists have formed a think tank called the 'Prescients', and they appear in a timely deus ex machina fashion to take Holly's granddaughter and Rafiq to safety in Iceland. Atemporal Marinus admits that the Horologists have had to become 'more interventionist politically' (590), and they reappear in Zachry's story in *Cloud Atlas* as the final beacon and protector of advanced civilization. The 'Prescients' therefore replace *Ghostwritten*'s concern with causality and 'pre-ghostwritten forces', and *Cloud Atlas*'s account of historical patterns and deterministic human behaviours by suggesting that Horologists, in prompting ameliorative human action, offer a counterweight to the carnivorous force of power as the structuring agent of history.

In conclusion, while *Ghostwritten*'s account of ecological crisis differs from *Cloud Atlas* and *The Bone Clocks*, all three texts imagine environmental destruction on a global scale through tropes that transcend historical and geographic difference and in terms that question the gap between knowledge of environmental degradation and ameliorative political action. Against the implicit political pessimism of this viewpoint, the transmission of resistive actions through storytelling or copies in *Cloud Atlas*, the irreverent ending of *Ghostwritten* and the appearance of the Prescients in *Bone Clocks* are together the utopian seeds that reinforce the importance of individual acts of narration and resistance. In *The Bone Clocks*, 'precognition' or prophetic visions are described as 'a flicker of glimpses. It's points on a map, but it's never the whole map' (479), and likewise Mitchell's speculative future imaginaries are flickers or assemblages of the current political conditions, discourses and anxieties that inform narratives of global ecological crisis.

Works cited

Barnard, R. (2009), 'Fictions of the Global', *Novel: A Forum on Fiction*, 42(2), 207–15.
Begley, A. (2010), 'David Mitchell, The Art of Fiction No. 204', *The Paris Review*, 193(Summer). Available online: http://www.theparisreview.org/interviews/6034/the-art-of-fiction-no-204-david-mitchell (accessed 26 October 2018).
Clayton, J. (2013), 'Genome Time: Post-Darwinism Then and Now', *Critical Quarterly*, 55(1), 57–74.
Garrard, G. (2004), 'Apocalypse', in *Ecocriticism*, Oxford: Routledge, 85–107.
Harvey, D. (2005), *A Brief History of Neoliberalism*, Oxford: Oxford University Press.
Heise, U. (2008), 'Among the Everywheres: Global Crowds and the Networked Planet', in *Sense of Place and Sense of Planet: The Environmental Imagination of the Global*, Oxford: Oxford University Press, 68–90.
Jameson, F. (1998), 'The Antinomies of Postmodernity', in *The Cultural Turn: Selected Writings on the Postmodern 1983–1998*, London: Verso, 50–72.

Knepper, W. (2016), 'Toward a Theory of Experimental World Epic: David Mitchell's *Cloud Atlas*', *ariel: A Review of International English Literature*, 47(1–2), 93–116.
Lively, A. (1999), 'Inside Every Psychopath Is a Jazz Buff Trying to Get Out', *The Observer*, 8 August. Available online: http://www.theguardian.com/books/19 99/aug/08/guardianfirstbookaward1999.guardianfirstbookaward (accessed 26 October 2018).
Logan's Run (1976), (Film) Dir. Michael Anderson, USA: Metro-Goldwyn-Mayer.
Macdonald, G. (2013), 'Research Note: The Resources of Culture', *Reviews in Cultural Theory*, 4(2), 1–24.
Malthus, T. R. ([1798] 2009), *An Essay on the Principle of Population*, London: J. Johnson; Project Gutenberg.
Martin, M. (2010), 'David Mitchell', *Barnes & Noble*, 25 June. Available online: https://www.barnesandnoble.com/review/david-mitchell (accessed 26 October 2018).
Marx, K. (1978), 'The Grundrisse', in R. C. Tucker (ed.), *The Marx-Engels Reader*, 2nd edn, London: W. W. Norton & Company, 221–93.
Medovoi, L. (2010), 'The Biopolitical Unconscious: Toward an Eco-Marxist Literary Theory', *Mediations*, 24(2), 122–39.
Mezey, J. H. (2011), 'A Multitude of Drops: Recursion and Globalization in David Mitchell's Cloud Atlas', *Modern Language Studies*, 40(2), 10–37.
Mitchell, D. (1999), *Ghostwritten*, London: Sceptre.
Mitchell, D. (2004), *Cloud Atlas*, London: Sceptre.
Mitchell, D. (2011), 'The Siphoners', in Mark Martin (ed.), *I'm with the Bears: Short Stories from a Damaged Planet*, London: Verso, 129–43.
Mitchell, D. (2014), *The Bone Clocks*, London: Sceptre.
Moore, J. W. (2003), 'Capitalism as World-Ecology: Braudel and Marx on Environmental History', *Organization & Environment*, 16(4), 431–58.
Moore, J. W. (2010), 'Cheap Food & Bad Money: Food, Frontiers, and Financialization in the Rise and Demise of Neoliberalism', *Review: A Journal of the Fernand Braudel Center*, 33(2/3), 225–61.
Moore, J. W. (2015), *Capitalism in the Web of Life*, London: Verso.
Moore, J. W. and T. Keefer (2011), 'Wall Street Is a Way of Organizing Nature: An Interview with Jason Moore', *Upping the Anti: A Journal of Theory and Action*, 12(May), 39–53.
Morton, T. (2010), *The Ecological Thought*, London: Harvard University Press.
Naughtie, J. (2007), 'David Mitchell', *Bookclub Radio 4*, 6 March. Available online: http://www.bbc.co.uk/programmes/b007mdcg (accessed 26 October 2018).
Nixon, R. (2011), *Slow Violence and the Environmentalism of the Poor*, Cambridge: Harvard University Press.
Ng, L. (2015), 'Cannibalism, Colonialism and Apocalypse in Mitchell's Global Future', *SubStance*, 44(1), 107–22.
Parker, J. A. (2018), 'Mind the Gap(s): Holly Sykes's Life, the "Invisible" War, and the History of the Future in *The Bone Clocks*', *C21 Literature: Journal of 21st-Century Writings*, 6(3), 1–21. Available online: https://c21.openlibhums.o rg/article/doi/10.16995/c21.47/ (accessed 26 October 2018).
Ross, A. (1991), *Strange Weather: Culture, Science and Technology in the Age of Limits*, London: Verso.

Ross, A. (1993), 'The Chicago Gangster Theory of Life', *Social Text*, 35, 93–112.

Schulz, K. (2014), 'Boundaries Are Conventions. And *The Bone Clocks* Author David Mitchell Transcends Them All', *Vulture*, 25 August. Available online: http://www.vulture.com/2014/08/david-mitchell-interview-bone-clocks-cloud-atlas.html (accessed 26 October 2018).

Shaw, K. (2018), '"Some Magic Is Normality": Fantastical Cosmopolitanism in David Mitchell's *The Bone Clocks*', *C21 Literature: Journal of 21st-Century Writings*, 6(3), 1–19. Available online: https://c21.openlibhums.org/article/doi/10.16995/c21.52/ (accessed 26 October 2018).

Smith, N. (2007), 'Nature as Accumulation Strategy', *Socialist Register*, 43, 1–21.

Soylent Green (1973), [Film] Dir. Richard Fleischer, USA: Metro-Goldwyn-Mayer.

Vermeulen, P. (2012), 'David Mitchell's *Ghostwritten* and the "Novel of Globalization": Biopower and the Secret History of the Novel', *Critique: Studies in Contemporary Fiction*, 53(4), 381–92.

Wallerstein, I. (2004), *World-Systems Analysis: An Introduction*, Durham: Duke University Press.

Wark, M. (1994), *Virtual Geography: Living with Global Media Events*, Bloomington: Indiana University Press.

Wilder, T. (1963), *The Bridge of San Luis Rey*, New York: Washington Square Press.

9

The Bone Clocks and the mud of humanity: The Anthropocene *Bildungsroman*

Chris Koenig-Woodyard

Chapter summary

Extrapolating Franco Moretti's notion that the *Bildungsroman* is an 'anthropocentric space', I argue for a new critical perspective of genre: Mitchell's *The Bone Clocks* (2014) is an example of what I designate as the 'Anthropocene *Bildungsroman*'. The genre furnishes Mitchell with a narrative space in which he interleaves the realistic and the fantastic as he depicts sixty years in the life of the novel's central character, Holly Sykes. Straddling the realism of Mikhail Bakhtin's 'national-historical' chronotope and Ramona Fernandez's body-centred 'somatope', I argue that the genre of the Anthropocene *Bildungsroman* is shaped by the jointly realistic-fantastic anachronotope.

Introduction

David Mitchell's *The Bone Clocks* (2014) is an Anthropocene *Bildungsroman*, a genre that amalgamates the Anthropocene – the

10,000-year-old geological epoch we currently live in – and the *Bildungsroman*, the novel of education and formation. The novel spans sixty years of Holly Sykes's life from 1984 to 2043, from age fifteen to seventy-five. Covering approximately one decade each, the novel's six chapters are narrated in the first person, with the first and final by Holly and the middle four by different male characters. The story bears the hallmarks of the *Bildungsroman*, and as Holly 'comes of age', Mitchell depicts her meeting, befriending and loving, as well as grieving the deaths, of friends and family, which include the bewitching Miss Constantin, who visits seven-year-old Holly in the middle of the night; her young brother Jacko, who disappears when Holly, at fifteen, runs away from home; university student Hugo Lamb, with whom she has a romantic relationship when she is twenty-three; childhood friend Ed Brubeck, whom she lives with in her thirties, and with whom she has a daughter; novelist and creative-writing teacher Crispin Hershey, with whom she forms a deep friendship when she is in her late forties; the centuries-old Marinus, a Horologist, who reveals to fifty-seven-year-old Holly that there is a war between the supernatural Horologists, who protect humanity, and the vampiric Anchorites, who consume human souls; and her granddaughter, Lorelei, with whom she resides in Ireland during the 'Endarkenment', when the world has collapsed ecologically, politically and socially.

My reading of the *Bildungsroman* is shaped by three critical tenets about the theoretical elasticity of the genre. The first: the generic designation is orismologically pliable. Orismology is the science of defining technical terms and '*Bildungsroman*' is one of the most 'defined, redefined, reconstructed and contested subgenres in literary study' (Feder 2014: 18). The second: historically, the *Bildungsroman* evinces 'a plot of masculine self-formation that both shapes and is shaped by national historical time' (Esty 2011: 24). Mitchell, however, is part of a 'lineage' of authors – including, among others, George Eliot, Virginia Woolf, Antonia Byatt, Margaret Drabble and Ursula Le Guin – whose works interrogate 'the ideological underpinnings of the *Bildungsroman* as a genre of male destiny and heroic modernization' (Esty 2011: 24). And the third: it is 'a tradition among critics of the Bildungsroman to expand the concept of the genre', rendering it more a 'conceptual tool' than 'a recognized historical and theoretical genre' (Abel, Hirsch and Langland 1983: 13–14). Thus, I refunctionalize the genre through a speculative explication of Mitchell's interleafing of realism and fantasy in *The Bone Clocks*. If, as Patrick O'Donnell argues, the 'archaeological anthropology' of Mitchell's writing explores the 'material and social dimensions of human cultures' (2015: 10), I mount a reading of the novel that traces the development of the *Bildungsroman*, as Franco Moretti argues, as an 'anthropocentric space' (1987: 12).

Cultural geology and the novel: The Anthropocene *Bildungsroman*

In 'The Bildungsroman and its Significance in the History of Realism', Mikhail Bakhtin argues that the *Bildungsroman* is a 'biographical novel of emergence' (1986: 24) in which a human emerges 'in real historical time, with all of its necessity, its fullness, its future, and its profoundly chronotopic nature' (1986: 23). Bakhtin's 'national-historical' chronotope determines the cultural and aesthetic corporeality of the genre (1986: 25); indeed, 'chronotopes are the engines for the making of genre' (Fernandez 2014: 1123). The chronotope delineates 'genre and generic distinctions' (Bakhtin 1981: 84) and the 'national-historical' chronotope of the nineteenth-century realistic novel and the *Bildungsroman* 'is an optic for reading texts as x-rays of the forces at work in the culture system from which they spring' (Bakhtin 1981: 425–6). I extend Bakhtin's 'chronotope' Anthropocenically and explore the generic, even the genetic or geological-literary, border between realism and fantasy in *The Bone Clocks*.

The 'Anthropocene' (a term coined in 2000 by atmospheric chemists Paul Jozef Crutzen and Eugene F. Stoermer) refers to the geological epoch of human beings from 10,000 BCE to the present day (Crutzen and Brauch 2016: 211). It aligns with the Holocene era of the last 12,000 years, a period of increased global warming that accelerated the conclusion of the last Ice Age, the Quaternary (110,000 to 12,000 BCE). Although Crutzen suggests that the Anthropocene begins with the steam-engine-driven industrial revolution of the late eighteenth century (2016: 211), a number of other dates have been used to mark the commencement of the epoch: the development of farming in 11,000 BCE; advances in farming techniques and the origins of rice production in 8,000 BCE and 6,500 BCE, respectively; the rise of 'New-Old World' colonialism, 1492 to 1900s CE; and the rise of nuclear warfare and industrialized chemical development and consumption in the 1940s (Lewis and Maslin 2015: 174). In his 'early-anthropogenic hypothesis', William Ruddiman proposes that the Anthropocene dates to 8,000 BCE (2003: 262), a 'period of human history', as Dipesh Chakrabarty notes, that sees the development of 'the institutions of civilization – the beginning of agriculture, the founding of cities, the rise of the religions we know, the invention of writing' (2009: 208).

The Anthropocene, thus, covers the epoch in which an exponentially growing human population has steadily technologized the cultivation (and depletion) of natural resources on a global scale with dire environmental consequences. *The Bone Clocks* is a novel of the 'new cultural geology' (McGurl 2011: 383) that engages what Wai Chee Dimock calls 'deep time': the 'threads of deep time' that give human beings 'a civil society woven of continents and millennia' (2006: 22) and a 'deep field of kinship, more robustly expressive of our humanity than our own life span' (2006: 58–9).

Mark McGurl offers a similar view of Dimock's deep time and argues that an awareness of the Anthropocene generates literary works that portray a humanism of 'transnational sympathy and identification' (2012: 534). In *The Bone Clocks*, Mitchell develops a longue durée story about 'the shape of literature against the history and habitat of the human species, against the "deep time" of the planet Earth' (Dimock 2006: 6).

The metatextual *Künstlerroman*

The Bone Clocks is a text of texts, a *Bildungsroman* of *Bildungsromane*, in which Mitchell explores the narrativization of humanity's physical and cultural reality – Dimock's 'deep field of kinship'. One of the central texts within the text is Holly's 'spiritual memoir', *The Radio People* (Mitchell 2014: 298). A mix of paranormal *Bildungsroman* and cathartic elegy, it covers close to forty years of her life, from 1968 until its publication in 2014, and was a form of 'therapy' for Holly, helping her to cope with her brother Jacko's disappearance (383). Although Holly's book focuses on 'the Radio People', the 'voices' she heard as a child (16), she does not fully document her psychic powers or interactions with the supernatural figures, the Anchorites. She tells Marinus that when Jacko went missing she had a 'daymare' in which she saw the Anchorite Miss Constantin (45): 'I left it out of *The Radio People*, it just read like a bad description of an acid trip. But it happened' (455). Holly is never comfortable with the 'psychic powers' that allow her to 'channel' the voice of another 'sentience' (352), and the book's popularity attracts many 'fake Jackos' (383) who seek to exploit her success: 'If I could unwrite that wretched book,' she remarks, 'I would' (440).

There are a handful of other *Bildungsromane* in *The Bone Clocks*. Crispin, for instance, states that one of his creative-writing students is composing 'a Mormon *Bildungsroman*-in-progress about a Utah boy escaping to a liberal East Coast college where sex, dope, and a creative writing program provoke existential angst' (389) – an example of a subgenre of the academic novel, the MFA novel. Aspiring novelist and book reviewer Richard Cheeseman offers a second *Künstlerroman*, the story of a writer's 'coming of age': 'My hero is a Cambridge student called Richard Cheeseman, working on a novel about a Cambridge student called Richard Cheeseman, working on a novel about a Cambridge student called Richard Cheeseman' (106). The metafictional collapse of the author-text fourth wall is humorous because Cheeseman is composing the very style of novel that Mitchell writes. Indeed, the duplicative *mise en abîme* structure of the gambolling novel-within-a-novel-within-a-novel configuration mirrors Mitchell's playfully postmodern aesthetics, the consociating Russian doll narratives and characters that populate the project of interconnected novels that he calls his 'Über-book' (Schulz, n.p.).

Cheeseman's *Künstlerroman* emblematizes the methodology of *The Bone Clocks*. The inter-nested author-characters include Cheeseman, Crispin and Mitchell himself because, as he confesses, Crispin 'is me' (Armistead 2014: n.p.). As Mitchell ventriloquizes himself into *The Bone Clocks*, he frames a hermeneutic space in which to examine the chronotopic elements of the *Bildungsroman*. Cheeseman, for instance, is not a fan of Crispin's David-Mitchell-esque style. In his review of Crispin's novel *Echo Must Die*, he quips that to castigate '*Echo Must Die* [as] "infantile, flatulent, ghastly drivel" would be an insult to infants, to flatulence, and to ghasts alike' (294). The 'fantasy subplot', 'State of the World pretensions' and the 'writer-character' of *Echo Must Die*, moreover, make the novel 'a decomposing hog' (294–5). Similarly, the reviewer Maeve Munro criticizes Crispin for his author-character: '*Echo Must Die*'s protagonist is, like yourself, a novelist, yet in your memoir *To Be Continued* you dub novels about novelists "incestuous"' (295). Cheeseman and Maeve disparage Crispin for the very meta-aware and hybridic *Künstlerroman* mode that Mitchell himself employs. Just as Crispin evades Maeve's charge of artistic hypocrisy, he ducks his editor's concerns about the hybridity of his new novel with a conciliating calculation about its genre(s). Crispin's (and Mitchell's) novel(s) about a 'psychic woman who hears voices' is, Crispin reckons, 'one-third fantasy. Half, at most … think *Solaris* meets Noam Chomsky via *The Girl with the Dragon Tattoo*. Add a dash of *Twin Peaks*' (364). These comments synecdochically capture Mitchell's self-aware treatment of the *Bildungsroman* and its potential for the Anthropocenic expansion of the chronotope of the realistic through the fantastic.

Human mud and icebergs: The Glaciology of characterization

Mitchell describes *The Bone Clocks* as a 'novel preoccupied with human mud' – an earthy image of the realistic chronotope. The novel is about 'human mud because, as you age, your life gets muddier': 'The reason we love the books we love – it's the people. It's the human mud, the glue between us and them, the universal periodic table of the human condition. It transcends' (Mason 2010). *The Bone Clocks* is full of mud. In chapter one, as Holly ventures into the Kent County of Charles Dickens's *Great Expectations* (1861 [1998]), she observes that 'the Thames is riffled and muddy blue today, and I walk and walk and walk away from Gravesend towards the Kent marshes' (20). In the final chapter, Holly, now seventy-five, serves another character a mug of 'muddy home brew' (605).

Mud, moreover, is a fitting metaphor for the generic hybridity and the 'fractal' narrative style of *The Bone Clocks* (Harris 2015: 148). Mitchell develops the story of Holly's life through a kaleidoscope of multiple perspectives that rotate around her in alternating mirrored and diverse generic patterns. In each of the novel's four middle chapters, Mitchell offers overlapping narratives of first-person focalization that are distinct generic chronotopes. Her life is sculpted from realistic and fantastic muds and modes rooted in magic realism: young adult romance, vampire narrative, social realistic novel, supernatural thriller, spiritual memoir, literary lampoon and science fiction, among others. Mitchell devises a *Bildungsroman* of Holly's life that is an 'almanac of the possible yet primal human relationships' (Armistead 2014: n.p.). In a speech on the history of the novel, Crispin argues that such a form is well suited to portraying human relationships and the 'beauty, truth, and pain of the world' by 'uniting the personal, the past, and the political'. This involves the 'narrative tricks' of 'Dante and Chaucer, Shakespeare and Molière, Victor Hugo and Dickens, Halldór Laxness and Virginia Woolf, Alice Munro and Ewan Rice': 'Psychological complexity, character development, the killer line to end a scene, villains blotched with virtue, heroic characters speckled with villainy, foreshadow and backflash, artful misdirection' (379). Mitchell extends the chronotopic connection between the 'personal, the past, and the political' through characterization – the aesthetic heart of the *Bildungsroman* – as Hugo Lamb observes, at one point, of a television show he is watching: 'Each character gets deepened by a backstory – a good Chaucerian mix' (187).

Such character development is the very goal Crispin has in mind when he instructs his creative-writing students to compose their characters' 'potted life histories' by writing 'five letters from five leading characters, to yourself'. The letters should address the characters' loves, fears, desires, superstitions, passions, secrets and regrets; sexual, religious and political beliefs and attitudes; and physical, psychological and emotional demeanour. 'Only one-tenth' of the letters' contents, Crispin calculates, will appear in any finished narrative (389–90), a fraction that Holly echoes when she comments that 'people are icebergs, with just a bit you can see and loads you can't' (28). Mitchell's iceberg image is a compelling conglomeration of several literary and psychological sources. Holly's comment recalls Samuel Taylor Coleridge's 'Rime of the Ancient Mariner' (1798), Mary Shelley's *Frankenstein* (1818) and, even, Charlotte Brontë's *Jane Eyre* (1847) – Jane paints a watercolour of 'an iceberg piercing a polar winter' that includes figure of death (Brontë 1999: 196–7). Moreover, Mitchell's iceberg evokes Ernest Hemingway's 'theory of omission', the maxim for his minimalist writing style and development of character in which only 'one-eighth of it (is) above water' (1932: 192). The iceberg also connects with psychoanalysis: Donald A. Laird's description of the human mind as an iceberg – 'the mind is really much like an iceberg. Nine-tenths of an iceberg is below the surface of the ocean' (1922: 893) – which is chronically misattributed to Sigmund Freud.

If a human is like an iceberg, the *Bildungsroman* is well suited to plumbing the glaciological depths of human identity and existence. Indeed, the iceberg serves as a metonym for the Anthropocenic, the iceberg-like dimensionality of Holly's character that is an 'almanac' of her roles and relationships. She is a 'mother, sister, daughter, widow, writer, friend' (523). She is also a 'mystic lady turned Irish egg farmer' and a 'singular young lady [who] is all grown-up ... menopausal, cancerous, and fallen in with quite the wrong sort' (524). As the iceberg-like *Bildungsroman* of Holly spans the chronotopes of the realistic (the tip of the iceberg) to the fantastic (the large portion of the iceberg that draughts underwater), Mitchell reconstitutes the chronotope of the conventional *Bildungsroman* as a narrative of a postmodern fragmented self. Holly's 'self', as Linda Hutcheon argues of the postmodern self, is 'a flux of contextualised identities' shaped 'by gender, class, race, ethnicity, sexual preference, education, social role, and so on' (Hutcheon 1988: 59). Holly, however, is not solely positioned as a subject according to the dictates of realism, fragmented as she is; rather, in *The Bone Clocks*, she emerges as a figure of the fantastic who transmogrifies history into more Anthropocenic and mythological temporalities: she looks like 'Little Red Riding Hood's grandmother' and is a 'psychic' (556, 283–5).

From chronotope to somatope: Maximalism and the Über-book

The Bone Clocks's Anthropocenic scope expands Bakhtinian chronotopicity from the national to the global through the ontological integration of realism and fantasy. Ramona Fernandez finds Bakhtin's chronotope 'evocative' but argues that his insistence that humanity 'is always intrinsically chronotopic' fails to explore the 'relationship between the chronotope and the human body' (2014: 1124). The fragmented postmodern self that stands at the centre of the Anthropocene *Bildungsroman* is, as Fernandez adapts the chronotope, a 'somatope' – from the Greek *soma* for 'body' and *tope* for 'place' (2014: 1122–4). 'In somatopic narratives,' Fernandez argues, 'the body' makes 'meaning and directs the plot' because it is 'almost always morphing or under contention'. The somatope is 'the fulcrum of the narrative, and the narrative is enslaved to its representations of the body' (2014: 1125). The meta-aesthetics of Mitchell's Anthropocene *Bildungsroman* and his propensity for the *Künstlerroman* generate 'somatopic narratives' that are 'engines of intertextual reference' with 'seemingly endless iterations/ replications, cuts and recuts, remakes of remakes, spin offs of spin offs, copycat after copycat' (2014: 1125).

The Bone Clocks is a somatopically minded novel that reveals Mitchell's chronoscopic interest in 'permutations of mortality' (Armistead 2014: n.p.). The Anchorite Miss Constantin remarks as much to Hugo – that 'mortality is inscribed in your cellular structure' – when she initially offers him the opportunity to join the Anchorites and to 'defer death in perpetuity'

(101–2). The somatopic transmogrifies the Goethe-Dickens lineage of the *Bildungsroman*, modelled on a chronotope of realism, into a Postmodern mode that interweaves realism and fantasy – or, as Hugo remarks, when he is tempted to enter into a 'Faustian pact' and join the Anchorites (198): 'telepathy is as real as telephones' (206).

When asked in a 2015 interview about the merging of 'human cultural history and geological/evolutionary timescales' in his novels (Harris 2015: 14–15), Mitchell responds that in future novels he will reveal that the 'origins of the transmigrating Atemporals' involves 'Anthropocene memory' (Harris 2015: 16). Mitchell links the Anthropocene and the fantastic: 'I've always been a maximalist world-builder ("macrography" is the word of the week) and always loved the big space operas, the wide open spaces of the maps of Middle Earth, the infinitudes of scale' (Harris 2015: 16). Indeed, as he explains in a 2014 interview, the already-macrographic scale of his novelistic universe will continue to expand geologically: an upcoming novel will be 'set 250 million years in the future' (Schulz 2014).

As the maximalist and macrographically-minded Mitchell aggregates chronotopes and somatopes, plots, themes, characters, intertexts and genres across his novels, his books comprise 'chapters' in what he dubs 'an *Über*-book' and 'each new novel causes the previous one to shape-shift' (Schulz 2014). The Anthropocene *Bildungsroman* in Mitchell's work, then, is codicologically and narratologically tectonic in nature; it is a global genre, and Mitchell is, as Kathryn Schulz argues, a 'pangaeic writer' and a 'supercontinental writer': 'What is for geologists a physical fact … is, for Mitchell, a metaphysical conviction' (2014).

The 'V-Word': Trans-corporeal characters

In *The Bone Clocks*, Mitchell's elision of the physical and metaphysical politicizes human-scalar metrics of time. Indeed, in many ways, the novel is an ecological elegy of the Anthropocene as characters observe the destruction of the earth by humans. Hugo, for instance, dates a woman who belongs to a commune called Rivendell, from Tolkien's *The Hobbit* (1937): it is a 'postcapitalist, postoil, postmoney … outpost of the future' (136). In chapter five, set in the postcapitalist, postoil and postmoney year of 2043, Marinus reflects that 'these woods are remnants of the old forest that covered Ontario for most of the Holocene Era. The trees' war against subdivisions, agro-forestry, sixlane highways, and golf courses is more or less lost' (412). In a companion scene, Marinus's elegy turns dystopian: the 'Earth's population is eight billion, mass extinctions of flora and fauna are commonplace, climate change is foreclosing the Holocene Era' (500). Elsewhere, Ed reads 'Ballard's novel *High Rise*' in which 'civilization' devolves into 'primal violence' (270). Two single-sentence vignettes similarly depict the dystopian as Mitchell composes Anthropocenic micro-novels.

In March 2016, Crispin pens 'a story about a gang of feral youths who roam the near future, siphoning oil tanks of lardy earth mothers' that is proleptically aware of future events in 2043 (307–8). In the second vignette, Mitchell models a feminist deconstruction of the post-Anthropocene: one of Crispin's students composes 'a Utopia about life after a plague destroys every male on earth' (389).

This sequence of *mise en abîme* vignettes runs the generic gamut from the Anthropocene to the post-Anthropocene, including the 'petro-melancholic' dystopia (LeMenager 2011: 25) of the *Mad Max* movies (1979–2015), as well as the gyno-topias of Charlotte Perkins Gilman's *Herland* (1915) and Brian K. Vaughan's graphic novel series *Y: The Last Man* (2002–8). As he offers micro- and macro-graphical dystopian visions of the Anthropocene, Mitchell imbricates an eco-lament of the epoch into his generic augmentation of Bakhtian chronotopicity; or as Jo-Ann Parker sees it, *The Bone Clocks* is a 'novel of the Anthropocene' in which Mitchell explores 'humanity's destructive impact on our planet' (Parker 2018: 3). Casey Shoop and Dermot Ryan similarly observe of *Cloud Atlas* that the novel 'recontexualize[s] the anthropocentric narratives of human time that have brought us to a perceived moment of historical crisis' (2015: 95).

In *The Bone Clocks*, Mitchell envelops the story of Holly's life within a *Bildungsroman* that is shaped by the 10,000-year Anthropocene. His characters, with their accretive 'mettages', are constitutionally more geological and mythological than biological (434). The Anchorites and Horologists, however, employ different methods to achieve their atemporality that, as Marinus notes, has 'terms and conditions' (440). Founded in the '1210s', by a Thomasite monk in Switzerland, who was charged with 'witchcraft' for 'delving into matter, noumena, logos, mind, (and) the Soul' (452–3), the Anchorites are 'apex predators' who treat humanity as a 'food supply – its salmon farm' (401–2). They 'consume the psychovoltaic souls' (489) of human children with psychic abilities (like Holly), preventing the 'cellular subdivision' of 'aging' (451–6). They are, in a word, 'the V-word', 'vampires' (452).

The humanistic mission of the Horologists is to 'assassinate' the Anchorites in order 'to cure these Carnivores of their predatory habits' (489, 484). A Horologist is a soul, a non-corporeal spirit-form, that can inhabit 'unknowing' human hosts (512), taking form as a 'Sojourner' or a 'Returnee' (483). Sojourners can 'move on to a new body when the old one's worn out' (483), while Returnees live in a 'spiral of resurrections' (451) as they successively 'transmigrate' (479), or 'transubstantiate', into human hosts until their host's death (538–9). The 'Atemporal and psychosoteric' cosmology of the Horologists is jointly chronotopic and somatopic (450): when their human host dies, a Horologist returns to 'the Dusk' (451) and forty-nine days later, he/it/she wakes as a child 'in a body of the opposite gender' and 'on another landmass', making each resurrection 'a lottery of longitudes, latitudes, and demography' (432). This joint chronotopicity-somatopicity revolves around what Stacy Alaimo calls the 'trans-corporeal', an ontological and, I would argue, Anthropocenic state refracted through the lens of the fantastic in which 'the human is always inter-meshed with the more-than-human world' (2010: 2).

In *The Bone Clocks*, Mitchell configures the trans-corporeality of the Horologists Anthropocenically: Marinus is '1,400 years' old (462), Xi Lo is 'twenty-five centuries old' and Esther Little is, in 1871, 'seven millennia old' (434). When Marinus first meets Esther in 1871, she resides in Moombaki, and from 1871 until 2025, the soul known as Esther successively sojourns into the bodies of six characters: Moombaki, Esther Little, Ian, Holly, Unalaq and Ōshima (423, 25, 59, 495, 499 and 507). In 1984, Esther claims 'asylum' and is trapped in a repeating two-minute loop in Holly's 'memories' (492) for 'forty-one years', from June 1984 until April 2025 when she dies in a battle with the Anchorites (495, 523). Describing Esther as having 'a face of many stories' (408), Mitchell anthologizes the Anthropocenic age of the atemporal Horologists in the 'long names' of their sequential 'meta-lives' (445): their 'true name(s)' and the names of all of their human 'hosts' (432). By 1871, Moombaki-Esther's long name is 'a history of her people, a sort of Bayeux Tapestry that bound myth with loves, births, deaths; hunts, battles, journeys; droughts, fires, storms; and the names of every host within whose body Moombaki had sojourned' (436). The chronotope-stretching Atemporality of Mitchell's characters is Anthropocenic: Esther is, by my reckoning, 7,154 years old when she perishes in 2025. The long names are onomastic-biographical palimpsests with opaque but always-already discernible traces of all previous lives observable beneath the text of the current human host. They represent the Anthropocene *Bildungsroman* in miniature as the discourse of the *bio-* (of one life) only partly covers the ever-present underlying, iceberg-like, narrative of the *anthropos-* (all of humanity).

The 'Script': An atemporal palimpsest

At the heart of *The Bone Clocks* there is, indeed, a palimpsest – although there is no term in the vocabulary of textual criticism that accurately describes 'the Script' (61). It is, to adapt Julia Kristeva's term, a genotext: a 'process' that articulates 'structures that are ephemeral', including 'matrices of enunciation, which give rise to discursive "genres" (and) "psychic structures"' (1986: 121). If the genotext is 'language's underlying foundation', the more finite phenotext 'obeys rules of communication and presupposes a subject of enunciation and an addressee. The genotext, on the other hand, is a process; it moves through zones that have relative and transitory borders' (1986: 121). I adapt Kristeva's terminology, shifting it away from a discussion of the semiotic and symbolic nature of language and apply it to a consideration of genre.

The Script can be viewed as the genotext to the numerous phenotexts in *The Bone Clocks*. The Script is a genotextually stratified series of phenotexts that form a palimpsest in which the multiple phenotextual narratives of Holly's life accrete successively with superseding texts never fully erasing preceding texts. The young poet Soleil Moore, for instance, informs Crispin that he is 'in the script' (300), qualifying later that he is 'of the Script' – that he 'wrote' himself 'into the Script' with his book 'The Voorman Problem' (400). The Script is a somatopic textless text of 'intertextual performativ(ity)', as Fernandez sees it (2014: 1125), an Anthropocene *Bildungsroman* and *Künstlerroman* about humanity that includes, among others: Cheeseman's reviews and novels, Holly's *The Radio People*, Ed's award-winning journalism, Crispin's novels, the work of his creative-writing students and Soleil's poetry.

If, as I have argued, *The Bone Clocks* is a text of text, a *Bildungsroman* of *Bildungsromane*, the genotextual Script operates at the level of genre, guiding and shaping the constituent elements of narrative: setting, plot, agon, and protagonists and antagonists. Like the Horologists, the Script is non-corporeal, with unknown origins. In chapter five, Holly asks Marinus about the Horologists, wondering, 'Why do Atemporals exist?'; did they 'evolve' or were they 'made'?; and 'Was it something that happened to you, in your first life?' (512). The Horologists do not know, and Holly's questions highlight a political and ideological friction between scales of time in the novel as the deep history of geology conflicts with Christianity. If, as Constantin taunts Holly before the battle between the Anchorites and Horologists, 'God's dead' (525), Holly's comment later in the novel, that 'there is no God but the one we dream up' (574), captures a key shift in the epistemological and ideological underpinnings of Bahktin's chronotope in *The Bone Clocks* from human-scripted ideological narratives to geological and cosmological discourses. The genotext of the Script registers the mixed chronotopic-somatopic temporality of the Anthropocene *Bildungsroman* genre as dialectically dynamic. The Anthropocene *Bildungsroman* is a generic mode that emerges as anachronotopic from the synthesis of the binaries of the chronotope of the realistic and the somatope of the fantastic.

The 'M-Word': Magic realism and anachronotopicity

Mitchell constructs the anachronotopicity of *The Bone Clocks* through a multilinear and interweaving of atemporality that shapes the supernatural disposition of the Anchorite and Horologist characters in the novel: analepsis or 'scansion' – the 'frame-by-frame' reading of a person's memories (418, 493); metalepsis and ellipses (breaks or gaps in time): characters are 'hiatus(ed)' and 'redact(ed)' which are, respectively, the 'freez(ing)', or suspension, of time (485), and the 'wip(ing)' of 'memories of what happened' (492); and synchronicity or 'coincidence' (22). Perhaps the most pervasive anachronotopic mode is prolepsis or, as Marinus says, 'the Script loves foreshadow' (495). These are (seemingly) precognitive 'glimpses' of future events (287). In chapter five, set in 2025, for instance, Esther responds to Holly's comments about the scarcity of books that 'Books'll be back,' because once the 'power grids start failing in the late 2030s ... the future' will look 'a lot like the past' – to which Holly remarks: 'Is that, like ... an official prophecy?' (502). Atemporality in *The Bone Clocks* is cosmologically charged because its anachronotopicity positions the Anthropocene *Bildungsroman* as more fantastic and Blakean (and, by extension, romantic) than realistic and Pythagorean. When Holly runs away from home at the start of *The Bone Clocks*, she says that she will not miss studying 'Pythagoras triangles' in school (4). Her comment captures in miniature the chronotope of orderly and mathematical realism in *The Bone Clocks*. The speculative cosmology of William Blake contrasts this chronotopicity, as Mitchell suggests when Crispin meets the poet Soleil. She presses Crispin to read her volumes of poetry, *Soul Carnivores* and *Your Last Chance* (399), that expose the existence of the Anchorites and remarks, in response to Crispin's dismissive attitude, that 'nobody wanted William Blake's work either' (300).

Soleil's connection to Blake illuminates the anachronotopicity of the atemporal and the fantastic as constituent elements of the Anthropocene *Bildungsroman* in *The Bone Clocks*, elements which Crispin anatomizes during a lecture on the history of the novel as a genre:

> We work in a physical space ... but we also write within an imaginative space. Amid boxes, crates, shelves, and cabinets full of ... junk, treasure, both cultural – nursery rhymes, mythologies, histories, what Tolkien called 'the compost heap'; and also personal stuff – childhood TV, homegrown cosmologies, stories we hear first from our parents, or later from our children – and, crucially, maps. Mental maps. Maps with edges. And for Auden, for so many of us, it's the edges of the maps that fascinate. (380)

The imaginative and physical spaces – the physical, on the one hand, and the psychical, the mythological and the cosmological, on the other – adumbrate the fantastic realms and figures that lie beyond the realistic. Mitchell explores the imaginative space of the novelistic form through magic realism, generating the generic hybridity of the novel through a pendular aesthetics as he vacillates between the realistic and the fantastic. Crispin maps the atemporal geography of the Anthropocene imagination – its 'lottery of longitudes (and) latitudes', as Marinus says – with a paradigm of geo-anachronotopicity that sees the Anthropocene *Bildungsroman* oscillate from the muddy and realistic chronotopes of Dickens to the mountainous and fantastic somatopes of Shelley's *Frankenstein*. Holly and Hugo do, after all, end up in the Swiss Alps at Mont Blanc, the fantastic domain of Lord Byron's *Manfred* (1817) and Victor Frankenstein's creature (56).

'Transwhateveritis': The aesthetics of 'Weird Shit'

In *The Bone Clocks*, Mitchell offers several phrases, images, metaphors and tropes that capture the vacillating realistic-fantastic anachronotopicity of the Anthropocene *Bildungsroman*. It is, for instance, a novel of 'weird shit' – Holly's term for her 'daymares' and the 'radio people' (16–22); and, as Hugo says, 'weird shit needs theories and I have three' (147). Hugo explains his encounters with (and the ontology of) Miss Constantin as a hallucination, as a hoax, or as an ontological, cosmological de-/illusion of global proportions in which the 'real' world is not real. The third theory is 'plausible, *if* you live in a fantasy novel. Here, in the real world, souls stay inside the body. The paranormal is always, *always* a hoax' (148). For a time, he, and, to varying degrees, other characters in the novel, struggle with the shifting sands of realistic-fantastic anachronotopicity. Hugo's invective about the Anchorites – or 'Whateverthefuck they are' (203) – echoes Holly's exasperated description of the chronotopic instability – the weirdness – of transubstantiation, which she dismisses as 'transwhateveritis' (455).

In the novel, 'weird' appears thirty-one times and stands as a Lovecraftian cypher that structures the supernatural arc of the novel as Mitchell intertwines realism and fantasy. Indeed, in *The Bone Clocks*, Mitchell offers a study in the phenomenology of the weird as characters, and, in turn, readers, are led through a Coleridgean willing suspension disbelief to a Tolkien-like secondary belief. For instance, following his explanation of 'psychosoterics' (450), Holly asks Marinus if he is referring to 'technology? Or …' but her thoughts trail off. Marinus completes the epistemological ellipsis, knowing that Holly means 'the M-word': 'magic' (516). In a scene that evinces a similar typographical self-awareness, Ed remarks that he has 'always put inverted commas around Holly's "psychic stuff"' (287). Ed does not develop a Tolkien-like secondary belief, although he reaches a conditional willing suspension of disbelief: after observing Holly channel a 'voice', Holly states that Ed never 'started believing' in her psychic powers, only that 'he stopped disbelieving' (383).

Conclusion – or 'once upon a time'

Perhaps the most hermeneutically illuminating phrase that Mitchell uses in *The Bone Clocks* to capture the realistic-fantastic anachronotopicity of the Anthropocene *Bildungsroman* is the ubiquitous invocation of many fantastic narratives: the 'nursery rhymes, mythologies' and the 'stories we hear first from our parents,' as Crispin notes – 'once upon a time', an invocation that recurs in all of Mitchell's novels (most frequently in *number9dream*).

In *The Bone Clocks*, Mitchell associates the phrase with the novel's four male narrators and Holly: When Hugo first encounters Miss Constantin, he asks if she has been to La Fontaine Sainte-Agnes in Switzerland, to which she responds 'Once upon a time' (100); Ed jealously watches Holly at her sister's wedding 'laughing at a red-carnation young male's joke', remarking that 'once upon a time I could make her laugh like that' (229); Crispin comments on his waning writing career that 'once upon a time, the Kingdom of Midlist wasn't a bad place to earn a living: middling sales, middling advances, puttering along. Alas, the kingdom is no more' (373); Marinus, in a slight modification of the phrase, remarks, 'I felt like Lucas Marinus once did' (439) – his name in *The Thousand Autumns of Jacob de Zoet*. Lastly, in the dystopian Endarkenment of the novel's final chapter, Holly remarks that 'once upon a time "my body" meant "me", pretty much, but now "me" is my mind and my body is a selection box of ailments and aches' (569).

Two of the instances of 'once upon a time' in particular highlight the realistic-fantastic anachronotopicity of Mitchell's shift form Dickens to *Frankenstein* in *The Bone Clocks*. In the first of the two, Holly, only hours into her efforts to run away from home, notices a 'WELCOME TO THE ISLE OF GRAIN' sign and remarks that 'it's not a real island, mind. Once upon a time, perhaps' (29). This is an Anthropocenic moment that merges the geological, the realistic and the fantastic in an intertextual matrix. Holly travels the marshes of Kent where Dickens himself resided and where much of the early action of *Great Expectations* is set; indeed, she follows the route that Pip and Herbert take late in the novel. They 'struck across the marsh in the direction of the Nore' as they travel the length of the Isle, towards Sheppey, where they see the 'Nore' – the sandbanks off of the coast (Dickens 1861 [1998]: 463). The 'Isle of Grain', it is worth noting, has been an on-and-off again island throughout its history, as residents have alternately constructed and removed connecting land masses to either build up roads or open a waterway for shipping traffic (Gorton 1833: 2.118). Thus, the Isle becomes an Anthropocenic symbol of human efforts to move the mound of mud that is the earth to meet their capitalist needs.

The second instance of 'once upon a time' shifts from the mud of Dickens's *Bildungsroman* to the mountains of Switzerland – that is, to the domains of dark, or supernatural, romanticism. In chapter two, when Hugo first encounters Miss Constantin, he asks if she has been to 'Mont Blanc' in Switzerland (56, 99), to which she responds, 'Once upon a time' (100). The Alps are the site of the Anchorites' ancestral chapel, a place that Constantin has, of course, been to many times, including during the Anchorite-Horologist battle in chapter five and, prior to the battle, during Hugo's initiation into the Anchorites.

For his initiation, Hugo is driven deep into the Alps, in to a valley that houses 'the Thomasite Monastery of the Sidelhorn Pass' which is surrounded by 'thirty kilometers of glacier and crevasses' (202–3). Once there, he surveys the landscape and notes that, except for the paved road he travelled on, 'there are no other signs of the twentieth century' (204). In response to his query about why the Anchorites brought him to this specific location, Pfenninger responds, 'It seems apt' (204). The Alps are apt, I would contend, at the level of genre – at the level of the Anthropocene *Bildungsroman*. The mountains, along with the Kent County of Dickens's *Great Expectations* that Holly travels through, emblematize, respectively, the chronotope of the realistic and the somatope of the fantastic – the geo-literary and aesthetic poles that the anachronotopicity of the Anthropocene *Bildungsroman* fluctuates between in *The Bone Clocks*. The geologically diverse atemporality of the novel – from its mud to its mountains – fittingly captures the surreal archi*tex*ture of anachronotopicity, which is, perhaps best represented by Mitchell's portrayal of the Anthropocene as a kind of geological character in *The Bone Clocks*. While touring the glaciers and landscape of Iceland during one of his book tours, Mitchell anthropomorphically charges the Anthropocene – its geological and fantastic dimensionality; Crispin notes that a 'mossy boulder' in the deep valley of the Ásbyrgi, 'looks like the head of a troll's head' (366) that is 'on its side and brooding over an ancient wrong' (373).

Works cited

Abel, E., M. Hirsch and E. Langland (eds) (1983), *The Voyage In: Fictions of Female Development*, Hanover: University Press of New England.

Alaimo, S. (2010), *Bodily Natures: Science, Environment, and the Material Self*, Bloomington: Indiana University Press.

Armistead, C. (2014), David Mitchell on *The Bone Clocks*, Guardian Books Podcast. First broadcast 26 September. Available online: https://www.theguardian.com/books/audio/2014/sep/26/david-mitchell-bone-clocks-podcast (accessed 1 October 2016)

Bakhtin, M. M. (1981), *The Dialogic Imagination*, Austin: University of Texas Press.

Bakhtin, M. M. (1986), *Speech Genres & Other Late Essays*, Austin: University of Texas Press.

Brontë, C. (1999), *Jane Eyre*, ed. Richard Nemesvari, Peterborough: Broadview.

Chakrabarty, D. (2009), 'The Climate of History: Four Theses', *Critical Inquiry*, 35(2), 197–222.

Crutzen, P. J. and H. G. Brauch (eds) (2016), *Paul J. Crutzen: A Pioneer on Atmospheric Chemistry and Climate Change in the Anthropocene*, Cham: Springer.

Dickens, C. (1861 [1998]), *Great Expectations*, ed. Graham Law and Adrian J. Pinnington, Peterborough: Broadview.

Dimock, W. C. (2006), *Through Other Continents*, Princeton: Princeton University Press.
Esty, J. (2011), *Unseasonable Youth*, Oxford: Oxford University Press.
Feder, H. (2014), *Ecocriticism and the Idea of Culture*, Farnham: Ashgate.
Fernandez, R. (2014), 'The Somatope: from Bakhtin's Chronotope to Haraway's Cyborg via James Cameron's *Dark Angel* and *Avatar*', *The Journal of Popular Culture*, 47(6), 1122–38.
Gorton, J. (1833), *Topographical Dictionary of Great Britain and Ireland, Compiled from Local Information, and the Most Recent and Official Authorities*, 3 vols., London: Chapman and Hall.
Harris, P. A. (2015), 'David Mitchell's Fractal Imagination: *The Bone Clocks*', *SubStance*, 44(1), 148–54.
Hemingway, E. (1932), *Death in the Afternoon*, London: Charles Scribner.
Hutcheon, L. (1988), *A Poetics of Postmodernism*, London: Routledge.
Kristeva, J. (1986), *The Kristeva Reader*, New York: Columbia University.
Laird, D. A. (1922), 'Is Your Mind Like an Iceberg?', *The Forum*, 68, 893.
LeMenager, S. (2011), 'Petro-Melancholia: The BP Blowout and the Arts of Grief', *Qui Parle: Critical Humanities and Social Sciences*, 19(2), 25–56.
Lewis, S. L. and M. A. Maslin (2015), 'Defining the Anthropocene', *Nature*, 519, 171–80.
Mason, W. (2010), 'David Mitchell, the Great Experimentalist', *The New York Times Magazine*, 25 June. Available online: http://www.nytimes.com/2010/06/27/magazine/27mitchell-t.html?_r=0 (accessed 1 October 2016).
McGurl, M. (2011), 'The New Cultural Geography', *Twentieth Century Literature*, 57(3–4), 380–90.
McGurl, M. (2012), 'Posthuman Comedy', *Critical Inquiry*, 38(3), 533–53.
Mitchell, D. (2014), *The Bone Clocks*, Toronto: Alfred A. Knopf.
Moretti, F. (1987), *The Way of the World*, London: Verso.
O'Donnell, P. (2015), *A Temporary Future*, New York and London: Bloomsbury.
Parker, J. A. (2018). 'Mind the Gap(s): Holly Sykes's Life, the "Invisible" War, and the History of the Future in The Bone Clocks', *C21 Literature: Journal of 21st-Century Writings*, 6(3), 1–21. doi: https://doi.org/10.16995/c21.47.
Ruddiman, W. F. (2003), 'The Anthropogenic Greenhouse Era Began Thousands of Years Ago', *Climatic Change*, 61, 261–93. Available online: http://stephenschneider.stanford.edu/Publications/PDF_Papers/Ruddiman2003.pdf (accessed 1 October 2016).
Schulz, K. (2014), 'Boundaries are Conventions. And *The Bone Clocks* Author David Mitchell Transcends Them All', *Vulture*, 25 August. Available online: http://www.vulture.com/2014/08/david-mitchell-interview-bone-clocks-cloud-atlas.html (accessed 1 October 2016).
Shoop, C. and D. Ryan (2015), '"Gravid with the Ancient Future": *Cloud Atlas* and the Politics of Big History', *SubStance*, 136(44.1), 92–106.

10

David Mitchell as world-builder: *The Bone Clocks* and *Slade House*

Wendy Knepper

Chapter summary

With the publication of *The Bone Clocks* and *Slade House*, David Mitchell has reconstituted his oeuvre as a single, sprawling tale about a world uncannily like our own, yet fantastically other. This chapter considers the author as a world-builder whose irrealist story of cosmological warfare renders perceptible, and therefore open to critique and change, the unequal world of combined and uneven development. The literary world maps and challenges overlapping histories of oppression and violence, even as it constructs a pluralistic, more-inclusive account of the world as a historical reality and space of dissent and affiliated resistance. In crafting another world, Mitchell engages in world-making activities that strive to enact change in the world by disseminating the stories and cultures of the dispossessed to a global readership.

Introduction

In the face of capitalist crisis and an uncertain global future, Ursula Le Guin argues that we need creative writers who are 'visionaries – the realists of a larger reality' (2014): those who 'can see alternatives to how we live now ... to other ways of being, and even imagine some real grounds for hope' (2014). Such remarks provide a fitting introduction to David Mitchell as an imaginary world-builder who critiques our global order, even as he strives to imagine the world as other by awakening alternatives latent within history and culture. With the publication of *The Bone Clocks* (2014) and *Slade House* (2015b), Mitchell has reconstituted his oeuvre as an epic 'Übernovel' (Finney 2015) – a 'biblioverse' (Hopf 2019: 183) or a 'sprawling macro-novel' (Finney) – that chronicles the history of an imaginary world from its tribal past through trading networks, empire and global capitalism to a post-apocalyptic future. Across his oeuvre, Mitchell's unfolding tale of global transformation 'attempts to reckon with humanity' (Kirsch 2017: 13) to expose 'the cardinal sins of our times – cruelty, exploitation, inequality' (Kirsch 2017: 103). Yet, these global realities are confronted through a fantastical story of cosmological conflict in a supernatural shadow world, where an invisible war pits soul-destroying and life-sustaining forces against one another in a struggle over human and planetary life.

As a world-builder, Mitchell draws on various modes and genres of irrealism to author 'an imaginary world, composed of fantastic, supernatural, nightmarish, or simply nonexistent forms' to 'critically illuminate aspects of reality' (Löwy 2010: 223). *The Bone Clocks* and *Slade House* capitalize on a popular cultural appetite for tales of vampirism and the undead in the global cultural marketplace, whether in the form of neo-Gothic works, such as Stephenie Meyers's *The Twilight Saga* (and its adaptation), the post-apocalyptic horror of *The Walking Dead* TV series or the dark fantasies of J. K. Rowling, Neil Gaiman and George R. R. Martin, to name a few examples. Where some fantasy authors invent new languages, cultures, histories or geographies to critique reality and/or imagine alternatives, Mitchell tends to draw on pre-existing geographies, cultures, languages and histories to offer a more encompassing view of the world. Stories of vampires, supernatural threats and daemonic forces from around the world, both contemporary and archaic, combine in a narrative that tracks and resists inequality throughout a long global history of uneven development; at the same time, a Buddhist-derived cosmology mixes together tales of ghosts, reincarnated souls and transient spirits to craft a planetary counter-narrative about individual and affiliated struggles to challenge violence. Irrealism works to re-immerse readers in the historical struggle over transformation, such that the art of world-building inaugurates radical political forms of 'world-making' (Cheah 2008: 36) that move beyond the critique of inequality to reincorporate and disseminate the worldviews and stories of the dispossessed to a global readership. From the shadows of the otherworld, an alternative view of our world emerges.

David Mitchell as world-builder

Mark J. P. Wolf describes imaginary worlds as 'realms of possibility, a mix of familiar and unfamiliar, permutations of wish, dread, and dream and other kinds of existence that can make us aware of the circumstances and conditions of the actual world we inhabit' (Wolf 2012: 17). While all literature involves some form of world-building (even that which aspires to social realism), the activity is most often associated with the creation of alternative realities, such as through fantasy, particularly when it involves the creation of maps, the crafting of fresh cultures and languages, magical abilities, supernatural incidents and cosmic struggles. This kind of high fantasy appealed to Mitchell early on as a child occupied in trying to fill in the spaces of Tolkien's maps and continues to influence him now as a reader of fantasy, ghost tales and Gothic fiction.

When the author refers to world-building, he cites J. R. R. Tolkien as the 'ultimate world-builder' (Keating 2014) and George R. R. Martin, author of *A Song of Ice and Fire* (adapted as *Game of Thrones*), as 'a world-building genius' (Keating 2014). But it is perhaps Ursula Le Guin who is his strongest influence, with her Taoist philosophical understanding of the world as a union of opposites, such as action and inaction, light and dark and the quest for balance for a soul in conflict and a world at war. Of her, he writes: 'I wanted to spend my life – crafting worlds as real, as full and as irresistible as hers, or die trying' (Mitchell 2018). Clearly, Earthsea, Middle Earth and Westeros are among the imaginary worlds that have shaped Mitchell's ideas and practices as a world-builder. Significantly, these high fantasies represent warring cultures of social transformation, with Tolkien's fiction as an allegory of the events of the Second World War, Martin's on the War of the Roses and Le Guin's as a more oblique critique of the mythologies of war, drivers of conflict and struggles for power in the world.

By contrast, Mitchell's cosmological fantasy renders perceptible various histories of violence, drawing them into a common field of representation and critique. Historically, Mitchell's work registers and politicizes economic and armed conflicts, including the Gulf War (*The Bone Clocks*), conflict in Rhodesia (*Slade House*) and trade-related conflicts in Japan (*Thousand Autumns*). But these historical allusions are subsumed within a cosmology that pits vying atemporal forces against one another in a battle for the human soul, such that the supernatural re-politicizes violence. *Thousand Autumns* and *Slade House* tell stories of Gothic enclosures, where evil forces committed to the acquisition of wealth and consolidation of power imprison and destroy others, often targeting the most vulnerable members of society. *The Bone Clocks* depicts a world where an 'invisible war' (Mitchell 2014: 52) among unseen forces is taking place, where the soul-destroying Anchorites battle the life-sustaining Horologists through a series of conflicts that erupts in open warfare at the Temple of the Blind Cathar. To date, Mitchell's Über-novel has tracked world-systemic transformation through premodern tribal formations, trade networks, empire and global capitalism to an uncertain post-apocalyptic future that collapses once more into tribal groupings and struggles. Mitchell's world-building practices rival the incomplete processes of globalization, but they also create an imagined, altered space of reflection on world-historical transformation.

Ghostly visitations, fantastical intrusions, portals between worlds, cosmological immersions and shifts among various worldly and otherworldly 'realities' express the complex realities, the seen and unseen forces, that shape global life. Examples include Neil Brose's encounter with a little girl and postcolonial hauntings in *Ghostwritten* (see Dunlop 2011: 208–14); the apparition of a ghost of Akiko Kato's son as well as the visitation by a divinity (housed in Dr Voorman) in *number9dream*; the trope of cannibalistic consumption and reincarnation of souls in *Cloud Atlas*; the encounter with a ghost boy on the ice in *Black Swan Green*; *The Sunken Garden* opera with its supernatural encounters; *Wake*, another opera, with its post-traumatic hauntings, following the Enschede fireworks disaster; and the Sadeian enclosure of the monastery in *Thousand Autumns*. Such apparitions and incidents un-repress and work through traumatic histories as well as reveal alternative realities, whether through a 'fantastical cosmopolitanism' that gives voice to 'imaginative cultural protestation' (Shaw 2018: 1) or tales of 'worldly spirits' that 'help us think', more ethically, 'in the more complex vein of the world rather than the reductive frame of the globe' (Trimm 2018: 24). Mitchell remarks on the somatic and political effects of irrealism on readers:

'I create realities, we all do. Like the Slade House, there's a door, which is a book, and you go through that door and it's Narnia, it's not real, but if it's not real, how can we care about it so much, how can it affect your heart rate and adrenal glands?' he says. 'Maybe we can look at the word "real" in different ways.' (Nanda 2015)

Mitchell's world-building activities stake claims for literature as a simulation that acts upon real readers – affecting their hearts, minds and bodies – to renew the world.

Mitchell's irrealism is far from escapist. Instead, this radical political form of writing 'seeks to play an active role in shaping development by problematizing its position and interventions in the world' as it works to get to the roots of inequality and imagine alternatives (Knepper 2016: 98). This is a form of 'world-literature' (with a hyphen), defined by the Warwick Research Collective (WReC) as *'the literature of the capitalist world-system'* (WReC 2015: 15, emphasis in original) that registers and mediates the 'combined unevenness' of international development (WReC 2015: 49). Both the form and content of such a literature register the ways in which capitalism draws the world together in a combined global reality but does so only partly or unevenly. As a result, such a world constitutes a contradictory 'amalgam of archaic with more contemporary forms' (Leon Trostky cited by WReC 2015: 10), one shaped by complex and differential histories, both capitalist and pre-capitalist, as well as perhaps anticipatory of post-capitalist futures. Politically, such fictions participate dynamically to proffer an interactionist account of world culture as the site of a 'ceaseless struggle for power' (WReC 2015: 56). Irrealism plays an important role because of its capacity to recover 'both the specific history of the present and the alternative histories that might have been but were not yet, yet that (paradoxically) still might be' (WReC 2015: 72). Temporal and cultural skewering is thus to be expected as irrealist writing contorts to reveal the fullness of history: to restore to consciousness the dispossessed and to reawaken moribund cultures.

As an irrealist, Mitchell mobilizes the voices and forms of the (semi) periphery and core to register combined and uneven development, but he also intervenes creatively to recombine cultural and historical resources in ways that challenge histories of violence and dispossession. For instance, in 'A Possibly True Ghost Story' (2015a), Mitchell claims to have had a ghostly encounter while living in Japan, which brings Eastern and Western traditions, both modern and ancient, together. Significantly, Mitchell's ghost story is haunted by the imperialisms of the Anthropocene era: a time inaugurated by the horror of nuclear bombing in 1945. He describes how the very material terror of atomic bombing produced the horror of history, Hiroshima, with its dead and radiated bodies, with an estimated number of 90,000 to 166,000 deaths in total. Mitchell observes, 'In the Japanese context, this also means a vast number of restless ghosts denied the Buddhist funerary rites required for a smooth passage to the next world' (2015). His encounter with this spirit, to whom he introduces himself in faltering Japanese, generates fear: 'I was scared by my visitor in a way I hadn't been scared before, and haven't been scared since. ... My fear that night in Kabe was more like an ongoing, low-level electrical shock, and if it resided in any organ it was my skin' (Mitchell 2015). This metaphysical terror registers his anxieties about living with the aftermath of Hiroshima as well as his profound anxieties as a foreigner in Japan.

Mitchell's numinous narrative is shaped by a Buddhist awareness of the soul's transition into death, a cosmology that more generally informs his view of the soul's rebirth through time and space. This ghostly encounter produces a new sense of the universality of world culture: 'Maybe these imaginings were a factor in what follows, or maybe "my" section of the river was what Irish mystics call "Thin Places", where the screen between this world and an eternal one is thin, less a wall and more a membrane. I didn't know then and I don't know now' (Mitchell 2015). Mitchell attests to the significance of liminal spaces, the Gothic encounter between the here and now that refuses to conform to a chronological or linear sense of time and irreal realities, including a reawakening of the voices of the dead in the realm of the living. Speaking to his Western readers, his ghost tale ends with the admission that it was hardly like the terror of 'Oh, Whistle, and I'll Come to You, My Lad' or 'The Monkey's Paw', references that speak to the incursions of the supernatural into quotidian life as well as the otherness and global interconnectedness of British society, whether through Templar history or the reach of Empire. The material world of 'the now' dissipates and rematerializes as a space of multiple, overlapping and co-existing temporal and cultural realities.

Eric Hayot observes that literary worlds 'no matter how they form themselves, are among other things always a relation to and theory of the lived world, whether as a largely preconscious normative construct, a rearticulation, or even as an active refusal of the world-norms of their age' (2012: 44–5). I contend that Mitchell's writing takes the form of 'critical irrealism', or what Michael Löwy refers to as 'nonrealist works of art' that 'contain a powerful critique of the social order' (2010: 211). Furthermore, Mitchell's Über-novel incarnates a fantasy world that 'offers alternative ways of explaining and coping with reality' (Mendlesohn and James 2012: 217); this irrealist fiction strives to express 'realities we have never seen or dreamed, by making speakable realities that might previously have seemed only idiosyncratic or incommunicable' (Bowlby 2010: xxi). As a world-builder, Mitchell projects the dominant narrative of global transformation into an otherworld, even as he works to map and disseminate an alternative view of our troubled world. Such a radical political fiction is well on its way to becoming a world-making agent of change in the world.

Warring cultures of development in *The Bone Clocks*

Slade House and *The Bone Clocks* critique and challenge the violence of combined and uneven development through irrealist inscriptions of conflict and resistance. *The Bone Clocks* documents an invisible war between the Anchorite forces of predacity and the Horologist defenders of sustainability, which erupts in a supernatural showdown in a church of the Cathar, demanding a perilous flight through a labyrinth to escape with one's soul and life intact. *Slade House* combines the haunted house narrative with the vampire tale to track global history from the Victorian period to the contemporary neo-liberal era. Both fictions have received favourable to less positive and mixed reviews (Collins 2014; Skidelsky 2014; Thompson 2014; Wood 2014). *The Bone Clocks* won the Best Novel at the 2015 World Fantasy Awards and was nominated for the Booker Prize. Yet, Robert Collins refers to the novel as a 'third-rate fantasy' (2014), while James Wood argues that 'weightless realism' and 'weightless fantasy' are at odds in this 'theological allegory', which undermines human creativity and agency (2014). Meanwhile, *Slade House* has been described as *The Bone Clocks*'s 'naughty little sister in a fright wig': 'Vending-machine horror tropes, believable characters, wild farce, existential jeopardy, meta-fictional jokes: into the cauldron they go' (Jensen 2015). The unevenly mixed modes and styles of these fictions seem to unsettle some readers, perhaps far more than the terrors depicted within the story world.

In my view, Mitchell's cosmology functions as a global allegory for combined and uneven development: pitting an imaginary shaped by capitalist accumulation and consumption (Anchorite) against a more encompassing, interactionist and dynamic view of uneven development within and beyond the capitalist world-system (Horologist). In *The Bone Clocks* and *Slade House*, Mitchell mobilizes perceptions, encoded within Gothic terror and sensation fiction, to re-immerse readers in the struggles of world history. Significantly, irrealist forms, like the Gothic and sensation fiction, encode the very 'problem' of capitalist consumption through their themes, action and plotting, every bit as much through their circulation and readerly consumption. Yet such narrative forms intervene politically to provide representation for the dispossessed and marginalized. Moreover, Mitchell renders perceptible the warring forces at work in an era of global capitalist transition, relating individual conflicts to a more expansive field of struggle over the ends and means of collective development. Mitchell marshals cultural forms shaped by inequality, even violence, to challenge the dominant narrative of development and inaugurate a more pluralistic world-cultural imaginary.

In *The Bone Clocks*, Holly embodies a modern-day Gothic heroine of the sort found in sensation fiction. When it emerged in the mid-nineteenth century, sensation fiction involved a 'catholic mixture of modes and forms, combining realism and melodrama, the journalistic and the fantastic, the domestic and the romantic or exotic' (Pykett 1994: 4). Likewise, Holly's coming-of-age story features everyday realism mixed with fantasy, a fantastical romance with a journalist, a plot that leads to a labyrinth and cosmological intrusions. In this embattled coming-of-age story, she finds herself at the centre of a Manichean struggle as Horologists seek to defend her from Anchorite attacks, such that the fearful tale of female development is commensurate with a broader struggle for sustainable international development. In the first section documenting her youth, 'A Hot Spell', Gothic contexts, themes and subtexts are quickly established. Holly lives in Gravesend, Kent, a town whose very name invokes the dead, which has been popularly (even if not accurately) interpreted as the site of burial for those who fell prey to the Bubonic Plague in 1665. It is associated with Dickensian hauntings, both through the author's life history and works, including *The Pickwick Papers*, *Great Expectations*, where it features as a proposed escape route for the criminal Magwitch, and *David Copperfield*, where it serves as a kind of threshold space for emigration to a new life in Australia. *Frankenstein* and *Heart of Darkness* (and Holly's parents own a pub called Captain Marlow) also refer to the town, thus reinforcing its links to Gothic monsters and the evils of mercantile capitalism as well as colonialism. As the death place and burial site of Pocahontas, this is a place undoubtedly associated with violence and oppression.

In Gravesend, a place of cultural hauntings, Holly hears the otherworldly voices of what she calls the 'Radio people', has a paramour who compares himself to Dracula (14) and is visited upon by a spectral woman, Immaculée Constantin. The latter is a soul vampire whose blue eyes and fair appearance recollect Sheridan Le Fanu's description of Laura as Gothic heroine/visitant (the angel deceived by her double) in *Carmilla*, the eponymous heroine/killer (the deceiving 'angel') of *Lady Audley's Secret* or the blonde female vampire (the angel as daemonic other) in Bram Stoker's *Dracula*.

As a person with psychic gifts, Holly is an attractive prey to soul vampires who want to fuel their immortality by consuming her spiritual energy. From her young brother Jacko, who is endowed with the gift of precognition, Holly receives a map of a 'diabolical' labyrinth and instructions on how to escape from this perilous space in the future (7–8). As a precaution against soul vampirism, Dr Marinus, himself a reborn soul or 'Returnee', attempts to protect Holly from harm by tamping her forehead Chakra or 'Third Eye' (a centre of wisdom for cosmic consciousness in Buddhist belief) so as to dullen this receptor for psychic energy. Another spectral figure reveals her secret name, Esther Little, and enters into a pact with Holly, exchanging green tea (perhaps a reference to Sheridan Le Fanu's 'Green Tea', a drink that serves to unseal the inner eye and unleashes haunting) for the use of her soul as a space of secret sanctuary. Later, Holly is attacked by Rhimes, another vampire, but defended by a renanimated corpse of a murder victim. Invoking Talking Heads' *Fear of Music* (1979) as its dark pop musical backdrop (3), the opening sequence to *The Bone Clocks* proffers a surfeit of supernatural and terrifying incident, reawakening Gothic sensationalism in contemporary world contexts.

Holly's conflicted romantic history is sensationalistic, for this realistic-yet-fantastical heroine forms relationships with lovers who are Gothic (Vinny, compared to Dracula), diabolical (Hugo Lamb, a lover turned soul vampire) and war-torn (Ed Brubeck, a war reporter). In two of these instances, Mitchell employs the vampiric motif to critique world-systemic pressures that constrain subjectivity. Saverio Tomaiuolo observes that one of 'the most famous political uses of the vampire' occurs in Karl Marx's *Capital*, where he compares capitalism to a vampire: 'Capital is dead labour, that vampire-like, only lives by sucking living labour, and lives the more, the more labour it sucks' (2009: 103). Likewise, the Anchorites live by sucking life from others for their own profit, and they live for an extended life span by consuming souls, and the more they live, the more souls they decant and drink or 'suck back'. Two victims of the vampiric Rhimes are Marxist activists, both of whom point out that a secret class war is taking place: '"An invisible war's going on", says Heidi ... "and all throughout history – the class war. Owners versus slaves, nobles versus serfs, the bloated bosses versus the workers, the haves versus the have-nots"' (52). For Holly, a working-class heroine, the romance with 'posh' Hugo Lamb takes a Gothic turn only when he explicitly chooses to become a vampire: when he turns his back on love, on Holly, he decides to profit from the lives of others, to consolidate his power as an initiate of the Anchorites.

World cultural histories, texts and forms are reanimated within Mitchell's Über-novel as a world-literary space that awakens fresh interpretive evaluations by reanimating earlier texts and forms in contemporary contexts. For example, a foray into Walpurgis, the name of a dance club in Mitchell's work, is echoed by allusions to Goethe's *Faust* and Thomas Mann's *Magic Mountain*. Lamb's Faustian pact (187) (to extend his mortal life span by consuming the lives of others) is conveyed through references to other irrealist fictions. Lamb's escape in a blizzard parallels the experiences of Hans Castorp in Mann's work. Castorp forgets the insight that 'love stands opposed to death' (Mann 1999: 496) and *'for the sake of goodness and love, man shall let death have no sovereignty over his thoughts'* (Mann 1999: 496, emphasis in original). By contrast, Lamb eventually recalls feelings of love when he and Holly face death (519–20). The Dickensian motif of a haunted Christmas, with Lamb as its potentially 'love-drunk, reformed-Scrooge' (186), reinforces the themes of economic disparity and class division. Somewhat paradoxically, Mitchell's materialist critique of inequality and oppression arises from a vampiric aesthetic that posits the reader as a voracious consumer of texts within the global literary marketplace, including his own Über-novel, for Lamb, Marinus, Hershey and others reappear elsewhere in the author's oeuvre.

Violence emerges as a problem within the imagined world as well as the world-literary field of struggles among competing irrealist traditions. Slavoj Žižek claims that any effective critique of violence needs to confront the relationship between subjective and objective forms of violence, the latter including both the symbolic violence of language and cultural forms and the systemic violence of economic and political systems (2009: 1). Yet, Žižek argues that there is a 'catch' because 'subjective and objective violence cannot be perceived from the same standpoint' (2009: 2). However, Mitchell's fantasy of invisible warfare enables a unified critique of violence to emerge because it represents systemic, symbolic and subjective conflicts through a metafictional cosmology that pits Anchorites who seek to prey upon individual life against Horologists who seek to preserve and sustain it. Mitchell's representation of a world in crisis corresponds to Immanuel Wallerstein's observation that 'the modern world-system is in structural crisis and has entered into a period of chaotic behaviour' (2000: 251), driven by 'an enormous political struggle between two large camps: the camp of those who wish to retain the privileges of the existing inegalitarian system ... and the camp of those who would like to see the creation of a new historical system that will be significantly more democratic and egalitarian' (2000: 267). That systemic conflict shapes Mitchell's numinous narrative as it mediates between a Gothic-derived (Anchorites) camp that seeks to profit from inequality and a Buddhist-inspired (Horologists) camp that seeks to construct a more democratic and egalitarian order. For the characters (subjects) of this imagined universe, life is now constituted as an endless struggle to survive repeated threats of violence in a seemingly unending global battlefield.

But the narrative also challenges violence through its self-conscious remediation of fantasy and turn towards global allegory. Invented terms are used to describe this literary universe, such as banjax, the blind Cathar, psychovoltage, metalife, animacide, Anchorites and Horologists. This lexicon immerses the reader in a fantasy world of invented language, but equally one could argue that these slightly ludicrous terms seem to parody fantasy's propensity for invented languages and thus create a sense of critical distance. That sense of estrangement paves the way for an allegorical reading of the Anchorites and Horologists as representatives of competing visions of development. The Anchorites (mortal immortals) consume souls like fuel and power their existence by consuming those of others: as such, they seem to embody the predatory dimensions of combined and uneven development. By contrast, the Horologists or Atemporals, who are not dependent on the consumption of souls for their immortal existence, incarnate two alternative accounts of development through their return as Returnees or Sojourners. As Patrick O'Donnell notes, the Returnees 'transmigrate their souls from body to body, "ingressing" to each body in the form of a memory of the past conjoined with the soul of the new body' (2015: 161), resulting in an 'incrementally layered consciousness' (2015: 161). For their part, the Sojourners embody uneven and combined development, as different souls come to co-exist, resulting in a multilayered and pluralistic world soul who can acknowledge simultaneous temporalities and non-linear formations of history. The human hope for survival depends upon a recognition of the unseen realities of world-historical struggle and entry into the field of battle to defend the body and soul against global destruction.

Holly's coming-of-age experience takes the form of an initiation that enables her, and by extension the reader, to map and critique global violence. In world-systemic terms, *The Bone Clocks* presents a linear story of female development, showing how global capitalism menaces the life of the feisty adolescent, troubled lover, mystical author, supernatural warrior and protective mother-figure. Yet, at the same time, alternative temporalities, irreal events and cross-cultural influences disrupt the linearity of Holly's life story. An example of temporal disruption occurs in 'An Holorogist's Labyrinth (2025)', when Holly finds her way out of a menacing labyrinth by seizing a golden apple that operates as a portal between the otherworld of dark fantasy and the globalized world of world-systemic conflicts. Significantly, the golden apple 'belongs' to a futuristic fantasy world in 2025 as well as the 'real' world of long historical development. The apple appears in Agnolo Bronzino's Mannerist painting, entitled 'Venus, Cupid, Folly and Time' (circa 1544–5), and antecedent embodiments in Asia and Africa (533). This fantastical fruit – a symbol of absolute beauty in Greek mythology, of divine knowledge in the Bible, of supreme political power (as the *kizil elma*) in Ottoman/Turkish legend – embodies the pluralistic realities, the variant cultural perspectives, of world history. The golden apple may save Holly from certain death, but it cannot redeem time as it throws her back into a world hurtling towards an Endarkenment: a dark reality that results from a failure to act as guardians of planetary life (533). Mitchell's fable of global violence charts the conflicts of strife and love, perhaps embodying an Empedoclean cosmology, but it also serves as a 'wake-up call' to the realities of a global crisis that may well devastate the future of the planet and its children.

In this global feminist tale of international development, Holly emerges as a spokesperson for the dispossessed and guardian for those who are most vulnerable to global violence. As a medium for the 'radio people' and world author, Holly transmits and records an otherworldly literature that stakes claims for alternative and composite tales of global life that both predate and postdate the contemporary capitalist moment. As a guardian and mother, she willingly sacrifices her life for the next generation, when she agrees that Marinus should use his powers of 'suasion' to save the children under her protection and leave her to struggle to survive in a precarious and chaotic environment. Arguably, Mitchell fails to envision a future beyond the confines of a patriarchal culture that fetishizes female suffering and maternal sacrifice, as it has already done for millennia. Yet, this irrealist *Bildungsroman* takes Holly's (mis)adventures as the basis for its social critique of a world shaped by the combined oppressions of economic exploitation, patriarchal oppression and environmental devastation. This heroine is keenly aware of her place in world history as well as the perils that she will suffer when she chooses to safeguard the life of a child over her own. Consequently, Mitchell offers an intersectional feminist critique of violence, even as he affirms a woman's agency and right to choose the terms of her own life and death.

Slade House: A portal to alternative realities

Slade House offers another instalment in the unfolding tale of the unseen violence that shapes global life: this time by rendering perceptible the hidden history of twin soul vampires and serial killers, Norah and Jonah Grayer, whose lives begin in the Victorian age and extend into our postmillennial era. *Slade House* takes Edgar Allan Poe's 'The Fall of the House of Usher' as its subtext for the haunted house, the deathly twins and the fears concerning the encrypted or hidden body that is both dead and alive. Where the House of Usher is fearful from the start, Slade House is at first appearance a welcoming, well-tended home. However, it gradually declines as its embodied state comes (like the House of Usher) to manifest the conditions of its inhabitants, the twins, Norah and Jonah, who serve as doubles for Poe's siblings, Roderick and Madeline Usher. But *Slade House* also updates Poe's haunted house narrative by inserting elements more commonly associated with the fin de siècle Gothic, in works such as *Dracula* and *The Picture of Dorian Gray*. This is entirely appropriate, for the Grayer twins are soul vampires, thus analogues to the blood-consuming entities of Bram Stoker, and are rather like Dorian Gray; their fair appearance masks a ghastly reality of the hidden body contained in secret in the house. Unlike the Usher siblings, the Grayers are members of the lower classes who rise to fortune, mostly by exploiting their own paranormal gifts for profit, as Fred Pink (aka Jonah) later reveals in his tale of their itinerant lifestyle (146–77). As Marinus observes, their predatory behaviour belongs to a long history of world-systemic oppression that links 'feudal lords to slave traders to oligarchs to neocons' (230). Where Dracula traverses Europe, the twins traverse the world to practice and enhance their dark art, thus working to globalize the Gothic before domesticating it once again in Britain.

Fred Botting and Justin D. Edwards argue that the Gothic intervenes in a globalized world to register 'the anxieties that arise from national, social and subjective dissolution' and construct 'an otherness that screens out the excesses of anxiety, while turning the mirror back on itself … globally, darkly, monstrously' (2013: 23). *Slade House* certainly incorporates global violence, but it also mobilizes cosmological, numinous and irrealist forms, thus working to establish a counter-narrative to terror. Told through five serial instalments, the narrative traces the dark forces that run through global history, including accounts of its ramp-up phase in the late nineteenth and early twentieth centuries, its late capitalist and postcolonial transitions and eventual emergence of neo-liberalism. Each story maps its own moment in an unfolding world-literary Gothic, engaging with the smaller, more intimate, dramas of individual lives within a given decade. Significantly, the novel mediates the typical story of the grand haunted country house. Set in the suburbs, the house appears and reappears as an increasingly shabby and illusory embodiment of capitalist privilege. Each portal-like entry into Slade House affords an entry into a fantastical view of history as the Grayer twins draw their victims into a simulated world reality or 'orison', where 'reality folds in, origamilike, and darkens to black' (185). Global and local, residual and emergent cultures of development uneasily recombine and coalesce through the simulated realities of *Slade House* as a site of temporal distortion and simulation: an irrealist space in which the world's historical and cultural realities dematerialize and rematerialize.

Episode (chapter) one, 'The Right Sort', foregrounds the violence arising from inequality through its allusions to class hierarchies in this story about the socio-economic challenges that constrain the life of a single mother and her child, Nathan, who has Asperger Syndrome. Told from Nathan's perspective, this supernatural tale represents another way of seeing, hearing and feeling the world, heightened because he has taken two of his mother's Valium tablets (4). Mitchell registers the Gothic and fantastical dimensions of this world through references to 'Dungeons & Dragons' (4), *Godzilla* (4) and Asterix's magical potion (8). The narrative itself takes the upper-class tradition of the hunt, the chase of the fox and hounds, as the basis for its tale of death and destruction. Significantly, Nathan experiences a simulated reality, when he experiences a visit to his father in colonial Rhodesia. The year in which this story is set, 1979, represents a period of turmoil and crisis leading up to the 1980 formation of the Republic of Zimbabwe and election of Robert Mugabe. The spectre of imperial and future dictatorial violence to come converges with the child's fantasy of reunification with the father and the conflicting loyalties of a child of divorce. When he swallows coffee from a mug, his nose feels 'like a gas mask' (32), and the mug, in turn, gulps him down. The child's feelings of suffocation eerily echo the Rhodesians' own historical trauma of the First World War under German gas attacks. Too late, the child realizes that this Gothic horror 'vision' (33) is an intrusion to distract him from his own historical moment of devastation (33). Norah's reference to this fantasy as a corny 'ersatz mishmash' (35), is comparable to Edgar Rice Burroughs's Tarzan fantasy of colonial Africa (35). Jonah counters that the fantasy is a kind of projection of the child's own imagined world of the Bushveld (35), thus foregrounding the ideological trap of colonial fantasies. The symbolic and systemic devastation of the child's soul registers the violence of war and empire, both within Africa and the world unevenly combined to illustrate the truth of the slogan on the Grayer's creepy grandfather clock: 'TIME IS', 'TIME WAS', 'TIME IS NOT' (27).

Likewise, *Slade House*'s subsequent tales interlock to reveal a larger irrealist story about unevenly combined temporalities of violence, victimhood and resistance: both worldly and otherworldly. Episode two, 'Shining Armour (1988)', alludes to the Rolling Stones' 'Emotional Rescue', which invokes Gothic romanticism with its lyrics about a knight in shining armour who will come to the emotional rescue of his lady. For Gordon Edmond, the victim of this episode, macho fantasies of playing the role of the heroic knight, who saves the damsel in distress, prove to be his undoing: he falls prey to Norah Grayer who has taken on the guise of Chloe Chetwynd, a modern-day version of the 'Belle Dame Sans Merci' from John Keats's Gothic poem of a beautiful but fatal love interest. Reference to the troubles in Ireland (39) and police brutality during the Brixton riots (43) feature in this racist's and misogynist's tale of domestic violence. Ironically, his efforts to 'exorcise Julia's ghost' (41), a reference to the ex-wife he battered (40), lead to the destruction of his soul. Self-consciously, this fantasy tale references and deconstructs the interlinking mythologies of knighthood and patriarchal imperialism. Realism and fantasy intrude upon one another.

This irrealist tale self-consciously combines and remediates various numinous forms to disseminate fresh perceptions of world culture. For instance, the third episode, 'Oink Oink (1997)' represents a 1990s 'Goth' culture shaped by the cultural influences of *Rocky Horror Picture Show* (101), *The Monkey's Paw* (102), *The Wizard of Oz* (102), *Star Wars* (109), *The Incredible Hulk* (109) and *The Exorcist* (111); its paranormal investigation, in the style of the *Blair Witch Project*, documents the malaise associated with economic migration (106) as well as the far greater oppressions suffered by 'an AIDS orphan or North Korean or Shell Oil wife's maid' (107). References to the petrol industry echo the environmental concerns thematized in episode one of *Slade House*, when Nathan's father refers to his son as a Kraken, an intertextual allusion to John Wyndham's fantasy of global warming (29). These interlinked incidents contribute as well to Mitchell's larger narrative of environmental critique in *Cloud Atlas* and *The Bone Clocks*. Chapter three references Crispin Hershey's novel *Dessicated Embryos* from the *The Bone Clocks* (108), thus invoking the larger cosmological 'realities' of Mitchell's Über-novel. Episode four, 'You Dark Horse You (2006)', queers the global Gothic as the unfolding story is continuously interrupted by Freya Timms's text exchanges with her lover, Avril. Like others before her, Freya falls prey to the Grayer's schemes, that is until her sister Sally's ghost arises and, armed with the silver fox-head hairpin from Nathan's mother, wounds Jonah and saves Freya's soul from destruction – though not her body from death (190). The hairpin itself was a gift from Nathan's father, brought back from Hong Kong following the Second World War (4), a reminder of a happier time of peace and love, both lost. As a weapon, an ornament, a sign of love, the hairpin pulls together various tresses of history to form an unevenly combined counter-narrative of historical resistance to violence.

Slade House challenges violence through its affective strategies, worlding of the numinous and non-linear, oddly combined temporalities. In episode one, Nathan bears witness to the destruction of his own '*Beautiful*' soul (36), a motif repeated when other souls are decanted and revealed in all their splendour. The recurring appearance of the 'Cold bright star white' (36, 82), a moth, at the moment of the soul's destruction opens up cross-cultural interpretations of the irreal: the white moth can variously symbolize the death (China), life (Japan) or disrupted and restless existence (Jamaica) of the soul. Likewise, Mitchell remediates the trope of portraiture in Gothic fiction, which Kamilla Elliot describes as 'rife with animated portraits, appearing as "bodies" animated by ghosts' (2012: 41). By enabling these portraits to speak, even as their souls are being consumed, the victims claim agency in the face of oppression. Moreover, the portraits defy the Gothic by regaining life as '*part of* the chain of images that constitute identity' (Elliott 2012: 39, emphasis in original), this time by establishing affiliations among the 'victims' through time. Cultural objects reappear like spectral reminders of a ghostly past now intruding on the realities of the present. As she is dying, Freya recognizes a Maori jade pendant, a gift she once gave to her sister (190). Its spectral return attests to the presence of her sister: to memories and affiliations that survive beyond the violence of the present. Known to the Maori as a Pounamu carving, this jade necklace signifies the importance of transgenerational memory. Significantly, the re-apparition of the jade pendant unevenly combines the memory of peripheral culture with the personal memory of sisterly love. Resistance is thus freshly articulated through the multiple affiliations of interlinked temporalities, which form a counter-narrative to the 'realities' of global capitalist consumption as incarnated by the all-consuming vampires in the attic.

Appropriately, this testament to the importance of transgenerational memory precedes Marinus's arrival on the scene in 'Astronauts (2015)', the final episode. In *Slade House*, as in *The Bone Clocks*, Marinus the Horologist appears as a Returnee who has been reborn time and time again, thus becoming a bearer of cross-cultural and multigenerational memories of global life. In Mitchell's biblioverse, Marinus appears in *The Bone Clocks*, *Slade House* and *Thousand Autumns*, as well as Mitchell's libretti. Marinus the Returnee emerges as a trans-racial, genderqueer witness to the vast scale and unity of this literary universe; the course of his/her 'metalife' forges unpredictable pathways through global history and, in turn, discloses alternative mappings of temporality. Through cycles of death/revival, Marinus embodies resistance as a form of resilience, evidenced in struggles to overcome dire setbacks and defeat. Marinus challenges violence thanks to an ability to track and analyse the relationship between its drivers and processes through time (223; 229). Nonetheless, in *Slade House*, the apparent victory over Norah Grayer is belied by the fact that this soul vampire rematerializes in the body of an unborn child. Mitchell, the world-builder, cannot exorcise the spectre of a dark global future driven by global capitalist predacity. Yet, this world-making fiction seeds radical hope by re-incarnating solidarity through intertwined acts of resistance that coalesce over time to create a space for otherness in the future.

Towards a radical politics of dissent and affiliated resistance

David Mitchell's sprawling macro-novel re-incorporates global history through its irrealist representation of occulted global realities. Together, *The Bone Clocks* and *Slade House* re-stage the 'horror show' of combined and uneven development with its interlocking and overlapping oppressions. Global Gothic tales of soul vampirism register the realities of world-historical predacity through the extraction of profit and consumption of life; meanwhile, tales of haunting, of rebellious spirits, revive and disseminate the stories of the dispossessed to register dissent and establish coalitions of resistance to the dominant matrices of power. As such, irrealist genres and forms do not take flight from reality but un-repress the actualities, possibilities and alternatives latent within world history. What has been consigned to fantasy or lost to oblivion returns to the world in the form of a more encompassing reality. Such fictions revive and replenish an impoverished global imaginary by awakening moribund, repressed, sometimes nearly obliterated, accounts of worldhood. Mitchell's art of world-building takes a radical political turn through its world-making efforts to redress the impoverishments of a global culture diminished by the violence of combined and uneven development. Between the world of the story and the story of the world, Mitchell stakes out a field of unceasing struggle over the fate of humanity and the planet at this critical and precarious juncture in history. Even as his epic macro-novel projects a global future of crisis and collapse, his world-building activities remind readers of alternative realities, of possibilities, in a history that remains open to change through dissent and affiliated resistance.

Works cited

Botting F. and J. D. Edwards (2013), 'Theorising Globalgothic,' in Glennis Byron (ed.), *Globalgothic*, Manchester: Manchester University Press, 11–24.

Bowlby, R. (2010), 'Foreword', in M. Beaumont (ed.), *A Concise Companion to Realism*, Malden: Wiley-Blackwell, xiv–xxi.

Cheah, P. (2008), 'What Is a World? On World Literature as World-Making Activity', *Daedalus,* 137(3), 26–38.

Collins, R. (2014), 'How on Earth did David Mitchell's Third-Rate Fantasy Make the Man Booker Longlist?', *The Spectator*, 06 September 2014. Available online: https://www.spectator.co.uk/2014/09/the-bone-clocks-by-david-mitchell-review/ (accessed 01 July 2016).

Dunlop, S. (2011), 'Speculative Fiction as Postcolonial Critique in *Ghostwritten* and *Cloud Atlas*', in S. Dillon (ed.), *David Mitchell: Critical Essays*, Canterbury: Gylphi, 201–23.

Elliot, K. (2012), *Portraiture and British Gothic Fiction: The Rise of Picture Identification 1764-1835*, Baltimore: The Johns Hopkins University Press.

Finney, B. (2015), 'The David Mitchell Übernovel: Brian Finney Reviews "Slade House"', *Los Angeles Review of Books*, 05 December. Available online: https://lareviewofbooks.org/article/the-david-mitchell-ubernovel-brian-finney-reviews-slade-house/ (accessed 07 July 2016).

Hayot, E. (2012), *On Literary Worlds*, Oxford: Oxford University Press.

Hopf, C. (2019), 'Creating a Fictional Universe: An Interview with David Mitchell', in C. Hopf and W. Knepper (eds), *David Mitchell: Contemporary Critical Perspectives*, London: Bloomsbury, 183–94.

Jensen, L. (2015), '*Slade House* by David Mitchell Review – Like Stephen King in a Fever', *The Guardian*, 29 October 2015. Available online: https://www.theguardian.com/books/2015/oct/29/slade-house-david-mitchell-review (accessed 01 July 2016).

Keating, S. (2014), 'David Mitchell: "Who Cares If a Book Is Highbrow or Lowbrow: Is It Any Good or Not?"', *The Irish Times*, 27 October 2014. Available online: http://www.irishtimes.com/culture/books/david-mitchell-who-cares-if-a-book-is-highbrow-or-lowbrow-is-it-any-good-or-not-1.1977387 (accessed 07 July 2016).

Kirsch, A. (2017), *The Global Novel: Writing the World in the 21st Century*, New York: Columbia Global Reports.

Knepper, W. (2016), 'Towards a Theory of Experimental World Epic: David Mitchell's *Cloud Atlas*', *ariel: A Review of English Literature*, 47(1–2), 93–126.

Le Guin, U. (2014), 'Ursula K Le Guin's Speech at National Book Awards: "Books Aren't Just Commodities"', *The Guardian*, 20 November. Available online: https ://www.theguardian.com/books/2014/nov/20/ursula-k-le-guin-national-boo k-awards-speech (accessed 01 July 2015).

Löwy, M. (2010), 'The Current of Critical Irrealism: "A Moonlit Enchanted Night', in M. Beaumont (ed.), *A Concise Companion to Realism*, Malden: Wiley-Blackwell, 211–24.

Mann, T. (1999), *The Magic Mountain*, trans. H. T. Lowe-Porter, London: Vintage Books.

Mendlesohn, F. and E. James (2012), *A Short History of Fantasy*, Faringdon: Libri Publishing.

Mitchell, D. (2014), *The Bone Clocks*, London: Sceptre.

Mitchell, D. (2015a), 'A Possibly True Ghost Story from David Mitchell', *Literary Hub*, 24 September 2015. Available online: https://lithub.com/a-possibly-true-ghost-story-from-david-mitchell/ (accessed 07 July 2016).

Mitchell, D. (2015b), *Slade House*, London: Sceptre.

Mitchell, D. (2018), 'Ursula K Le Guin by David Mitchell: "She was a Crafter of Fierce, Focused, Fertile Dreams"', *The Guardian*, 25 January 2018. Available online: https://www.theguardian.com/books/2018/jan/25/ursula-le-guin-davi d-mitchell-earthsea (accessed 01 February 2018).

Nanda, A. (2015), 'David Mitchell on Ghosts and the Paranormal', *The Straits Times*, 20 December 2015. Available online: http://www.straitstimes.c om/lifestyle/arts/david-mitchell-on-ghosts-and-the-paranormal (accessed 07 July 2016).

O'Donnell, P. (2015), *A Temporary Future: The Fiction of David Mitchell*, London and New York: Bloomsbury Academic.

Poe, E. A. (2003), 'The Fall of the House of Usher', in D. Galloway (ed.), *The Fall of the House of Usher and Other Writings*, London: Penguin, 90–109.

Pykett, L. (1994), *The Sensation Novel: From* The Woman in White *to* The Moonstone, Plymouth: Northcote House Publishers.

Shaw K. (2018), '"Some Magic Is Normality": Fantastical Cosmopolitanism in David Mitchell's *The Bone Clocks*', *C21 Literature: Journal of 21st-Century Writings*, 6(3). Available online: https://doi.org/10.16995/c21.52 (accessed 15 October 2018).

Skidelsky, W. (2014), '*The Bone Clocks* by David Mitchell', *The Observer*, 07 September 2014. Available at: https://www.theguardian.com/books/2014/s ep/07/bone-clocks-review-david-mitchell-lot-of-fun-booker (accessed 07 July 2016).

Thompson, D. (2014), '*The Bone Clocks*: David Mitchell's Almost-Perfect Masterpiece', *The Atlantic*, 02 September 2014. Available at: https://www.the atlantic.com/entertainment/archive/2014/09/review-david-mitchells-bone-cloc ks-the-cloud-atlas-authors-meta-masterpiece/379445/ (accessed 01 July 2016).

Tomaiuolo, S. (2009), 'Reading between the (Blood)lines of Victorian Vampires: Mary Elizabeth Braddon's "Good Lady Ducayne"', in M. Brock (ed.), *From Wollstonecraft to Stoker: Essays on Gothic and Victorian Sensation Fiction*, Jefferson: McFarland, 102–19.

Trimm R. (2018), 'Spirits in the Material World: Spectral Worlding in David Mitchell's *Ghostwritten* and *Cloud Atlas*', *C21 Literature: Journal of 21st-Century Writings*, 6(3). Available online: https://doi.org/10.16995/c21.63 (accessed 15 October 2018).

Wallerstein, I. (2000), 'Globalization or the Age of Transition? A Long-Term View of the Trajectory of the World System', *International Sociology*, 15(2), 251–67.

Warwick Research Collective (2015), *Combined and Uneven Development: Towards a New Theory of World-Literature*, Liverpool: Liverpool University Press.

Wolf, M. J. P. (2012), *Building Imaginary Worlds: The Theory and History of Subcreation*, New York and London: Routledge.

Wood, J. (2014), 'Soul Cycle: David Mitchell's "The Bone Clocks"', *The New Yorker*, 08 September 2014. Available online: http://www.newyorker.com/magazine/2014/09/08/soul-cycle (accessed 01 July 2016).

Žižek, S. (2009), *Violence*, London: Profile Books.

Creating a fictional universe: An interview with David Mitchell

Courtney Hopf

Courtney Hopf: With the publication of your first novel, *Ghostwritten*, you established a reputation for writing about life in our globalized world, both through epic tales that traverse time and space as well as through intimate fictions that explore the impact of world events on various subjects and communities. But it has also become clear, perhaps most especially with *The Bone Clocks*, that you are creating a fictional universe with its own distinctive history, recurring characters, world events and global culture. Could you tell us a bit about your approach to creating a fictional world/universe?

David Mitchell: I read Richard Dawkins's *Climbing Mount Improbable*, in which he talks about how the eye evolved, because the old creationist argument was, well, if evolution's a series of tiny steps, something is either an eye or it's not an eye. Or it may have been something about wings – the argument being that one ten-thousandth of a wing has no advantage, it's no good for anything, so how could evolution have evolved wings, when only a full wing was any good? And the answer is, of course, wings evolved from other things. Half a wing is good if you're a reptile and it's working as a radiator. And it's a little bit like that, the first stage of the Über-book.

Courtney Hopf: So the growth of the Über-book was a process of evolution.

David Mitchell: Exactly. The Über-book/multiverse/biblioverse (yes, how about 'biblioverse'?) has grown book by book. I think I put Suhbataar the Mongolian gangster from *Ghostwritten* into *number9dream* because I thought it was cool how Haruki Murakami had the Sheep Man and a character called Noboru Watanabe appear in several of his novels. No motive further-reaching than 'cool', really. Around the same time, I read Hermann Broch's *The Sleepwalkers*, where characters you never expected to reappear show up in a different milieu. Then with *Cloud Atlas* I discovered the pleasure in 'reverse-resurrecting' a minor character from an earlier book – the elderly Luisa Rey, who calls into Bat Segundo's radio show in *Ghostwritten* – and giving her a lead role. Knowing her future lends a poignancy to the reader's relationship with her younger self. In other words, they bring luggage. *Black Swan Green* would lack something without Eva Crommelynck's presence; and her presence is made weightier by her origins in *Cloud Atlas*. *Jacob de Zoet* was trickier, as it predated anything else I'd written, but I managed to get a young Mr Boerhaave from *Cloud Atlas* in and this time 'pre-planted' a conditional immortal, Marinus, who I knew would bloom into something bigger in the next book. I like how *The Bone Clocks* makes the case that the book before it is not only an historical novel, but also a fantasy novel – that soul extraction for immortality storyline, according to *The Bone Clocks*, isn't the lethal feverish nonsense of mad crypto-Shinto monks – it's real, and it works! And only backwards do we understand why Marinus was so sympathetic to slaves and women – he had been them – and why he was so nonchalant about his own death – he knew that 49 days later, he'd be waking up again.

By this point, it had dawned on me that I was making my own mapless Middle Earth, or Earthsea, by default and book by book. That pleased me enormously, as it lets me be the maximalist I dreamed of being when I was a kid, but also the 'minimalist' writer making each book an island unto itself, very different to others, that I want to be as an adult. I 'did a Luisa Rey' with Hugo Lamb in *The Bone Clocks* – a minor character in *Black Swan Green* – who becomes the joint second major lead and gave Jonny Penhaligon's sister a medium-sized role in *Slade House*. That moon grey cat has been a regular visitor from *Black Swan Green* onwards and seems immune to the laws of physics and time, but that's cats for you. These days I also think of the Biblioverse as my own rendering in text of the Universe. People do drift in and out of our lives, then unexpectedly return sometimes, bringing with them luggage from the old days, but also new stuff, readjusted roles and contexts. Don't you find?

Courtney Hopf: Certainly, the pleasure of encountering a character you once knew is the same as unexpectedly running into an old friend. If you had to describe your 'biblioverse' to someone unfamiliar with it, what would you say?

David Mitchell: It's a world made up of and by and for my books. It's a mad old rambling house with a new extension added on every time I publish, though which is the main house and which the extension or wing becomes obscured over time. It's a large stage of time and space made mostly of blur and possibilities and potential, but with small islands of detail and clarity where my novels occur. I don't feel as if

I'm really building it, though I suppose I am: it feels more like my books are building it themselves. It's the sum of which my books are a part. Then I'd change the subject and offer the person a cup of tea.

Courtney Hopf: That image of a massive stage on which islands of action occur was in my mind as well. And that largeness of scope is something that I wanted to talk about because it *is* big – the novels are big, the world is big, the potentialities are big, you can literally take it anywhere, and I've wondered about that with regard to the global emphasis that you seem to have – from the very beginning with *Ghostwritten* you had this global reach in your work. Would you say that part of that big-ness was also an effort to create a more global literature, something that moves beyond the Western traditions that you grew up with and read – to break out of the borders of Middle Earth, as it were?

David Mitchell: It's a question of which comes first, the horse or the cart. I did and do want to scoop up and haul in, like with a drift net, as much of the world as I can, and represent it in words, in text, in fiction. But it's not that I was clever enough to devise this as the method through which to do that. It's a happy consequence of not wanting to write about English people in England having marital problems. I'm hungry to put in as much of the world that excites me and just gives me that breathless feeling of, oh, I want to do that, and that, and that, I want to write about that and then I could do that ... I'm just hungry to get in as much of that as I can. And this form of the multi-novel novel, the multi-novel opus, as I've linked books more and more, it's presented itself as the optimum way of doing that.

Courtney Hopf: As an Englishman who spent many years in Japan and now lives in Ireland, to what extent are you invested in understanding and representing 'Englishness'?

David Mitchell: I don't think it would sound evasive to say that when a novel wants me to do that or needs me to do that to work, then I'm interested in it. I suppose there's a bit of it with Crispin Hershey, and *Black Swan Green* is a really English novel. I think in terms of what I want to achieve with my career, it's just a sense that if I know there's something there that's going to be really good if I get it right and that's got some Englishness in it, like the class system, I'll focus on that, but then if I'm writing about 12th-century Vikings, which I might be doing next, obviously it's irrelevant.

Courtney Hopf: So then what makes you choose those Vikings? If you're not coming from a place of saying 'I want to tackle Britishness' or 'I want to tackle globalization', how do you decide, when you have an entire world and all of time to draw upon, which stories you want to tell? Where are the Vikings coming from in all of that?

David Mitchell: They are ... I have a reasonless attachment to them. The North Atlantic just, it kind of stirs me, like music, like some music can stir you. Why does Sibelius's *Andante Festivo* just, whoosh! do that to the hairs on my forearm – no idea, but it does, in a way that something, Haydn, doesn't, really. In a way that even Sibelius's symphonies don't, really, if I'm honest. It's just that one piece, whoosh, that just does it for me. So, so what's the why? I don't really know, I suppose it's because I'm me, it kind of wows me in a way that it might not wow another writer.

Courtney Hopf: Is it entirely reasonless though? The Vikings traversed the world, just like your fiction.

David Mitchell: Global explorers, yes; major players in the history of early Europe; initially pagans, later Christian evangelists; the best boat builders of their day; seemingly capable of tenderness to their own, the creation of proto-novels *and* casual, implacable barbarity. I don't admire the violence, but the coexistence of civilization and a fondness for rape, pillage and genocide is intriguing.

Courtney Hopf: I'm going to tell a little story to introduce this next question, so bear with me. Back at the conference where we met, seven years ago, at St. Andrews, I gave a paper called 'Narratology and the Mitchell Multiverse.' And I argued that what your oeuvre is doing is actually propagating multiple worlds, because otherwise Luisa Rey was an impossibility; she existed on a different narrative level from the other texts in *Cloud Atlas*. And afterward, you came up during the coffee break to talk to me and you said Luisa had always kind of bothered you, and you were wondering if you could write something in a future novel that implied she was 'real' and would 'fix' the problem. And I said, well, it doesn't matter, this is literature, and people can be both textual constructions and real at the same time. They can be alive and dead at the same time. So I'm wondering now, as your Über-book has grown and mutated and nearly doubled in size since that time, what do you think about those gaps and inconsistencies today? Are they ... burdens? Are they challenges? Are they something you're happy for readers to just play around with and attempt to figure out?

David Mitchell: I have thought about this, and I remember our conversation as well, and it continued to bother me. And it goes beyond just the growth and size of the Über-novel; what also happens is that earlier versions get outdated. For example, there was the story 'The January Man', in the Granta collection, that got a good hefty rewrite in *Black Swan Green*. So the question is, 'The January Man', is that elbowed out?

Courtney Hopf: Yes, 'is that "canon"? What do we do with that?' It forces the question of what fervent fans of your work are supposed to make of those shifts.

David Mitchell: The answer is in fandom and the Bible. There's the canon and Apocrypha. And some things can start off in the canon, but a later rewrite or muscling out, or an ontological shift whereby someone was actually dreaming it, elbows it into Apocrypha. However, I'd rather think of Luisa Rey as real, really. It's just that I haven't really got round to telling anyone that yet, but I think I will.

Courtney Hopf: Can you unpack a little why it's so important to you that Luisa be 'real'?

David Mitchell: I know she isn't real on our level of reality, of course (which we might call LOR Zero) – I'm deluded but not that deluded. But I want her to belong to the next level of reality down – LOR1. I don't want her main residence to be a play within a play or a tale within a tale or a film within a novel, or anything (LOR2) like that. The suspension of disbelief doesn't reach that far, so the fear and joy we feel for her is rather pale and performative. That's why a lot of postmodern fiction feels a little sterile, I think – who gives a damn about a character who's drolly flaunting their own fictionality? They make you feel like a mug for caring.

Courtney Hopf: Fair enough. And so the answer is that these gaps are indeed challenges, spaces you want to fill in eventually.

David Mitchell: They are. I want consistency, it's somehow a part of the deal. It's cheating not to. A multiverse is a possible answer, but I quite like the neatness of it being a universe, whose raggedy bits certainly give it the semblance of a multiverse, so that is one rabbit hole I could go down and find an answer there, but I think I prefer the idea of delivering the neatness of a universe, where inconsistencies are solved, sometimes through rather Heath Robinson-like inventions, but nonetheless solutions are there.

Courtney Hopf: It's interesting that you are so committed to the universe model, because multiverses seem to be everywhere in popular culture right now – particularly in comics and television. You said once in another interview that you'd learnt a lot about storytelling from the world-building of comics like *2000AD*. What, specifically, have you learnt from comics?

David Mitchell: It's just a fine model of long-form drama. There's Judge Dredd, and they do ten or fifteen-week stories, all set in the same universe, but the stories are distinct, so already we have a macroworld that exists that everything contributes to. But a series, like a box set, like a *season*, within a box set, you have medium length narrative arcs there, and a single episode also has to have a satisfaction as well, so you have micro-arcs and medium arcs, all contributing to the macro arc. Comics need to do that to sell, there's a commercial imperative on them, to getting that right, and I think that was a good thing for my 12-year-old self to have imbibed. I'm doing something a little bit like that as an adult. Chapters need to have a beginning, middle and end, even if the end is another beginning. And then the novel itself also needs to work, and then they are all contributing to the greater Über-book.

Courtney Hopf: I think there are some interesting connections between the seriality of comics and what you're doing, which I would never classify as serials because there needs to be a kind of linearity and teleology to a serial, whereas you're bouncing back and forth in different times and spaces. But because of how your world is ... compounding, each time you meet a character it's compounded, each time you see a reference it's compounded, it's functioning in a similar way.

David Mitchell: Yes, seriality. It's cheeky to not declare it, but then I've discovered I don't need to, and I kind of don't want to, because I don't want to put people off and have them thinking, 'well I can't read *The Bone Clocks* unless I read *Jacob de Zoet*.' Since I don't need to declare it, I don't, which kind of tickles me slightly.

I never thought about this before, really, but there was a character in *2000AD* that I probably learnt a lot from. He was called the Stainless Steel Rat, and he was a sort of thief. He was a human but that was his nickname, he was a metaphorical rat. He's an anti-hero who you actually do root for. He's an outsider in this perfect, futuristic world, he doesn't belong, he's a non-conformist, he's a dissident. And he gets recruited by a kind of FBI and interstellar MI5 of the future, because he's close to the criminals they're trying to catch, and he was formerly a criminal, but he's turned to the light side, mostly.

Great character, just great, but then I discovered the Stainless Steel Rat wasn't invented by *2000AD*'s writers, they were serializations from novels, by an American science-fiction writer called Harry Harrison. And they were strong novels. And without knowing what I was doing, I bought the novels, and read them, and compared them to the same civilizations represented in the comic. It forced me to notice and question: What bits are crucial? What's the plot and the character? What happens to the themes and ideas as the forms change? Where and how are all these elements transferred to the comic book? Why are they important?

What a useful activity for my teenage self to be doing. The Stainless Steel Rat's real name is Jim Digrizz, and his recruiter and boss was this English, slightly Churchillian figure called Inskipp. And occasionally Inskipp and Jim Digrizz would just have a conversation about society and non-conformism and criminality and justice. They were never very long, but without them it would have been Batman nonsense. Not interesting Batman but the TV, 'kapow' Batman that was totally devoid of ideas. And those ideas would stick. Possibly they were early lessons for me on the necessity of the vitamin of ideas in fiction.

Courtney Hopf: I think this is just one of those examples that show what a wonderful art form comics are.

David Mitchell: Yes, of course there's a lot of mass-produced, formulaic, unloved – even by the people who made them – trash, but the good stuff is art, and excellence is excellence, whatever genre you find it in.

Courtney Hopf: In your fiction, especially *Cloud Atlas*, you explore the possibilities for storytelling through the use of various and evolving technologies. But it seems to me that you are also interested in experimenting with technology yourself as a writer. What did you learn about your creative process as you adapted your Twitter story 'The Right Sort' into the first chapter of *Slade House*?

David Mitchell: What works sequentially on the screen of a smartphone doesn't work on the page as well, or in the same way. One idea early on was just to reproduce the tweets of 'The Right Sort.' Thank you very much, that's my first chapter, all done. That's a fifth of my advance already earned. But no, that really wasn't going to work. I printed it out and realized no, this is going to have to be totally redone. And actually why wouldn't I? Why oblige myself to stick to the limitations of the tweet form when I've got the page?

I thought of this metaphor before I rewrote it, but it applied even more afterwards. A tweet narrative is – and this is an idea that's nicked from Nabokov's *Speak, Memory*, when he's talking about his very early memories – a tweet form narrative is like you're on a train looking through a window in a snowy landscape, moving through a sequence of tunnels, and there's nothing and then a burst of light, and you can see a lot, and then nothing, burst of bright, see a lot, then nothing, but once you have, you can't go back to it, it's gone. A page of text, though, is like you're a balloonist, looking down on the landscape, and you can see a little ways, to the top of the page, the bottom of the page, you can walk backwards, you can chew it over, you can make assonance work throughout a paragraph, you can ... design the page, you can break it into modules, so you have space where you want it. Page design is a profession for a reason. And especially in the laptop generation of writers, I think it is not unusual to think about page design actually while you're writing. There's something really annoying about having a word go over the end of the line and just disappearing, to the point of, sometimes, just making something shorter so it fits in.

David Peace, a friend of mine who is a British writer and lives in Tokyo, is published by Faber, and he's fixed his laptop font size and line spacing so that it looks exactly as it will do on the published page. Now it's a bit daft, this, because things are going to be proofread, you're going to lose things and you're going to gain things – I know that, but I still want it to look right when I write it. Anyway you get to think about a lot when it's on the page. So this is what I learnt when I was recalibrating 'The Right Sort' into the first chapter of *Slade House*.

Courtney Hopf: You've tackled the coming-of-age story in a few different ways now – you've done a Japanese teenager in *number9dream*, an English teenager in *Black Swan Green*, and you've done the life of a woman with Holly in *The Bone Clocks*, a novel some academics are calling a postmodern *Bildungsroman*. What would you say attracts you particularly to this mode of storytelling?

David Mitchell: Isn't that cluster of years when you stop being a kid and start being an adult fascinating? How could that not be fascinating? The most fascinating bit of a caterpillar's lifespan is when it's in the pupa. It's amazing, you're part kid, part adult, what a weird being you become for a while. And how extraordinary your perception becomes, and how nervy the world is of you, being not quite sure how to treat you. What rights to give you, or your responsibilities. It's a fascinating time, but I think, again it's about intentionality. Whatever you do, if you have a character who's a teenager your book will be called a *Bildungsroman*, you just can't avoid the title, it's going to be put on there. And it's not necessarily with Eiji that I wanted to write one, it's just that he's that age, so the book gets called that. Nothing to do with me!

Courtney Hopf: So it's more the attraction to that age itself than what it might allow you to do in fiction.

David Mitchell: I don't see myself as making any formal contribution to the archive of human literature called the *Bildungsroman*. Not at all. It's interesting, it is a fascinating time, and publishers and critics and academics want to label that – it's a reflex. We like labels.

Courtney Hopf: Absolutely, we like to categorize.

David Mitchell: And on it goes. A character or protagonist's age is just begging for it, and people oblige.

Courtney Hopf: Well you've done a lot with male characters, and I feel like there was an interesting shift with Holly Sykes in *The Bone Clocks*. This is one of the more sustained times that you've entered the head of a female character …

David Mitchell: I had a go.

Courtney Hopf: Did you do anything in particular to get yourself into that head space?

David Mitchell: Not *really*. I'd never written a sustained female first-person character before so it was daunting but that daunting-ness was the attraction. I don't know if I pulled it off or not. Identifying and avoiding the most obvious pratfalls was one stage; that was one big part. When male writers try and over-compensate and start to talk about … reflex responses of parts of the female anatomy, for example, it's just embarrassing! You're just sitting there thinking, what, do female writers do that when they write male characters? I don't think so! Also, making her a tomboy, she's already a little bit male in her outlook; it's a bit of a tough, working-class milieu she's come from. I went to school with some girls like that. Short hair, mod jackets …

Courtney Hopf: She's a little bit Dawn Madden [from *Black Swan Green*], isn't she.

David Mitchell: Yes, yeah. I thought for a little while, could she *be* Dawn?

Courtney Hopf: Actually that could have worked, in terms of time period.
David Mitchell: I did think about it. But then she's in the wrong town. It didn't work geographically. There is ... oh it's a book I haven't done yet. There will be another *Black Swan Green* connection later. Otherwise no, I just showed that Holly chapter to my wife, who okayed it, and that's what gave me confidence. We are very different when it comes to childbirth and other things, but in many other ways we're not. And it's actually the similarities that are not sufficiently acknowledged by society. That's what causes the trouble.

Forgive me, but it seems that women subscribe to the entirely justifiable argument that just because one's reproductive organs are stored inside instead of outside, why does that make it fulfilling to spend years changing diapers? Why does it mean that you have a genetic propensity to want to look after elderly in-laws? What would I choose? So again, thinking like that, actually maybe it's not that tough to do, to write a plausible female character. Maybe there is more within me that I can just use.

Courtney Hopf: There are some really interesting ways that gender gets played with in your work, especially because of all the body-hopping that tends to happen with the transmigratory souls – sometimes those souls hop between bodies of different genders. And the transgender civil rights debate is so prominent in the cultural imaginary right now. Does any of this play across your mind as you're working with these constructions of plot and character?

David Mitchell: Partly my friendship with Lana Wachowski is conflated into this; we had some great late-night-through-to-early-morning discussions in Berlin when she was shooting *Cloud Atlas*. And she was the first transgender person I'd ever met, let alone the first one I've met and known well enough to talk about transgender issues with. And she told me so many interesting things, I think it needed an outlet.

Courtney Hopf: That makes sense. Especially given your friendship with Lana, does the representation, seeing a film version of *Cloud Atlas*, does that ever change how you see your work?

David Mitchell: Oh the characters, yes. The big thing is I can no longer remember how I visualized the characters. Timothy Cavendish has Jim Broadbent's face and body, and always will do. He can't not. The film feeds back. For example, for cinematic arc reasons, Lana gave Cavendish and Ursula a happy coming together in the film version, and I think in ... *The Bone Clocks*? Is that there? Certainly in something I have either recently written or will soon write, that happens in my own universe. It needs to fit, and so it will. There are a few other things like that to come. But yes, I want to absorb and own what film versions of my work might do – have done or might do in the future.

Courtney Hopf: So actively absorbing paratexts and adaptations to make them part of the canon instead of the Apocrypha. It feels like a rare stance for an author to take, to be comfortable with allowing other people's visions of your work to influence it.

David Mitchell: Yeah, it's doesn't bother me at all. Did you ever track down something I did called 'My Imaginary Vancouver'? [Ed.: Actual title is 'Imaginary City', Geist.com, 2010]

Courtney Hopf: No, I don't think so.

David Mitchell: I was invited to Vancouver for a festival, and they wanted a little piece on me. I'd never been to Vancouver at that point, so I just wrote about what I thought Vancouver might look and be like. I sat on the plane, and I was flying over, and I had no knowledge, I didn't Wikipedia it or anything like that, I just had these ideas about Vancouver. And I read it out to the audience when I arrived, to their pleasure and hilarity, because it was so very wrong, with maybe one or two things I got right. But then I just made the point that even cities we've never been to, they aren't vacuums; we've got little sketches and impressions in our minds, images drawn from other cities, from TV shows, a mention in a Neil Young lyric. It shows how the imagination not so much abhors a vacuum, but exists to fill them.

And how your imaginary city, in this case Vancouver, within five minutes of leaving the airport, has vanished, forever, and you can't get your imaginary Vancouver back, if you hadn't written it down beforehand. It's really gone. It's a very very gone thing indeed. Your imaginary perceptions of a city you've never visited *after* you've visited it. Deeply buried, probably annihilated by reality. That'd be a good title for something, I'm not sure what, 'Annihilated by Reality.'

Courtney Hopf: There's a real prevalence in your writing of characters with various forms of disability, and I know your son is autistic and you had your own struggles growing up with speech disfluency – is this just a case of your own life influencing what you want to write about? Or is there kind of a more concerted effort to bring in different forms of what it's like to be a human being?

David Mitchell: It is important because it's there with me in the first place and also an ideological wish to represent other sometimes underrepresented people in fiction, (a) for ideological reasons and (b) because it's interesting. It's really interesting. The more different the skin is to yours, the more interesting it is to be in it, and for us to learn what they know. In the same way it's worth studying French, for example, not for the academic ability but because it helps you see the world in a French way.

Courtney Hopf: It's strikes me that this is another way of talking about how jumping into different people's skin is what drives your writing. There's something very humanist about that, to me, that it's important to see the world through as many eyes as possible. It's political, too, and there is obviously a politics in your writing – environmental issues, predacity, slavery, corporate greed, these are all themes that are always *there* in your work. Do you see yourself, or by extension your writing, as political?

David Mitchell: Try putting all the world, or try putting as much of the world as you can into your books without putting politics into it. It ain't gonna happen, is it?

Courtney Hopf: But I do think there's a little difference between putting politics into it and writing *as* political, if that makes sense.

David Mitchell: Yes, or between it being there almost by default or you seeking to import it, or ... allowing it to arrive. Generally, with those two, for me it's the latter. I allow it to be there because it would be perverse and odd to try to strike it out. And if it is going to be there then do it properly. Maybe in a weird and hopefully not too clever way it's actually both. I'm writing about power relationships, I'm writing about countries, sometimes, about the hold that a corporation can exert upon its host society. Those things are in the world and so into the book they come, but once they are there, well, you can't have it there and not think about them, not analyse, not give voice to those political relationships. So, in the beginning, I allow it to be there in a somewhat placid way, but then once I notice it's there, maybe I'm more interested in actively exploring it.

So, I don't see myself particularly as a political writer per se. I've been invited to give my views about Brexit, say in an Irish paper, but apart from being deeply depressed I don't know what to say, I would just be recycling what I've been reading in *The Guardian*, in *The New Statesmen* or *Prospect*. And I know there are other people who do it more insightfully, do it more creatively, and who are used to it. I'll leave that to them and read them. Maybe I'm a sort of slow-time political writer, maybe I've got to wait until things have settled and read about them a year or five or ten years later and see how any given political issue exists, in a cluster of neighbouring political issues and understand things that way, rather in slow motion. It makes me pretty useless for writing about it; I don't work at journalism speed. I am deeply interested in the world and its political relationships and its politics and national politics and global politics and local politics as a force, but I never quite know what I think about the here and now in most cases.

Reality is so complex and messy, and it seems to enjoy frustrating clear, determined, persuasive, pithy opinions about it. My friend Hari Kunzru I'd be happier to say I'd describe as a political writer, and he may well think of himself that way; he may well give you a less hedged-about 'yes' than I'm giving you. He's a deeply intelligent, highly read, politically engaged man, and I know I'm not like that. I'll hear something someone says and I'll think, that's pretty persuasive and then I'll hear a counter-argument that says 'yes, but', and I'll think 'well actually there's quite a lot in that as well, so, hm'. I'm reluctant to take positions because there's often truth in any given thesis's hypothesis. And I don't want to lose sight of that. So, hence, I'm a slow-motion political writer, but not a white-hot of the moment one.

Courtney Hopf: You recently contributed the second piece of writing to the Future Library project, and in your statement on it you wrote about hope, saying 'its fruition is predicated upon the ongoing existence of Northern Europe, of libraries, of Norwegian spruces, of books and of readers.' So much of your work hinges on the tension between hope and devastation, optimism and pessimism. Ultimately, are you optimistic or pessimistic about the future?

David Mitchell: I've developed a really good answer to this which you may have come across before, but I'll give it you now because it's not flippant and I can't better it. On Mondays, Wednesdays, Fridays and Sundays, I'm optimistic. And on Tuesdays, Thursdays and Saturdays I'm pessimistic. And that's four against three. Despair is too easy. Cynicism is too easy. A sort of ... emo despair, it may be cool, but in the end it's just posturing. And what good is it to anybody, what's that going to build? What wrong ill, what misguided narrative is that going to fix? It's a close-run thing, but I'll be optimistic. Why bother, if you're not?

Courtney Hopf: Perhaps this is a related question to conclude with: as a non-religious person, what attracts you to creating a universe that is underpinned so strongly by the notion of the human soul being a real, tangible thing?

David Mitchell: I so want the soul to be real. I want that wriggle room in the death contract to exist. I want my loved ones to carry on in some form. Don't you? Me ceasing to be, okay, I can handle that, but our kids, my family, that's unbearable. Don't you think? Even for me, I want the chance to keep what I've learnt and to do better next time. The afterlives of the world's established religions seem mostly insulting to my God-given intelligence (insert smiley here) but the existence of the soul, this little dot of distilled us-ness, somehow seems more plausible. I don't feel self-delusional when I admit the possibility of the soul. I can be a content agnostic. You could drive a coach and horses through the logic in this answer, I know, but that's okay, we humans are contradictory beings, me as much as any. Incorporeal fingers crossed.

This is an edited transcript of an interview that took place at the University of Edinburgh on 30 June 2016.

FURTHER READING

I Works by David Mitchell

Novels

(1999), *Ghostwritten*, London: Sceptre.
(2001), *number9dream*, London: Sceptre.
(2004), *Cloud Atlas*, London: Sceptre.
(2006), *Black Swan Green*, London: Sceptre.
(2010), *The Thousand Autumns of Jacob de Zoet*, London: Sceptre.
(2014), *The Bone Clocks*, London: Sceptre.
(2015), *Slade House*, London: Sceptre.

Translations

Higashida, N. (2013), *The Reason I Jump: One Boy's Voice from the Silence of Autism*, trans. with K. A. Yoshida, London: Sceptre.
Higashida, N. (2017), *Fall down Seven Times, Get up Eight: A Young Man's Voice from the Silence of Autism*, trans. with K. A. Yoshida, London: Sceptre.
Miyazawa, K. (2012), 'The Earthgod and the Fox', *McSweeney's*, no. 42, 59–77.

Short Stories

(2003), 'The January Man', *Granta 81: Best of Young British Novelists*.
(2004), 'What You Do Not Know You Want', in *McSweeney's Enchanted Chamber of Astonishing Stories*, London: Vintage.
(2005), 'Acknowledgements', *Prospect Magazine*, 22 October.
(2005), 'Hangman', *New Writing 13*, ed. Ali Smith and Toby Litt, London: Picador.
(2006), 'Preface', *The Telegraph*, 29 April.
(2007), 'Dénouement', *The Guardian*, 26 May.
(2008), 'Judith Castle', *The Book of Other People*, ed. Zadie Smith, Penguin.
(2009), 'An Inside Job', *Fighting Words*, ed. Roddy Doyle, Stoney Road Press.
(2009), 'Character Development', *Freedom: Short Stories Celebrating the Universal Declaration of Human Rights*, Amnesty International.
(2009), 'The Massive Rat', *The Guardian*, 1 August.
(2010), 'Earth Calling Taylor', *Financial Times*, 30 December.
(2010), 'Muggins Here', *The Guardian*, 14 August.

(2011), 'The Gardener', *The Guardian*, 6 June.
(2011), 'The Siphoners', *I'm With the Bears: Short Stories From a Damaged Planet*, ed. Mark Martin, Verso Books.
(2012), 'In the Bike Sheds', *The Bookseller*, 20 June.
(2013), 'Lots of Bits of Star', *Kai and Sunny, 'Caught by the Nest'*, art exhibition.
(2014), 'The Right Sort', *Twitter*.
(2014), 'Variations on a Theme by Mister Donut', *Granta Magazine*, 127.
(2015), 'A Possibly True Ghost Story from David Mitchell', *Lithub*, 24 September.
(2016), 'My Eye on You', *Kai and Sunny, 'Whirlwind of Time'*, art exhibition.
(2017), 'A Forgettable Story', *Silkroad*, 30 June.

Essays and Articles

(2004), 'Enter the Maze', *The Guardian*, 22 May.
(2005), 'Japan and My Writing', *Japan Railway & Transport Review*, 42, 60–1.
(2005), 'Kill Me or the Cat Gets It', *The Guardian*, 8 January.
(2006), 'Let Me Speak', *The British Stammering Association*, 1 June.
(2010), 'Adventures in Opera', *The Guardian*, 8 May.
(2010), 'David Mitchell on Historical Fiction', *The Telegraph*, 8 May.
(2010), 'Once Upon a Life: David Mitchell', *The Guardian*, 8 May.
(2010), 'Imaginary City', *Geist*. Available at: http://www.geist.com/fact/dispatches/imaginary-city/
(2011), 'Foreword', *David Mitchell: Critical Essays*, Canterbury: Gylphi.
(2011), 'Lost for Words', *Prospect Magazine*, 23 February.
(2013), 'Learning to Live With My Son's Autism', *The Guardian*, 29 June.
(2014), 'David Mitchell on How to Write: "Neglect Everything Else"', *The Atlantic*, 23 September.
(2015), 'David Mitchell on Earthsea – A Rival to Tolkien and George RR Martin', *The Guardian*, 23 October.
(2015), 'I Have Created My Own Middle Earth', *The Guardian*, 17 August.
(2016), 'Ghost Stories Tap into Something Ancient and Primal', *The Guardian*, 12 July.
(2018), 'Start with the Map: A Writers' Lessons in Imaginary Cartography', *The New Yorker*, 13 September.
(2018), 'Ursula K. Le Guin by David Mitchell: "She Was a Crafter of Fierce, Focused, Fertile Dreams"', *The Guardian*, 25 January.

Libretti

(2010), *Wake*, Nationale Reisopera, Enschede.
(2013), *Sunken Garden*, English National Opera, London.

Other

(2014), 'Before the Dawn', With Kate Bush, monologue in live production.
(2014), 'The Right Sort: David Mitchell's Twitter Short Story', *The Guardian*, 14 July.

(2016), 'Dreizehn Arten das Stottern zu betrachten' or 'Thirteen Ways of Looking at a Stammer', Herausgeber: Stottern & Selbsthilfe Landesverband Ost e. V.
(2114), *From Me Flows What You Call Time* (Future Library Project, format unknown).

II Critical material

Books and special issues on David Mitchell

Dillon, S. (ed.) (2011), *David Mitchell: Critical Essays*, Canterbury: Gylphi.
Eve, M.P. (2019), *Close Reading with Computers Textual Scholarship, Computational Formalism, and David Mitchell's* Cloud Atlas, Stanford: Stanford University Press.
Harris, P. A. (ed.) (2015), 'David Mitchell in the Labyrinth of Time', *SubStance*, 44(1). Available at: http://substance.org/136-david-mitchell-and-the-labyrinth-of-time/
Harris-Birtill, R. (ed.) (2018), *David Mitchell. C21 Literature: Journal of 21st-Century Writings*, 6(3). Available at: https://c21.openlibhums.org/issue/39/info/
Harris-Birtill, R. (2019), *David Mitchell's Post-Secular World: Buddhism, Belief and the Urgency of Compassion*, London and New York: Bloomsbury Academic.
O'Donnell, P. (2015), *A Temporary Future: The Fiction of David Mitchell*, London and New York: Bloomsbury Academic.

Book chapters

Bayer, G. (2014), 'Cannibalizing the Other: David Mitchell's *The Thousand Autumns of Jacob de Zoet* and the Incorporation of "Exotic" Pasts', in Rousselot, E. (ed.), *Exoticizing the Past in Contemporary Neo-Historical Fiction*, London: Palgrave Macmillan, 103–19.
Boulter, J. (2011), 'Humanizing History: David Mitchell', in *Melancholy and the Archive*, London: Bloomsbury Publishing, 101–39.
Childs, P. and Green, J. (2011), 'The Novels in Nine Parts', in Dillon, S. (ed.), *David Mitchell: Critical Essays*, Canterbury: Gylphi, 25–48.
Childs, P. and Green, J. (2013), 'David Mitchell', in *Aesthetics and Ethics in Twenty-First Century British Novels*, London: Bloomsbury, 127–58.
Deckard, S. (2017), 'Capitalism's Long Spiral: Periodicity, Temporality and the Global Contemporary in World Literature', in Sarah Brouillette, Mathias Nilges and Emilio Sauri (eds), *Literature and the Global Contemporary*, Cham: Springer, 83–102.
Dillon, S. (2011), 'Introduction: David Mitchell's Universe: A Twenty-First Century House of Fiction', in Dillon, S. (ed.), *David Mitchell: Critical Essays*, Canterbury: Gylphi, 3–24.
Dunlop, N. (2011), 'Speculative Fiction as Postcolonial Critique in *Ghostwritten* and *Cloud Atlas*', in Dillon, S. (ed.), *David Mitchell: Critical Essays*, Canterbury: Gylphi, 201–24.

Edwards, C. (2011), 'Strange Transactions: Utopia, Transmigration and Time in *Ghostwritten* and *Cloud Atlas*', in Dillon, S. (ed.), *David Mitchell: Critical Essays*, Canterbury: Gylphi, 177–200.
Front, S. (2015), 'Eternal Recurrence in David Mitchell's *Cloud Atlas*', in *Shapes of Time in British Twenty-First Century Quantum Fiction*, Cambridge: Cambridge Scholars Publishing, 73–96.
Hopf, C. (2011), 'The Stories We Tell: Discursive Identity Through Narrative Form in *Cloud Atlas*', in Dillon, S. (ed.), *David Mitchell: Critical Essays*, Canterbury: Gylphi, 105–26.
Huber, I. (2014), 'Dreaming of Reconstruction: David Mitchell's *number9dream*', *Literature after Postmodernism: Reconstructive Fantasies*, London: Palgrave Macmillan, 181–214.
Lindner, O. (2015), 'Postmodernism and Dystopia: David Mitchell, *Cloud Atlas* (2004)', in Voigts, E. and Boller, A. (eds), *Dystopia, Science Fiction, Post-Apocalypse: Classics – New Tendencies – Model Interpretations*, Trier, Germany: WVT Wissenschaftlicher, 363–78.
Machinal, H. (2011), '*Cloud Atlas*: From Postmodernity to the Posthuman', in Dillon, S. (ed.), *David Mitchell: Critical Essays*, Canterbury: Gylphi, 127–54.
Matz, J. (2016), 'Impressionism after Film', in Nilges, M. (ed.), *The Contemporaneity of Modernism*, New York: Routledge, 91–104.
McCulloch, F. (2012), '"Around We Go": Transpositional Life Cycles in David Mitchell's *Cloud Atlas*', in *Cosmopolitanism in Contemporary British Fiction*, London: Palgrave Macmillan, 141–63.
McMorran, W. (2011), '*Cloud Atlas* and *If on a Winter's Night a Traveller*: Fragmentation and Integrity in the Postmodern Novel', in Dillon, S. (ed.), *David Mitchell: Critical Essays*, Canterbury: Gylphi, 155–76.
Posadas, B. T. (2011), 'Remediations of "Japan" in *number9dream*', in Dillon, S. (ed.), *David Mitchell: Critical Essays*, Canterbury: Gylphi, 77–104.
Schmitt-Kilb, C. (2010), 'Gypsies and their Representation: Louise Doughty's *Stone Cradle* and David Mitchell's *Black Swan Green*', in Helff, S. (ed.), *Facing the East in the West*, Amsterdam: Editions Rodopi, 293–308.
Schoene, B. (2009), 'The World Begins Its Turn with You, or How David Mitchell's Novels Think', in *The Cosmopolitan Novel*, Edinburgh: Edinburgh University Press, 97–125.
Shaw, K. (2017), '"A Multitude of Drops": The Global Imaginaries of David Mitchell', in *Cosmopolitanism in Twenty-First Century Fiction*, Cham: Palgrave Macmillan, 27–66.
Simpson, K. (2011), 'Or Something Like That: Coming of Age in *number9dream*', in Dillon, S. (ed.), *David Mitchell: Critical Essays*, Canterbury: Gylphi, 49–76.
Sims, C. A. (2013), 'David Mitchell's *Cloud Atlas*: Cloned AIs as Leader of an Ontological Insurrection', in Sims, C. A. (ed.), *Tech Anxiety*, Jefferson: McFarland & Company, Inc., 178–222.
Stephenson, W. (2011), 'Moonlight Bright as a UFO Abduction: Science Fiction, Present-Future Alienation and Cognitive Mapping', in Dillon, S. (ed.), *David Mitchell: Critical Essays*, Canterbury: Gylphi, 225–46.
Vermeulen, P. (2011), 'The Novel after Melancholia: On Tom McCarthy's *Remainder* and David Mitchell's *Ghostwritten*', in Middeke, M. and Wald, C. (eds), *The Literature of Melancholia*, London: Palgrave Macmillan, 254–67.

Journal articles

Anderson, T. R. (2017), 'Staggered Transmissions: Twitter and the Return of Serialized Literature', *Convergence: The Journal of Research into New Media Technologies*, 23(1), 34–48.
Barnard, R. (2009), 'Fictions of the Global', *Novel: A Forum on Fiction*, 42(2), 207–15.
Baucom, I. (2015), '"Moving Centers": Climate Change, Critical Method, and the Historical Novel', *Modern Language Quarterly: A Journal of Literary History*, 76(2), 137–57.
Bayer, G. (2015), 'Perpetual Apocalypses: David Mitchell's *Cloud Atlas* and the Absence of Time', *Critique*, 56(4), 345–54.
Beville, M. (2015), 'Getting Past the "Post-": History and Time in the Fiction of David Mitchell', *Sic: A Journal of Literature, Culture, & Literary Translation*, 1, 1–17.
Boulter, J. (2015), 'Posthuman Temporality: Mitchell's *Ghostwritten*', *SubStance*, 44(1), 18–38.
Burn, S. J. (2012), 'Reading the Multiple Drafts Novel', *MFS: Modern Fiction Studies*, 58(3), 436–58.
Childs, P. (2015), 'Food Chain: Predatory Links in the Novels of David Mitchell', *Etudes Anglaises*, 68(2), 183–95.
De Cristofaro, D. (2018), '"Time, No Arrow, No Boomerang, but a Concertina": *Cloud Atlas* and the Anti-Apocalyptic Critical Temporalities of the Contemporary Post-Apocalyptic Novel', *Critique*, 59(2), 243–57.
Diaman, C. (2016), 'Subaltern Framings of the Posthuman in Jeanette Winterson's *The Stone Gods* and David Mitchell's *Cloud Atlas*', *Metacritic Journal for Comparative Studies & Theory*, 2(2), 101–13.
D'haen, T. (2013), 'European Postmodernism: The Cosmodern Turn', *Narrative*, 21(3), 271–83.
Dillon, S. (2011), 'Chaotic Narrative: Complexity, Causality, Time and Autopoiesis in David Mitchell's *Ghostwritten*', *Critique*, 52(2), 135–62.
Dimovitz, S. (2015), 'The Sound of Silence: Eschatology and the Limits of the Word in David Mitchell's *Cloud Atlas*', *SubStance*, 44(1), 71–91.
Dimovitz, S. A. (2018), 'Schrödinger's Cat Metalepsis and the Political Unwriting of the Postmodern Apocalypse in David Mitchell's Recent Works', *C21 Literature: Journal of 21st-Century Writings*, 6(3). Available at: https://doi.org/10.16995/c21.50
Eve, M. P. (2016), '"You Have to Keep Track of your Changes": The Version Variants and Publishing History of David Mitchell's *Cloud Atlas*', *Open Library of the Humanities*, 10 August. Available at: https://olh.openlibhums.org/articles/10.16995/olh.82/
Eve, M. P. (2017), 'Close Reading with Computers: Genre Signals, Parts of Speech, and David Mitchell's *Cloud Atlas*', *SubStance*, 46(3), 76–104.
Eve, M. P. (2018), 'The Historical Imaginary of Nineteenth-Century Style in David Mitchell's *Cloud Atlas*', *C21 Literature: Journal of 21st-Century Writings*, 6(3). Available at: https://doi.org/10.16995/c21.46
Ferguson, P. (2015), '"Me Eatee Him Up": Cannibal Appetites in *Cloud Atlas* and *Robinson Crusoe*', *Green Letters*, 19(2), 144–56.

Frame, K. (2015), '"The Strong do Eat": David Mitchell and Herman Melville – A Study in Intertextuality', *Australasian Journal of American Studies*, 34(1), 17–29.

Hagan, B. (2009), 'David Mitchell's *Ghostwritten*: Ghosts, Doubles, and Writing', *Explicator*, 67(2), 84–6.

Harris, P. A. (2015), 'David Mitchell's Fractal Imagination: *The Bone Clocks*', *SubStance*, 44(1), 148–53.

Harris, P. A. (2015), 'Introduction: David Mitchell in the Labyrinth of Time', *SubStance*, 44(1), 3–7.

Harris, P. A. (2018), 'In the Labyrinth of Slow Time: "A Perturbation in the Deep Stream" and "A Perambulation in the Deep Stream"', *C21 Literature: Journal of 21st-Century Writings*, 6(3). Available at: https://doi.org/10.16995/c21.61

Harris-Birtill, R. (2015), '"A Row of Screaming Russian Dolls": Escaping the Panopticon in David Mitchell's *number9dream*', *SubStance*, 44(1), 55–70.

Harris-Birtill, R. (2018), 'Introducing the David Mitchell Special Edition of *C21 Literature*', *C21 Literature: Journal of 21st-Century Writings*, 6(3). Available at: https://doi.org/10.16995/c21.672

Hicks, H. (2010), '"This Time Round": David Mitchell's *Cloud Atlas* and the Apocalyptic Problem of Historicism', *Postmodern Culture: An Electronic Journal of Interdisciplinary Criticism*, 20(3). https://muse.jhu.edu/article/444704 (accessed 21 March 2019).

Hooks, S. (2015), 'Palter & Prescience – On David Mitchell and *Ghostwritten*', *SubStance*, 44(1), 39–54.

Hortle, L. (2016), 'David Mitchell's *Cloud Atlas* and the Queer Posthuman', *LIT: Literature Interpretation Theory*, 27(4), 253–74.

Knepper, W. (2016), 'Toward a Theory of Experimental World Epic: David Mitchell's *Cloud Atlas*', *ariel: A Review of International English Literature*, 47(1/2), 93–126.

Larsonneur, C. (2015), 'Revisiting Dejima (Japan): From Recollection to Fiction in David Mitchell's *The Thousand Autumns of Jacob de Zoet*', *SubStance*, 44(1), 136–47.

Larsonneur, C. (2016), 'Archipelagos of Apocalypse in David Mitchell's *Cloud Atlas* and *The Bone Clocks*', *Textus*, 29(1), 197–211.

Larsonneur, C. (2016), 'Weaving Myth and History Together: Illustration as Fabrication in David Mitchell's *Black Swan Green* and *The Thousand Autumns of Jacob de Zoet*', *Image & Narrative*, 17(2), 24–33.

Larsonneur, C. (2018), 'Oblique Translations in David Mitchell's Works', *C21 Literature: Journal of 21st-Century Writings*, 6(3). Available at: https://doi.org/10.16995/c21.53

Matz, J. (2017), 'Genre Beside Itself: David Mitchell's *The Bone Clocks*, Pulp Intrusions, and the Cosmic Historians' War', *Studies in Contemporary Fiction*, 58(2), 121–8.

McNally, L. (2011), 'Fictions of Composition in the Novels of David Mitchell', *Dandelion Journal*, 2(1). Available at: https://dandelionjournal.org/article/doi/10.16995/ddl.240/

Mezey, J. H. (2011), '"A Multitude of Drops": Recursion and Globalization in David Mitchell's *Cloud Atlas*', *Modern Language Studies*, 40(2), 10–37.

Mousotzanis, A. (2016), 'Network Fictions and the Global Unhomely', *C21 Literature: Journal of 21st-Century Writings*, 4(1), 1–19.

Ng, L. (2015), 'Cannibalism, Colonialism and Apocalypse in Mitchell's Global Future', *SubStance*, 44(1), 107–22.

Olson, C. (2012), 'The Nightmare of History: A Look at Time in the Novels of Eliade, DeLillo and Mitchell,' *Theory in Action*, 5(1), 81–102.

Parker, J. A. (2015), 'From Time's Boomerang to Pointillist Mosaic: Translating *Cloud Atlas* into Film', *SubStance*, 44(1), 123–35.

Parker, J. A. (2018), 'Mind the Gap(s): Holly Sykes's Life, the "Invisible" War, and the History of the Future in *The Bone Clocks*', *C21 Literature: Journal of 21st-Century Writings*, 6(3). Available at: https://doi.org/10.16995/c21.47

Polanki G. (2018), 'The Iterable Messiah: Postmodernist Mythopoeia in *Cloud Atlas*', *C21 Literature: Journal of 21st-Century Writings*, 6(3). Available at: https://doi.org/10.16995/c21.59

Rickel, J. (2016), 'Practice Reading for the Apocalypse: David Mitchell's *Cloud Atlas* as Warning Text', *South Atlantic Review*, 80(12), 159–77.

Selisker, S. (2014), 'The Cult and the World System: The Topoi of David Mitchell's Global Novels', *Novel: A Forum on Fiction*, 47(3), 443–59.

Schmitz E. (2018), '"No Man Is an Island": Tracing Functions of Insular Landscapes in David Mitchell's Fiction', *C21 Literature: Journal of 21st-Century Writings*, 6(3). Available at: https://doi.org/10.16995/c21.62

Schoene, B. (2010), '*Tour du Monde*: David Mitchell's *Ghostwritten* and the Cosmopolitan Imagination', *College Literature*, 37(4), 42–60.

Shanahan, J. (2016), 'Digital Transcendentalism in David Mitchell's *Cloud Atlas*', *Criticism*, 58(1), 115–45.

Shaw, K. (2015), 'Building Cosmopolitan Futures: Global Fragility in the Fiction of David Mitchell', *English Academy Review*, 32(1), 109–23.

Shaw, K. (2018), '"Some Magic Is Normality": Fantastical Cosmopolitanism in David Mitchell's *The Bone Clocks*', *C21 Literature: Journal of 21st-Century Writings*, 6(3). Available at: https://doi.org/10.16995/c21.52

Shoop, C. and Ryan, D. (2015), '"Gravid with the Ancient Future": *Cloud Atlas* and the Politics of Big History', *SubStance*, 44(1), 92–106.

Trimm R. (2018), 'Spirits in the Material World: Spectral Worlding in David Mitchell's *Ghostwritten* and *Cloud Atlas*', *C21 Literature: Journal of 21st-Century Writings*, 6(3). Available at: https://doi.org/10.16995/c21.63

Vermeulen, P. (2012), 'David Mitchell's *Ghostwritten* and the "Novel of Globaliza-tion": Biopower and the Secret History of the Novel', *Critique* 53(4), 381–92.

Walkowitz, R. L. (2015), 'English as a Foreign Language: David Mitchell and the Born-Translated Novel', *SubStance*, 44(2), 30–46.

Wegner, P. (2016), 'Romantic and Dialectical Utopianism in *Cloud Atlas*', *Science Fiction Film & Television*, 9(10), 114–18.

Newspaper reviews

General

Finney, B. (2011), 'Perfectly Plausible Worlds', *LA Review of Books*, 31 August.

Ghostwritten

Blincoe, N. (1999), 'Spirit that Speaks', *The Guardian*, 21 August.
Byatt, A. S. (1999), 'Wild Whirl of a Ghostly World', *Mail on Sunday*, 26(September), 7.
Kakutani, M. (2000), 'Caller no. 1', *The New York Times*, 17 September.
Lively, A. (1999), 'Inside Every Psychopath Is a Jazz Buff Trying to Get Out', *The Observer*, 8 August.
Mendelsohn, D. (1999), 'Big Blue Marble', *New York Magazine*, N.D.

number9dream

Francken, J. (2001), 'In Which the Crocodile Snout-Butts the Glass', *London Review of Books*, 7 June.
Iyer, P. (2007), 'David Mitchell', in 'The 2007 Time 100', *Time*, 03 May. Available at: http://content.time.com/time/specials/2007/time100/article/0,28804,1595326_1595332_1616691,00.html
Iyer, P. (2014), 'Juggling Worlds', *The New York Times Book Review*, 28 August. Available online: https://www.nytimes.com/2014/08/31/books/review/the-bone-clocks-by-david-mitchell.html
Kakutani, M. (2002), 'Books of the Times: Wandering Along the Border between Reality and Fantasy', *The New York Times*, 15 March.
MacFarlane, R. (2001), 'When Blade Runner Meets Jack Kerouac', *The Observer*, 11 March.
Poole, S. (2001), 'I Think I'm Turning Japanese', *The Guardian*, 10 March.
Waters, D. (2001), '*Number9dream* Fails to Rouse', *BBC News*, 12 October.

Cloud Atlas

Anderson, H. (2004), 'Time and Emotion Study', *The Observer*, 29 February.
Bissell, T. (2004), 'History is a Nightmare', *New York Times*, 29 August.
Byatt, A. S. (2004), 'Overlapping Lives', *The Guardian*, 6 March.
Macfarlane, R. (2004), 'Review: Fiction: *Cloud Atlas* by David Mitchell', *The Sunday Times*, 29 February.
Meloy, M. (2007), 'Cloud Atlas a Series of Virtuoso, Soaring Stories', *NPR*, 6 November.
Norfolk, L. (2004), '*Cloud Atlas* by David Mitchell: Islands of the Day Before', *The Independent*, 27 February.
Tait, T. (2004), 'From Victorian Travelogue to Airport Thriller', *The Telegraph*, 1 March.
Turrentine, J. (2004), 'Fantastic Voyage', *Washington Post*, 22 August.

Black Swan Green

Freudenberger, N. (2006), 'Wonder Year', *The New York Times*, 16 April.
Jones, T. (2006), 'Outfoxing Hangman', *London Review of Books*, 11 May.
Phillips, A. (2006), 'About a Boy Poet', *The Observer*, 16 April.
Poole, S. (2006), 'Life with the Hangman', *The Guardian*, 29 April.

Shriver, L. (2006), 'Down to Earth', *Financial Times*, 5 May.
Smith, A. (2006), 'Neither Sweet nor as Simple', *The Telegraph*, 14 May.
Swift, D. (2006), 'Ace in the Face or What?', *The Telegraph*, 21 May.
Thomas, S. (2006), '*Black Swan Green* by David Mitchell', *The Independent*, 6 May.
Zalewski, D. (2006), 'Thirteen Ways: A Portrait of Adolescence from the Puzzle Master of British Fiction', *The New Yorker*, 17 April.

The Thousand Autumns of Jacob de Zoet

Banks, E. (2010), 'Book Review: *The Thousand Autumns of Jacob de Zoet* by David Mitchell', *Los Angeles Times*, 4 July.
Charles, R. (2010), 'Book Review of *The Thousand Autumns of Jacob de Zoet*, a novel by David Mitchell', *Washington Post*, 30 June.
Eggers, D. (2010), 'Empire of Desire', *The New York Times*, 1 July.
Kyte, H. (2010), '*The Thousand Autumns of Jacob de Zoet* by David Mitchell: Review', *The Telegraph*, 2 May.
Linklater, A. (2010), '*The Thousand Autumns of Jacob de Zoet* by David Mitchell', *The Observer*, 9 May.
Tonkin, B. (2010), '*The Thousand Autumns of Jacob de Zoet*, by David Mitchell', *The Independent*, 6 May.
Wood, J. (2010), 'The Floating Library: What Can't the Novelist David Mitchell Do?', *The New Yorker*, 5 July.

The Bone Clocks

Boyagoda, R. (2014), '*The Bone Clocks*, by David Mitchell', *The Financial Times*, 5 September.
Collins, R. (2014), 'How on Earth Did David Mitchell's Third-Rate Fantasy Make the Man Booker Longlist?', *The Spectator*, 6 September.
Hingston, M. (2014), 'As Incongruous as David Mitchell's Novels Seem, *The Bone Clocks* Confirms they're All Deeply Connected', *The Globe and Mail*, 5 September.
Kavenna, J. (2014), '*The Bone Clocks* by David Mitchell, Review: "Painstakingly Kind to the Reader"', *The Telegraph*, 30 August.
Novitz, J. (2014), 'Rise of the Über-Book', *Sydney Review of Books*, 28 October.
Walton, J. (2015), 'Noble, Embattled Souls', *The New York Review of Books*, 3 December.
Wood, J. (2014), 'Soul Cycle', *The New Yorker*, 8 September.

Slade House

Boyne, J. (2015), 'Book Review: *Slade House* by David Mitchell', *The Irish Times*, 31 October.
Craig, A. (2015), '*Slade House*, by David Mitchell – Book Review: It's Not Just the Floors that Creak in this Haunted House', *The Independent*, 25 October.
Finney, B. (2015), 'The David Mitchell Übernovel: Brian Finney reviews *Slade House*', *Los Angeles Review of Books*, 5 December.

Flood, A. (2015), '*Slade House* by David Mitchell Review – Gleeful, Skin-Crawling Brilliance', *The Observer*, 1 November.
Jensen, L. (2015), '*Slade House* by David Mitchell Review – Like Stephen King in a Fever', *The Guardian*, 29 October.
Thomas, S. (2015), 'David Mitchell's *Slade House*', *The New York Times*, 11 November.

III Interviews

Beale, L. (2004), 'A Light is Shining on Author's "Cloud"', *Los Angeles Times*, 9 October.
Begley, A. (2010), 'David Mitchell, The Art of Fiction no. 204', *The Paris Review* 193.
Bradbury, W. (2016), 'Finding the Locus of David Mitchell', *The Japan Times*, 2 April.
Chalom, M. (2014), 'Interview with David Mitchell, Author', *The Harvard Crimson*, 25 September.
Harris, P. (2015), 'David Mitchell in the Laboratory of Time: An Interview with the Author', *SubStance*, 44(1), 8–17.
Jeffries, S. (2013), 'David Mitchell: "I Don't Want to Project Myself as this Great Experimenter"', *The Guardian*, 8 February.
Kellogg, C. (2012), 'An Interview with David Mitchell, the Author Behind *Cloud Atlas*', *Los Angeles Times*, 26 October.
Leong, L. Y, Morgan, D. and Duijsens, F. (2013), 'An Interview with David Mitchell', *Asymptote*, July.
Magras, M. (2014), 'David Mitchell, Unplugged', *Los Angeles Review of Books*, 22 October.
Martin, T. (2015), 'David Mitchell: 'Boredom Is a Geiger Counter for Me', *The Telegraph*, 18 October.
McWeeney, C. (2001), 'David Mitchell Discusses his First Novel, *Ghostwritten*', *Bold Type*.
Min, T. H. (2002), 'The Illusionist's Dream', *Quarterly Literary Review Singapore* 1(2), 2 January.
Naimon, D. (2015), 'A Conversation with David Mitchell', *Missouri Review* 38(2), 46–60.
Poole, S. (2014), 'David Mitchell: "I've been Calling *The Bone Clocks* My Midlife Crisis Novel"', *The Guardian*, 30 August.
Raja, N. (2005), 'Secret Architectures: A Conversation with David Mitchell', *The Agony Column*, 16 May. Available at: http://bookotron.com/agony/columns/2005/05-16-05.htm
Ruskin, Z. (2014), '"The Blank Screen is the Enemy": The Millions Interviews David Mitchell', *The Millions*, 29 October.
Schulz, K. (2014), 'Boundaries Are Conventions. And *The Bone Clocks* Author David Mitchell Transcends them All', *Vulture*, 25 August.
Sinclair, J. (2004), 'David Mitchell – the Interview', *BBC Local Nottingham*, February. Available at: http://www.bbc.co.uk/nottingham/culture/2004/02/david_mitchell_interview.shtml
Sooke, A. (2006), 'My Week: David Mitchell, Writer'. *The Telegraph*, 13 May.

Taunton, P. (2014), 'Bumping Into Your Memories: An Interview with David Mitchell', *Hazlitt*, 9 September.
Tonkin, B. (2014), 'David Mitchell Interview: "It's High Stakes: Do It Wrong and You've Got a Broken Book"', *The Independent*, 5 September.
Tweedie, N. (2013), 'David Mitchell: An Autistic Child? It's Parenting on Steroids', *The Telegraph*, 6 July.
Wilson, L. (2008), 'David Mitchell', in Tew, P., Tolan, F. and Wilson, L. (eds), *Writers Talk: Interviews with Contemporary British Novelists*, London: Continuum.

IV Filmography

Gill, M. (2013), *The Voorman Problem*, Manchester: Honlodge Productions.
Tykwer, T., Wachowski, L. and Wachowski, L. (2012), Warner Bros., *Cloud Atlas*.
Wachowski, L., Wachowski, L. and Straczynski, J.M. (2017), 'Polyphony' (season two, episode four), in *Sense8*, Netflix series.

V Websites

http://www.davidmitchellbooks.com/

INDEX

allegory   79, 113, 141, 167, 170–1, 174
anachronotope   159–60, 161, 162–3
Anchorites   3, 10, 109 n.5, 129, 143, 145, 150, 152, 155–6, 157–9, 161–3, 172, 173–4
Anthropocene   17, 143, 144, 169
  and *Bildungsroman*   149–52, 155–7, 159–63
'A Possibly True Ghost Story'   169–70
Apter, Emily   28
atemporality   156–60, 163
autism   3, 4, 7, 87–8, 192

Bakhtin, Mikhail   150–2, 155
Barker, Pat, *Regeneration*   89
biblioverse   4–6, 15, 166, 179, 183, 184, *see also* Über-book/Über-novel
Bildungsroman   2, 16–17, 190
  and *Black Swan Green*   86, 91
  and *The Bone Clocks*   150–63
  and *number9dream*   39, 43–4, 47–8
biopower/biopolitical   30, 34
Black Swan Green
  autobiography   7, 94
  as *Bildungsroman*   2, 86, 91
  and disability   16, 87–114
  Jason Taylor   5, 7, 16, 85–97
  narrative structure of   88–90
  Neal Brose   97, 138, 168
  reception of   86–7
Blake, William   160
Bone Clocks, The
  Anthropocene   17, 143–4, 149–63
  Crispin Hershey   150, 152, 153, 154, 157, 159, 160, 162, 163, 173, 178, 185

eco-crisis   134–5, 143–6, 156
Ed Brubeck   145, 150, 172
global development   170–5
Holly Sykes   123, 129, 143–6, 149–63, 171–5, 189–91
  irrealism of   170–5
  mortality   126, 128–9
  reception of   9, 10, 170
  somatope   155–9
  structure of   27 n.1, 102 n.2, 109 n.5, 150
book, technology of   56–8
Broch, Hermann   183
Brontë, Charlotte   154
Buddhism   111, 117–18, 122–130, 166, 169, 172, 173
Bush, Kate   4
Byatt, A. S.   8, 9, 150

Calvino, Italo   6
cannibalism   14, 78, 108, 109, 139, 141–2, 144, 168
capitalism   14, 71, 103
  and the environment   134–5, 137–9
  and *Ghostwritten*   23–6, 29–37, 45
  and irrealism   166–8, 172, 174
Caruth, Cathy   72, 73, 82
Cheah, Pheng   166
chronotope   151, 153–6, 158–9, 160, 163
climate change   27 n.1, 135, 142–5, 156
Cloud Atlas
  Adam Ewing   56–61, 71, 74, 76–82
  cannibalism   78, 139, 141–2, 168
  colonialism   59, 61, 108
  critiques of   7, 8

INDEX

environment 16, 63, 134–46, 178
  film 4, 191
  globalization 3, 11, 13, 63, 65
  Luisa Rey 62–3, 71, 134, 139, 141, 184, 186–7
  medicine 58–61, 80
  postcoloniality 15, 71
  postmodernism 10, 11
  predacity 70–1, 75, 139–41, 143–4
  racism 76–8, 80–1
  Robert Frobisher 62, 70, 71
  Rufus Sixsmith 62, 70
  slavery 3, 59, 76–7, 108
  Sonmi~451 7, 64–5, 70, 71, 74, 108, 137, 139, 141–4
  structure of 6, 56, 57–8, 71–2, 73–4, 86, 102 n.2, 126, 138, 141, 143, 186–7
  technology 16, 53–68, 189
  Timothy Cavendish 7, 63, 71, 136, 141–2, 191
  trauma 15–16, 69–82
  versions of 13, 57, 65–6
  as world-literary/epic 13, 55, 70
  Zachry Bailey 71, 74–6
cognitive mapping 8, 24–6, 28, 31–3, 35–7
Coleridge, Samuel Taylor 154, 161
colonialism 140, 151, 168, 171, 177
  and *Cloud Atlas* 59–60, 71
  and *Thousand Autumns* 102, 103, 104, 107, 108
comics 17, 187
  2000AD 187–9
  Judge Dredd 187
cosmology 1, 9–10, 157, 160, 166–7, 169, 171, 173, 175
cosmopolitanism 11, 12, 24, 29–30, 87, 104–5 n.3, 106, 168
counter-narrative 78, 166, 176, 178, 179
Coupland, Douglas 12
Cunningham, David 25

Dawkins, Richard 183
Deleuze, Gilles 33 n.3
Derrida, Jacques 104–7, 111, 113
  and *pharmakon* 58–65

description (Mitchell's use of) 28, 44, 65, 77, 78, 112, 123, 152, 172
Dickens, Charles 154, 156, 160, 171, 173
  Great Expectations 152, 162–3, 171
Dillon, Sarah 4, 11, 25, 107, 108
Dimock, Wai Chee 151–2
disability 7, 87–8, 93, 192
dissent 17–18, 47, 77, 165, 179–80
Dungeons and Dragons 5, 176

Earthsea 5, 167, 184
Edwards, Caroline 11, 24, 29 n.2, 32, 37, 105, 106
Eliot, T.S. 96
Empire (Hardt and Negri) 30, 33
epic 10, 13, 25, 55, 70, 79, 180, 183
ethics 13–14, 17, 40, 46, 50, 69–82
Eve, Martin Paul 13, 16

Falklands 86, 102 n.2
fantasy 5–6, 9, 17, 161, 184
  and *number9dream* 34–5, 43–4, 47–8
  and *Thousand Autumns* 103–4, 106, 108
feminism 104, 157, 175
Fernandez, Ramona 155–6, 159
fictional universe 1, 3–8, 14, 17, 136, 170, 174, 179, 183–94
film 6–7, 40, 44, 136, 140–1
  Blair Witch Project 177
  Chariots of Fire 91
  and *Cloud Atlas* 4, 57–8, 187, 191
  Exorcist, The 177
  and libretti 119–22
  Rocky Horror Picture Show, The 177
  Star Wars 7, 177
  Wizard of Oz, The 177
Forter, Greg 72, 73, 79
Freud, Sigmund 72, 79, 81–2, 154
future 1–3, 9, 10, 12–14, 28, 47
  and *The Bone Clocks* 156–60
  and *Cloud Atlas* 55, 64–5, 74, 80–1
  and the environment 134–46
  and irrealism 165–68, 175, 179
  and *Thousand Autumns* 105, 108–9, 111

INDEX

Future Library, The 3

genre 14, 154
genre-crossing 2–3, 40, 44, 50, 55, 86, 120–1, 149–51, 166, 179–80
geology/geologic time/mud 150, 151, 153–4, 156, 159, 160, 162, 163
Gesamtkunstwerk 117–18, 120–1, 128
ghosts/spirits 11, 15, 78, 146
  and *Ghostwritten* 24, 26, 32–3, 36
  and irrealism 167–70, 178–9
  and *Thousand Autumns* 103–5, 111, 114
Ghostwritten 2, 8, 23–37, 101–5, 108, 121, 135–8
  conspiracy 26, 27–9, 31, 33
  noncorpum 27–34, 109
  Quasar 27–31, 32, 35, 138, 143
  Zookeeper 31–5, 136–8, 143
globalization 11, 13, 15, 45, 63, 86, 135, 167, 185
  and *Ghostwritten* 23–37
  and *Thousand Autumns* 101–14
Goethe, Johann Wolfgang von 156
  Faust 173
Gothic 3, 14, 107, 166–7, 170–80
Guattari, Felix 33 n.3

Hardt, Michael 30, 33, 103, 105 n.3
Harris, Paul 12–13, 153, 156
Harris-Birtill, Rose 11, 12, 13, 15, 45, 48, 88
Hemingway, Ernest 154
Higashida, Naoki 7, 87
historical fiction 3, 101–2, 113
Hopf, Courtney 11, 16, 56, 57, 73, 119–20
Horologists/Horology 3, 10, 109 n.5, 143, 145–6, 150, 157–9, 162, 167, 170, 171, 173–4, 179
Hugo Lamb 129, 144, 150, 154, 155–6, 160–1, 162–3, 184
Hutcheon, Linda 46, 155

iceberg 153–5, 158
irrealism (and blurring of fantasy and realism) 165–80, 118, 123, 150–1, 155–6, 161

Ishiguro, Kazuo 9, 55
Iyer, Pico 4, 8

Jameson, Fredric 9, 24–6, 35, 39, 45, 50, 108, 138
Japan 3, 7, 123, 185
  and irrealism 167, 169–70
  and *number9dream* 28, 28, 30, 40, 44, 45–48
  and *Thousand Autumns* 101–14

Kai & Sunny 4, 88
Knepper, Wendy 13, 55, 58, 70, 76, 78, 82, 141
Kristeva, Julia 158
Künstlerroman 152–3, 155, 159
Kunzru, Hari 6, 14, 193

Langer, Lawrence 74
Le Guin, Ursula 5, 165, 167
Lennon, John 40, 48–9
liminality 92–5, 111, 169
Löwy, Michael 166, 170

magic realism 154, 159–60, 161
Man Booker Prize, The 2, 3, 170
Mann, Thomas, *Magic Mountain* 173
Maori 71, 74, 77, 79, 82, 108, 178
mapping 7–8, 11–13, 134–5, 137, 179, see also cognitive mapping
Marinus 3, 109, 111, 120, 122–4, 126, 128–9, 144–6, 150, 156–62, 172, 175–6, 179, 184
Martin, George R. R. 5, 167
Marxism 11, 23, 36, 54, 101, 104–6, 113, 140, 145, 172
'The Massive Rat' 88
metamodernism 42–3, 50
Mezey, Jason 13, 73, 141, 143
Middle Earth 5, 156, 167, 184, 185
Mitchell, David, see also cognitive mapping; mapping
  awards 3
  influences 4–8
  map-making 8, 12, 13, 134–5, 137
  oeuvre (overview) 2–4
  reception of 8–14

as world-builder 14, 17, 156, 166–70
Moore, Jason W. 134, 135, 142
Moretti, Franco 43, 150
Moriori 58, 69, 71, 74, 76–82, 108
Morton, Timothy 135, 137
'Muggins Here' 88
Murakami, Haruki 2, 6, 49, 183
music 89, 117–31, 137, 172, 185–6

Negri, Antonio 30, 33, 103, 105 n.3
number9dream 2, 39–51, 162
  Eiji Miyake 16, 39–40, 43–50, 190

O'Donnell, Patrick 12, 35, 37, 47–9, 55–6, 70, 86, 90, 105–6, 110, 150, 174
The Old Moon 2
'once upon a time' 161–3
oneworldedness 28–31, 33, 35
Orientalism 104, 107, 112

petro-melancholy 157
Poe, Edgar Allan, 'The Fall of the House of Usher' 175–6
politics (of writing) 10–11, 13–14, 113, 117, 179–80, 192–3
postcolonial 11, 15, 65, 71, 104, 168–9
postmodernism 11, 40–6, 50, 60
post-postmodernism 39–51
power 7, 10, 16, 18, 27 n.1, 28, 45, 47, 64, 77, 86–7, 108, 134–5, 139–41, 167, 179–80, 193
predacity 87, 108, 138–41, 143–4, 170, 179, 192
prosthesis 91–2, 95

queer 178–9, 191
quest narrative 39–51

racism 59, 76–9, 81–2
reality gap 23, 27, 27 n.1, 29–30, 34
real subsumption 24, 28, 29, 36–7
The Reason I Jump 4
resistance 3, 10, 16, 37, 48, 105, 146, 153
  and irrealism 170, 177–80

resource-angst 140–1
rhizome/rhizomatic 33, 33 n.3
'The Right Sort' 88, 189
Rorty, Richard 39–40, 50
Rushdie, Salman, *The Satanic Verses* 89
Russian Dolls 152

Schoene, Berthold 11, 108
Script, the 158–60
Shaviro, Steven 24, 37
Shelley, Mary, *Frankenstein* 154, 160, 161, 162
'The Siphoners' 142–3
Slade House 4, 121–3, 129, 175–9
  Norah and Jonah Grayer 175–9
soul
  battle over/stealing/violence to 3, 72, 120, 123, 129, 143–5, 160, 184
  and *The Bone Clocks* 170, 172, 174, 175
  cure/heal 62, 125
  and Mitchell as world-builder 166–170
  reality of (for Mitchell) 194
  and *Slade House* 175–9
  soul vampirism 150, 157, 179
  transmigration/rebirth of 14, 109–11, 139, 158, 161
space 5, 12, 82, 96, 104, 123
  and *The Bone Clocks* 149–50, 156, 160
  and *Ghostwritten* 26, 32–3, 35
  and *number9dream* 43–5
speech disfluency 85–97, 192
stammer/stutter 85–97
Stephenson, William 11, 24
Stoker, Bram, *Dracula* 172, 175–6
strange weather 137–8
Sunken Garden 4, 117–31
supernatural 3, 10, 63, 109, 110, 120, 122, 145, 152, 159, 161
  and irrealism 166–79
symbols and symbolism 85, 90, 95, 158, 162
  and *The Bone Clocks* 150, 152, 154, 159, 161, 162
  and irrealism 173, 174, 177, 178

and technology   63–4
    and *Thousand Autumns*   102, 111–12, 114

Tally, Robert   26, 34
Taoism   124, 167
technogenesis   54–5, 65–6
technology   16, 32, 53–66, 137, 161, 189
techno-Orientalism   45–6
Thousand Autumns of Jacob de Zoet, The   3, 101–14, 122, 129, 162
    Abbot Enomoto   104, 107, 109, 110
    Jacob de Zoet   101–4, 106–7, 109, 111–14
    Orito Aibagawa   101–4, 106–7, 109, 111–14
time/temporality   12–13, 87
    and *The Bone Clocks*   151–2, 156–62, 169, 174, 177, 178–9
    and *Cloud Atlas*   55, 62–5, 73–4, 141–2
    and *Ghostwritten*   33, 35–6
    and *Thousand Autumns*   104, 107–9, 112
Tolkien, J. R. R.   5, 156, 160, 161, 167
Toscano, Alberto and Jeff Kinkle   25, 34–5
totality/totalizing   23–37
transmigration/rebirth   14, 122–5, 128–9, 169
transubstantiation   156–8, 161
trauma   15–16, 30, 125, 168, 177
    and *Black Swan Green*   89–90, 92
    and *Cloud Atlas*   69–82
    and latency   71, 73–4, 78–9
tropical medicine   58–61

Über-book/Über-novel   4–5, 17, 118, 122, 128, 136, 152, 155–6, 166–7, 170, 173, 178, 183, 186–7, *see also* biblioverse; Hugo Lamb; Marinus

utopia/utopianism   23, 24, 26–7, 29, 32, 34–7

vampire/vampirism   154, 157, 166, 170, 172, 175–6, 179, *see also* soul
'Variations on a Theme by Mister Donut'   121
Vikings   185–6
violence   5, 10, 16, 17, 184–5
    and *The Bone Clocks*   156, 173–5
    and *Cloud Atlas*   59, 64, 72, 77, 79, 82
    and *Ghostwritten*   27–31
    and *Slade House*   177–9
virtual   57, 121–2
Voorman Problem, The   7, 159

Wachowski, Lana   4, 7, 191
Wake   4, 117–31
Wallerstein, Immanuel   13, 134, 173, *see also* world-system
warfare   1, 3, 10, 14, 71, 77, 150
    and the environment   136–8, 140, 145
    and irrealism   166–7, 170–5, 177, 178
    and *number9dream*   46–7
Warwick Research Collective   35, 168–9
Wilde, Oscar, *The Picture of Dorian Gray*   175–6
Wilder, Thornton, *The Bridge of San Luis Rey*   136
witness/bearing witness   71–3, 79, 82
world-ecology   134, 142
World Fantasy Awards   3, 9, 170
world-system   134, 141–2, 167–8, 171–6
    and *Ghostwritten*   24–5, 27, 29, 35–7

Yoshida, Keiko   87

Žižek, Slavoj   173

www.ingramcontent.com/pod-product-compliance
Lightning Source LLC
Chambersburg PA
CBHW052040300426
44117CB00012B/1904